Reputation and Image Recovery for the Tourism Industry

Edited by

Gabby Walters and Judith Mair

(G) **Goodfellow Publishers Ltd**

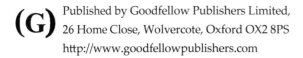

Published by Goodfellow Publishers Limited,
26 Home Close, Wolvercote, Oxford OX2 8PS
http://www.goodfellowpublishers.com

British Library Cataloguing in Publication Data: a catalogue record for this title is available from the British Library.

Library of Congress Catalog Card Number: on file.

ISBN: 978-1-911396-67-3

 Design and typesetting by P.K. McBride, www.macbride.org.uk

Cover design by Cylinder

Printed by Baker & Taylor, www.baker-taylor.com

Contents

Part 4 Organisational Crises and Crisis Communication

The authors

Cassiopée Benjamin, Département d'études urbaines et touristiques École des sciences de la gestion. Université du Québec à Montréal, Canada. benjamin.cassiopee@courrier.uqam.ca

Antonella Capriello, Associate Professor of Marketing, the University of Piemonte Orientale, Vercelli VC, Italy. Antonello.capriello@uniupo.it

Sean Chaidaroon, Senior Lecturer, Public Communication Program, University of Technology Sydney, NSW Australia. Sean.Chaidaroon@uts.edu.au

Nicholas Cradock-Henry, Manaaki Whenua Landcare Research, Lincoln, New Zealand. CradockHenryN@landcareresearch.co.nz

Kate M. Delmo, Lecturer, Public Communication, School of Communication, University of Technology Sydney, NSW Australia Kate.Delmo@uts.edu.au

Joanna Fountain, Department of Tourism, Sport and Society, Lincoln University, Lincoln, New Zealand. Joanna.fountain@lincoln.ac.nz

Gwyneth Howell, Associate Professor of Public Relations, School of Humanities and Communciation. Western Sydney University, NSW, Australia. g.howell@westernsydney.edu.au

Clemens Hutzinger, Department of Management Seeburg Castle University, Seeburgstrasse 8, A-5201 Seekirchen am Wallersee, Austria. clemens.hutzinger@uni-seeburg.at

Amy M Johnson, Department of Tourism, Event, and Sport Management, School of Health and Human Science, Indiana University-Purdue University Indianapolis, USA. amymjohn@iupui.edu

Po-Hsin Lai, Newcastle Business School, University of Newcastle, Newcastle NSW. Po-hsin.lai@newcastle.edu.au

Dominic Lapointe, Professor, Département d'études urbaines et touristiques, École des sciences de la gestion, Université du Québec à Montréal, Canada. lapointe.dominic@uqam.ca

Bingjie Liu-Lastres, Department of Tourism, Event, and Sport Management, School of Health and Hunan Science, Indiana University-Purdue University Indianapolis, USA. bliulas@iu.edu

Rohan Miller, Senior Lecturer in Marketing, The University of Sydney Business School, The University of Sydney, NSW, Australia rohan. miller@sydney.edu.au

Kaede Sano, Faculty of Tourism, Wakayama University, Wakayama City, Japan. kaede@wakayama-u.ac.jp

Bruno Sarrasin, Professor, Département d'études urbaines et touristiques, École des sciences de la gestion. Université du Québec à Montréal, Canada. sarrasin.bruno@uqam.ca

Richard Shipway, Senior Principal Academic, Bournemouth University, Bournemouth, UK rshipway@bournemouth.ac.uk

Simone Splendiani, Assistant Professor of Marketing, University of Perugia, Perugia, Italy, Splendiani80@gmail.com

Gabby Walters, Tourism Discipline, School of Business, University of Queensland, St Lucia, QLD g.walters@uq.edu.au

Wolfgang Weitzl, Department of Communication, University of Vienna, Althanstrasse 14, A-1090 Vienna, Austria. wolfgang.weitzl@ univie.ac.at

Nicholas Wise, School of Sport Studies, Leisure and Nutrition, Liverpool John Moores University. Liverpool, UK. N.a.wise@jmu.ac.uk

1 Introduction

Judith Mair and Gabby Walters

Tourism has always been impacted by crises and disasters, and no tourism destination is exempt (Beirman, 2006). Tourism is particularly susceptible to natural disasters (hurricanes, earthquakes and bushfires amongst others), which can cause sudden and immediate damage and destruction to destinations and their infrastructure, as well as longer terms issues with reduced visitor arrivals, leading to knock-on employment problems (Huang et al., 2008). However, there are other types of man-made crises that can also affect the tourism industry, including the actual or perceived threat of terrorism or political instability within a destination. Additionally, while some crises may affect entire destinations, others are more specific, affecting only particular industry sectors or organisations. Finally, not all challenges for destination marketers arise suddenly. Many destinations struggle to attract tourists because they are perceived to be unattractive for some reason, perhaps as a result of the long-running presence of heavy industry. The common thread linking these various crises, disasters and challenges is the unfortunate effect that they have on the reputation and image of the destination or organisation involved. Faulkner (2001: 136) defined a disaster as "a situation where an enterprise or a destination is confronted with sudden unpredictable catastrophic changes over which it has little control". A crisis, on the other hand, is considered to be "a situation where the root cause of an event is, to some extent, self-inflicted through such problems as inept management structures and practices or a failure to adapt to change" (Faulkner 2001, p.136). However, while there is an academic distinction between the term 'crisis' and 'disaster', they are often used interchangeably and in this book, both terms will be used.

Crisis and disasters that directly impact tourism can have extensive reputational implications for the organisations and destinations involved. It is critical that destination marketing organisations (DMOs) and chief executive officers (CEOs) communicate the right message in such circumstances to reassure the public that they have their best interests at heart. Often this is not done well. Every crisis and disaster is different, and knowledge is required to understand how different crises and disasters, whether they be at a destination or an organisational level, affect members of the public. Such insight provides managers with a clearer understanding of the most effective messaging and communication strategies post event. This book uses real life case studies to contextualise the relevant theories on tourism, marketing and communication, and unpacks examples of best practice to illustrate how carefully managed response strategies can ensure the future survival of an organisation. It is the 'go to' text for those seeking specific strategies and proven best practice techniques.

Although the book deals with a variety of types of crisis and disaster, and a range of contexts, nonetheless there are some common findings from the chapters. First, it is vital for destinations and organisations to be proactive in terms of crisis management – have a crisis management plan in place that is strategically designed to protect and recover reputation and image. It has been argued that organisations always operate in a pre-crisis phase (Fink, 2006), and this could apply to destinations too – being prepared is essential. Second, liaising with the media is crucial – ensure that the media receives a consistent message from all stakeholders that is honest and accurate, to prevent misrepresentation and to try to limit sensationalism. Third, use the recovery phase to critically assess the existing tourism product and marketing strategies – enforced down-time can be used wisely for a re-evaluation of current practices and offerings. Finally, social media continues to change the landscape of news and publicity – it is important to use social media to its best advantage as a way to provide a continual flow of consistent messages about a destination or organisation following a crisis or disaster.

Outline of contributions

This edited book is divided into four sections: the background; natural disasters; man-made crises; and organisational crises and crisis communication.

Section 1 - Background

This section sets the scene for the book and provides a detailed review of the theoretical concepts that are often drawn upon to enhance our understanding of how disasters and crises influence the image and reputation of tourism destinations and organisations. This chapter provides an introduction to the topic and discusses some definitions.

Chapter 2, by Walters and Mair, takes an in-depth look at the theoretical frameworks, models and concepts that underpin academic research in the areas of reputation and image recovery. In this chapter, the authors explore the applications of various consumer behaviour concepts such as emotions, risk perception, image formation, consumer involvement and information search. Following this, we discuss the influence of media reporting on image formation and reputation and the role that marketing communications can play in mitigating negative perceptions. Branding is introduced as a useful concept for destinations or organisations seeking to reinvent their image following long or short term reputational issues. Resilience is also discussed given its prevalence in two of the contributed works in this book and finally the chapter concludes by noting the relationship between effective service recovery strategies and reputation management following a critical event.

Section 2 - Natural disasters

As noted, tourism destinations are very vulnerable to the effects of natural disasters. Chapter 3, by Fountain and Craddock-Henry, examines the case of Kaikoura, New Zealand, which suffered a magnitude 7.8 earthquake in 2016. The chapter discusses how, despite damaged infrastructure and the depletion of the natural resources on which tourism in this destination depends, stringent efforts by committed locals led to ongoing improvements to the reputation and image of Kaikoura. Key recommendations from this chapter emphasise the importance of stakeholder collaboration and frequent, honest and positive communication with the media. This case study also shows that enforced 'down time' due to a natural disaster can be a valuable opportunity for DMOs to review a destination's product and positioning.

An earthquake (and accompanying tsunami) is also the topic of Chapter 4, by Sano, but in this chapter, Japan is the context. Sano examines the key strategies employed by destination marketers to attract both domestic and international tourists to Japan after the earthquake, and in light of the damage to the Fukushima nuclear power station and threat of ongoing radiation. In this case too, the importance of communicating accurate information emerged as a key recommendation, along with creating new tourism products that support sustainable development of disaster-affected areas. Sano also highlights the ubiquitous nature of social media and stresses that both the public and private sectors should understand the role that social media play in image and reputation recovery.

Finally in this section, Chapter 5 investigates the case of the island of Haiti, which has suffered from a series of natural disasters, including Hurricane Matthew in 2016. Using an analysis of the content of travel journal articles, Wise traces the direction of the narratives being created in the media, and demonstrates how the positive stories in the media are helping the industry recover. However, he also highlights that there are still points of concern in relation to Haiti's ability to recover, not just from natural disasters but also from its history of economic dependence on foreign aid and political uncertainty. Wise concludes by underscoring the need for destination managers to be aware of the importance of working with the media to ensure that the best possible stories of recovery are publicised, which may help to overcome some of the more negative images that people hold about the destination.

Section 3 - Man-made crises

This section considers those crises that can arguably be attributed to man-made causes. Such crises can be as devastating as natural disasters for the reputation and image of the tourism industry in a destination. Chapter 6, by Benjamin, Lapointe and Sarrasin, takes on the difficult subject of tourism and terrorism, and consider why some destinations recover relatively quickly from a terrorist attack while others suffer long-term reputational damage. Using a vulnerability-resilience framework, they seek to discover the determinants of destination resilience (any actions or elements that favour resilience) as well as the vulnerabilities that impede destination resilience. Case studies comparing Bali and Nepal are used to draw conclusions, including the importance of political stability as a key indicator of destination resilience. Additionally, the chapter suggests that there is a relationship between resilience and image – inward resilience in a destination contributes to a positive outward image portrayal. They recommend early recognition of the destination's vulnerabilities to prepare recovery strategies for potential terrorist attacks, and draw attention to the opportunities presented in the recovery phase to target new markets.

A different type of reputational problem is addressed in Chapter 7, as Lai and Walters examine the conflicting priorities of tourism destinations which rely on the development of industrial activities such as mining, energy and manufacturing, yet at the same time have natural and socio-economic landscapes that are attractive to visitors. Lai and Walters suggest that there are specific challenges associated with promoting places that often do not have a single identity or image, nor one single function and meaning. Using a participatory place branding approach, the chapter underlines the importance of engaging with multiple community stakeholders in consultation around place branding decisions, in order to understand the values and meanings stakeholders attribute to the destination, and enhance community support of a shared identity. Recommendations include the development of industrial tourism attractions that allow for a consistent brand image that will appeal to both investors and tourists, and working with both social media and traditional media to maintain the new brand image.

Chapter 8 investigates an issue that is garnering more and more public attention – that of waste and waste management, and its relationship with destination image and reputation. Drawing on examples of two destinations – Boracay and Naples – and applying learnings from these destinations to Bali, Miller and Howell suggests that while destination reputations can recede over time where issues are identified (in this case environmental and waste management problems), once these issues are satisfactorily addressed, the destination's reputation can be revised and rebuilt. The chapter proposes a range of recommendations, including issues that need to be addressed at the local level, such as improved waste infrastructure, perhaps using public-private partnerships; the development of an integrated island plan to manage transport, water, pollution, garbage disposal and environmental protection; and the introduction of a sustainability accreditation scheme. However, the authors also highlight the role of the international community in managing and minimising the ocean plastic problem. All of these are required to assist Bali and other 3S destinations who face ongoing pollution issues, to recover and rebuild their reputation.

The final chapter in this section examines the relationship between destination image and resilience and major sporting events. As Shipway and Miles point out, International Sports Events (ISEs) are viewed as attractive opportunities for developing nations seeking to enhance their global reputation and image. Chapter 9 uses case studies of events bid for by Qatar (2022 FIFA World Cup) and Cameroon (2019 African Cup of Nations) to illustrate the way that these countries have tried to use ISEs to improve their international reputations. However, for Qatar there have been ongoing issues with negative publicity around the treatment of foreign workers during the construction process and for Cameroon, the risks associated with political instability and the potential for natural disasters were considered so great that Cameroon was stripped of the rights to hold the event. Shipway and Miles draw on the notion of the reputation-resilience paradox and conclude that both the nations bidding for events, and those awarding the rights, have responsibilities to assess the resilience of potential host destinations before bidding for, or awarding events.

Section 4 - Organisational crises and crisis communication

In this section, the chapters examine reputation and recovery for various tourism organisations, including airlines and cruise lines, and considering the role of the media in times of organisational crisis.

Chapter 10 investigates the role of crisis communication, and proposes strategic approaches to crisis management communication for DMOs and tourism organizations. Capriello and Splendiani discuss three stages of strategically managing a disaster: prevention and preparedness, response, and recovery; and for each stage, identify the role that social media can play in public relations and communications. Arguing that advances in e-communications require a re-think of how best to preserve destination brands in the face of a crisis or disaster, they recommend a range of actions for destination managers. These include preparing or revising any current crisis communications plans to fully take into account the best way to use e-public relations; introducing a proactive social media monitoring team (where possible) to monitor and communicate prepared publicity material; communicating with key stakeholders to ensure a coherent message in dealing with any crisis or disaster; and encouraging tourists to promote the destination and the destination experience in the recovery stage.

Chapter 11 takes cruise lines as its focus and investigates current practices in the industry in relation to how cruise lines respond to major incidents such as ship sinkings, on-board disease outbreaks, severe weather and operational incidents. Liu-Lastres and Johnson draw upon Situational Crisis Communication theory to offer guidelines related to crisis response, the development and delivery of appropriate communications when responding to a crisis and strategic options for reputation management. The chapter findings suggest that although most cruise lines developed appropriate responses to the crises facing them, some were not acting in the best interests of the image and reputation of their organisations. Thus, a major recommendation of the chapter is that cruise lines need to be proactive in order to create the most effective crisis communication message, and have a coordinated and rehearsed crisis communication plan. Additionally, this contribution suggests that in the event of a crisis, cruise lines should re-connect with their loyal customers, as they are more likely to stay aligned with the cruise line during crisis times.

In Chapter 12, Delmo and Chaidaroon report on an aircraft disaster in South Australia. Naturally, airlines put a premium on the safety of travellers in their journey to and from destinations, and an air crash, particularly one with fatalities, puts extreme pressure on the airline. Using media framing as their lens, Delmo and Chaidaroon discuss the role of post-crisis investigations as sources of media stories, and conclude that the attribution of blame in media, as well as media sensationalism of the story, led to the eventual demise of Whyalla Airlines. The recommendations from this chapter include the importance of maintaining a culture of safety within an airline – while there are safety policies and mandatory safety practices, a lack of adherence to these policies in this case appears to have contributed to the negative media coverage. Additionally, airlines need to develop authentic messages that act as closure to the disaster – in this case study example, various different investigations and examinations continued for years. Finally, airlines should have a clear crisis communications and media plan to ensure that a supply of accurate information is provided to the media.

The final chapter in the book, Chapter 13, examines service recovery following a crisis or disaster. Hutzinger and Weitzl highlight the fact that many dissatisfied customers now automatically turn to social media to voice their complaints, a process known as negative e-word of mouth. This spreads awareness of the service failure far beyond only the customer involved and has implications for the reputation of the organisation. The chapter draws on the notion of the Service Recovery Paradox, which occurs when a service provider manages to increase the customer's satisfaction following a complaint to a higher level than their pre-failure satisfaction, and suggest that proactive webcare (anticipating problems and providing timely solutions) is essential for organisations when dealing with a service failure. Using an example of a service failure in a coffee shop, the chapter demonstrates that providing webcare not only improves the satisfaction of the complainant, but also improves the image/reputation of the organisation among those following the service recovery on social media. Recommendations suggest that organisations need to be aware of the wider positive effects of successful webcare, and ensure they develop effective recovery messages that are highly credible and take responsibility for causing the service failure.

References

Beirman, D. (2006). Best Education Network Think Tank V keynote address: "Marketing Tourism Destinations from Crisis to Recovery." *Tourism Review International*, **10**, 7–16.

Faulkner, B. (2001). Towards a framework for tourism disaster management. *Tourism Management*, **22**(2),135–147.

Fink, S. (1986). *Crisis Management*. New York: American Association of Management.

Huang, Y.-C., Tseng, Y.-P. & Petrick, J. F. (2008). Crisis management planning to restore tourism after disasters: A case study from Taiwan. *Journal of Travel & Tourism Marketing*, **23**(2), 203–221.

2 Theoretical foundations for the study of image and reputational management in tourism and hospitality

Gabby Walters and Judith Mair

Risk and reputation recovery in tourism should not be viewed as independent or isolated from other discipline areas. Frameworks, processes and theories cited in studies that explore tourism crisis recovery often include those from service recovery, public relations (PR) and communication, marketing, branding and consumer psychology. Many of the contributed case studies in this book demonstrate the use and application of these concepts, all of which are introduced and explored in this chapter. This chapter is organised into five sections. First, an understanding of the psychology behind consumer behaviour in times of crises is important to organisations and destinations seeking to maintain or recover their reputation. This chapter then begins by exploring the consumer behaviour concepts commonly employed by those seeking to better understand the impact of crisis and disasters on tourist demand. Following this, the influence of the media on the formation of tourists' image perceptions and subsequent behaviour is discussed. The next section discusses the role of marketing communications strategies and branding to the recovery process and in then we introduce the relationship between resilience and reputation and image recovery, a phenomena that features in two of our contributed cases yet remains understated in the current academic literature. The chapter concludes with a discussion on service recovery and its importance to image and reputation recovery within the tourism and hospitality sector.

Consumer behaviour

Consumer behaviour literature, theories and concepts have been used across the entire spectrum of crisis and disaster research to provide explanations for why tourists behave and respond the way they do. Crises and disasters are complex, diverse and variable in terms of extremity and their likely impact on consumers. On the other hand, how consumers respond is dependent on a wide variety of factors including personality, demographic background, cultural background, risk perception and previous experience or involvement in similar events – just to name a few. Of specific relevance to reputation and image management are consumer psychology concepts such as consumer emotion, consumer involvement, risk perception, image formation and information seeking behaviour. These are discussed below.

Emotions

How a tourist feels about a crisis or disaster will have a significant effect on their perceived image of the destination (Walters et al., 2015) and subsequent visitation intentions. One should note, however, that emotions can work for and against the image or reputation of a crisis-inflicted destination or organisation. For example, in the case of a terrorist attack, fear is a common response among tourists that then taints a destination's image in terms of its safety status (Walters, et al., 2018). Airline disasters provoke the traveller to question the safety of air travel and instil feelings of fear and even anger towards the airline involved (Henderson, 2006). Consumer anger is possibly the most detrimental emotion when it comes to reputation damage as angry consumers are more likely to vent their emotionally laden frustrations publically (Demeter et al., 2019). We learn however from research by Van der Meer and Verhoeven (2014) that that the use of emotional cues in an organisation's crisis response enhances the public's acceptance of messages, reduces feelings of anger, and subsequently minimises any damaging effects on the organisation's reputation. Sadness, on the other hand, despite being a negative emotion, does not necessarily lead to a negative evaluation of the destination/organisation. In the case of the Black Saturday bushfires that occurred in Victoria, Australia in 2009, the empathy and sadness felt among the tourist market towards the affected communities actually increased tourists' willingness to visit the region. The authors of this study, Walters and Mair (2012), therefore also advocate for the use of empathetic messaging when attempting to restore destination image following a disastrous event.

A commonly applied theory in the study of consumer emotions is cognitive appraisal theory (CAT). The idea behind this theory is that emotions are adaptive responses to environmental circumstances that directly relate to an individual's well-being (Moors et al., 2013). An appraised benefit can lead to positive emotions, whereas an appraised harm can lead to negative emotions. The felt emotions are determined by the interactions between events, an individual's perception about their own well-being, and the individual's expectations regarding his/her own ability to deal with the event (Moors et al., 2013). These variables, or appraisal criteria, play an important role in differentiating the kinds of emotions that occur in response to a crisis or disaster and subsequent behaviour (Watson & Spence, 2007).

It is important to note is that emotions overwhelm any rational mental processes necessary to fully evaluate a given situation (Etzioni, 1988). The occurrence or non-occurrence of an emotional response will depend on the level of exposure to the event and how important or relevant it is to the consumer – referred to in the consumer behaviour literature as involvement. How consumer involvement influences image formation and reputational status is discussed in the following.

Consumer involvement

Research indicates that the level of involvement consumers feel when processing information will influence the amount of effort, attention and cognitive elaboration towards the issue at hand (Celsi and Olson, 1988). In a general consumer behaviour context, product involvement is defined as "an unobservable state reflecting the amount of interest, arousal or emotional attachment evoked by the product in a particular individual" (Bloch, 1981: 12). According to Cai et al. (2004) how involved people are in their search behaviour will have a significant influence on their purchase decision. According to Teare et al. (1994), product involvement is likely to affect information search activities in particular as variables are inclusive of the consumer's receptivity to advertising and the type of cognitive responses generated during exposure to the available information sources. One of the key aims of tourism marketing communications is to evoke rich mental imagery that stimulates a desire within the target market to take a holiday at the featured destination. Depending on the level of involvement, these mental images are often accompanied by an emotional response that subsequently enhances the desire and the willingness to purchase (Walters et al., 2008). However, unfortunately, this path to involvement may also apply in the context of a disaster or crisis.

Involvement in a crisis or disaster context is demonstrated by the amount of attention, interest and care that the general public attribute to the event and the media coverage that surrounds it. Thanks to modern technology this news coverage is available via various sources 24 hours a day, 7 days a week. When a destination is affected by a disaster or crisis, sensationalised media commentary can at times undo the most successful marketing strategies by suggesting the area is dangerous, risky, depressing and – depending on the nature of the event – inaccessible. Such associations not only raise questions as to the destination's ability to provide a satisfactory tourism experience, but depending on one's level on involvement, may well result in enduring negative perceptions that are underpinned by emotional response. According to research by Walters and Clulow (2010) on the Black Saturday bushfires, the public were highly involved in the media coverage of the event for at least 2 to 3 days. While eventually the level of attention and interest in the fires faded, the consequent emotions and perceptions were enduring.

Risk perception

A perception that is particularly relevant to the works presented in this book is that related to risk. Risk perception is a standalone concept in consumer behaviour due to its prevalence in the consumer choice process. The extent of risk one associates with a destination or organisation will vary according to the person, the situation and the existing reputation (Schiffman et al., 2010). The tourism literature has demonstrated consistently that perceived risk has a significant influence on the image tourists hold towards, and their willingness to visit a destination (Sharifpour et al., 2014; Wong and Yeh, 2009; Sonmez and Graefe, 1998). The safety record of an airline for example would speak directly to the tourist's risk evaluation of flying with them. Risk perception and destination image are highly correlated (Lepp et al., 2011), which creates a problem for destination managers as in many cases, the perceived risk is unfounded. In their pre-post study on risk perception towards Oman, Al Rayami et al. (2017) revealed that visiting a destination first hand leads to a reduction in the risk perception of the destination held by travellers. However, given the influence of perceived risk on destination choice, it is not always viable to rely on managing unfounded risk perceptions through actual visitation.

One of the challenges destinations face when trying to manage unfounded risk perceptions following a disastrous event is what is commonly referred to as the 'spillover effect' (Walters et al., 2016). This is when a crisis or disaster in one specific location is perceived to affect a larger area that it in fact does. For example, violence in one country in the Middle East has led to a general labelling of the whole area as dangerous (Avraham, 2015). Similarly, natural disasters that have happened in one area of a country (e.g. bushfires in the Blue Mountains) have led to large parts of South East Australia being perceived as affected (Walters et al., 2016). The spillover effect has been widely acknowledged as problematic in a range of contexts including political instability (e.g. Sonmez et al., 1998; Avraham, 2015), disease (Wright, 2003); earthquakes (Huang et al., 2008); and bushfires (Walters & Mair, 2009).

This is particularly difficult for destinations dealing with a crisis or disaster, as tourists can wrongly assume (or be informed) that whole regions are inaccessible, dangerous, or otherwise unsuitable for visiting, when in fact the damage may be relatively limited and much of the destination may not be affected. Businesses operating within safe and/or undamaged areas of a destination are likely to find that tourists cancel or postpone visits because they are under the impression that the crisis or disaster has affected a much larger area (Walters et al, 2015). This leads to a double blow, where part of the destination is affected by the disaster, but the (unaffected) remainder of the destination suffers as a result of changes in visitation behaviour from tourists. For this reason, Henderson (2006) suggested that hotel and accommodation managers should communicate accurate information as to the conditions at destinations and the state of their specific properties. Henderson's research was conducted in the context of the Bali bombings of 2002; however, it applies equally to most other disaster contexts.

There is much to consider when trying to understand and respond to negative image perceptions that are underpinned by risk association – yet such intelligence is critical to the success of any reputation recovery strategy. Paradoxically, given the intangible nature of the tourism experience that does not allow pre-testing to occur, perception – whether it be positive or negative – is one's reality. Chapter 4 of this book, contributed by Kaede Sano presents an interesting case study that illustrates Japans' attempt to recovery its image following the Great Eastern Earthquake. While reputation and image recovery marketing strategies are discussed later in this chapter, the following section focuses on the formation of negative images and how consumers themselves seek to validate or eradicate any cause for concern.

Image formation and crisis and disasters

A negative image of an organisation or destination may be longstanding or periodic in nature. For example, destinations that experience high crime rates because of ongoing political or social instability may be disregarded by the tourist indefinitely. Destinations that endure a one-off disastrous event are generally only avoided temporarily as one's attention to the event wanes and the event itself becomes yesterday's news. Gartner (1994) describes the forces that influence these long or short term perceptions as 'image formation agents. These agents and how they influence a tourism consumer's image formation towards a specific destination or organisation are described in the table below.

Table 2.1: Gartner's image formation agents

Description	Example
Overt induced I	
Traditional forms of advertising such as print and online media where there is no question as to who is sending the message, i.e. the promoter, and why, i.e. to generate specific images towards the destination / firm.	Television advertisements promoting a specific destination – the goal being to construct the 'ideal' destination image
Overt induced II	
Promotional information passed on to potential tourists from tour operators or other members of the supply chain that may or may not have a direct affiliation with the destination or organisation. The key objective is to sell their own tourism product and not necessarily the destination as a whole. Consequently their representation of the host destination may or may not portray reality	Travel wholesalers promoting specific tourism experiences or accommodation facilities within a destination. The image formed by the consumer may not align with that which the destination wishes to portray
Covert induced 1	
The use of a third party spokesperson, e.g. celebrity endorser, to draw attention to the destination and/or overcome reputational issues. Emphasis placed on the credibility of the spokesperson whose characteristics or endorsement overshadows any psychological or social risk that the market may associate with the destination. Customer testimonials may be used if adequate funds for a celebrity are not available.	In the case of the Black Saturday bushfires, research revealed that the most effective recovery marketing message was one that was endorsed by a well-known celebrity who was recognised by the public as having an affiliation with the region (Walters and Mair, 2012). Negative perceptions are countered by the sense of trust the market holds towards the celebrity or third party spokesperson.

Covert induced II	
Again a third party representative in the form of a travel writer – i.e. journalist, blogger or opinion leader - informs the audience about the destination. Often the audience is unaware that the author has been commissioned by those attempting to promote the destination. There is no direct control over what is written however.	This agent comes with risks in terms of its effectiveness in mitigating negative destination image. Travel writers will often protect their own reputations by being bluntly honest as to the features or status of a destination. Consumers are more inclined to believe such agents due to the fact they are generally impartial to the goals of the destination promoters.
Autonomous	
Autonomous image formation agents comprise independently produced reports, documentaries and news articles. Media are considered to be the most common form of autonomous agents and have the most immediate effect on image formation. News media in particular alter images quickly.	News coverage of disastrous events or organisational crises is often drawn out and sensationalised to meet the supply pressures for 24/7 online and mainstream media news channels. Consumers now have more exposure than ever before to what is perceived as unbiased content – content that is known to have significant impacts on image formation.
Unsolicited organic	
When information about a destination is received irrespective of whether the recipient has requested it. Social media plays a significant part in the dissemination of unsolicited organic image formation agents.	When friends, colleagues, relatives or friends of friends inadvertently come across specific detail relating to a crisis or disaster whilst scrolling through their newsfeeds, how much attention is paid and the extent of influence such information has on their image formation towards the affected destination or organisation will depend on the credibility of the source.
Solicited organic	
This image formation agent is simply 'word of mouth' advertising. Again social media plays an important role in facilitating word of mouth activity and it is becoming common place for organisations to encourage and reward their consumers for sharing their preferences and positive consumer experiences online with their social networks.	Research has indicated that during and following a crisis or disaster, members of the public will often turn to social reference groups to seek clarification as to the actual events that took place and to source current information as to the event status. Here destinations and organisations have an opportunity to counter any negative images and reputational damage caused by sensationalist media reporting.
Organic	
The organic image formation agent has the highest credibility as it is based on actual experience or visitation.	This image agent allows consumers to form their image based on first-hand experience. This is particularly effective for destinations that face longstanding reputational issues or persistent scrutiny in the media that portrays them in a negative light.

Image formation and information search

It goes without saying that the image formation agents above would at some stage feature in the information search activities undertaken by tourists. Fodness and Murray (1997) describe information search as "a dynamic process wherein individuals use various amounts and types of information sources in response to internal and external contingencies to facilitate travel planning" (p.199). The tourism consumer's information search is a longer and more involved process than that accompanying the purchase of a tangible or physical product due to the intangible and multi-faceted components of the touristic experience. The digitisation of tourist information has led to a global shift in the way in which consumers acquire information, select, book and purchase their experiences. Social media platforms, travel review sites and online comparison and booking sites, for example, have increased the complexity of the information search process by disrupting the supply chain. More importantly however, these online platforms provide information gateways via which solicited and unsolicited image formation agents can reach their target audiences, regardless of whether they are actively seeking travel-related information.

The challenge for managers and marketers in times of crisis is to remain well-informed of the kind of solicited and unsolicited information being communicated to the public and how this in turn is influencing the destination/organisation's reputation. Regardless of what is actually occurring, what is important is what the market thinks is occurring. This is why it is crucial for managers to be vigilant in terms of monitoring the content, framing and tone of the mass media's reporting of a crisis and disaster and the commentary it is generating among their target markets. Careful monitoring of the dialogue that is taking place on social media will provide marketers with an idea of the market sentiment following any crisis or disaster or towards a destination. Social media not only serves as a useful information-sharing platform for consumers, but also a viewing platform from which marketing managers can access valuable market related insight (Dey et al., 2011). Capriello and Splendiani discuss the importance of E-communications to crisis management in Chapter 10. Such information can be highly useful to the development of marketing communications strategies that aim to counteract negative perceptions. The internet and news media have the power to alter images extremely quickly, particularly where large audiences worldwide watch repetitive scenes of an event (Tasci et al., 2007). Hence the following section extends our understanding of the role the media plays in influencing not only the public's perception of a crisis or disaster but also their decision process.

Media

According to Armstrong and Ritchie (2008), the global availability of media can rapidly lead to the formation of negative perceptions of a disaster-affected destination. However, Huang et al. (2008) claim that the mass media can cause anxiety and confusion among potential travellers, particularly when the reporting of crises and disasters has the potential to be sensationalist. It is common among researchers into post-disaster recovery in tourism destinations to highlight the role of the media in generating negative destination images (see for example Armstrong & Ritchie, 2008; Beirman, 2006; Lehto et al., 2008; Pearlman & Melnik, 2008; and Rittichainuwat, 2008); however, there is little research in this context to demonstrate empirically exactly how the media coverage causes such damage (Walters et al., 2016). Ghaderi et al. (2012) believed that the media had exaggerated the extent and the harmfulness of a crisis in Malaysia, and Peters & Pikkemaat (2005) highlight what they consider to be a major mistake made by the media following an avalanche in Austria, where the local community was blamed for the disaster. Finally, Walters et al. (2016) found that the use of sensationalist language and exaggeration in media reporting of a bushfire in New South Wales may have contributed to the estimated loss of over $100 million in tourism-related revenue experienced by this destination, thus providing supporting evidence for the role of the media in altering destination image.

There are several theoretical frameworks that can help to explain why the media can have such a devastating impact on destination image. Agenda setting theory (McCombs & Shaw, 1972) helps to explain that the way the media reports on issues shapes our perceptions of these issues: both in terms of what they choose to report on – which influences how important we think various issues are; and how they choose to report on them – which influences how we feel about these issues (McCombs et al., 1998). Birkland (1997) notes that the media deliberately covers some issues in depth with the intention of shaping public opinion, while other issues receive far less coverage, giving the impression to the public that they are of less significance.

In the context of a crisis or disaster, the media are likely to report on such events immediately and in depth, particularly where there has been significant damage and/or where lives have been lost. Mair et al. (2016) note that when a disaster strikes, initial media reports are more informative but as time goes by, the media need to find a story to keep the public's interest and this is where sensationalism can arise.

Linked to agenda setting is the notion of 'framing' – in this context, framing refers to the way that the media chose to cover a story, and this gives the reader insight into why an issue should matter to them, who might be responsible and what might be done (Nisbet & Mooney 2007). While reporting on these events is of course an important function of the media, it is the way in which the events are reported (the selected frame) that causes most damage to destination image. Editors and journalists make various decisions about how to frame a story, and these decisions have a significant influence on how the public respond to the story. Stories can be framed in a negative way (for example where poor outcomes, or blame for an event are highlighted), in a positive way (for example where heroes are hailed or community spirit is demonstrated) or through balanced reporting (where most of the information presented is factually accurate and unbiased). In the disaster context there appears to be a tendency for the media to use sensationalism to enhance readership and increase ratings. For example, in their research on the aftermath of Hurricane Katrina, Voorhees et al. (2007) highlighted a tendency among media reports to focus on the 'bad news', a finding substantiated by Walters et al. (2016) who also found a preponderance of negatively worded newspaper headlines in their context of a bushfire in NSW. Walters et al. (2016) also demonstrated widespread use of sensationalist language in their study, pointing to the use of metaphors, hyperbole, and highly emotive language. In Chapter 12, Delmo and Chaidaroon present lessons from a case that illustrates the media's misrepresentation of an Airline Disaster, that led to the decline of the regional airline's reputation to the extent the airline was left with no choice but to cease operating.

However, it is worth noting that while the media has been associated with having a negative effect on the destination image of various destinations suffering from crises or disasters, there is potential for the media to play a positive role in post-disaster recovery (Mair et al., 2016). An example of the way in which the media can be associated with recovery can be seen in Ciocco & Michael's (2007) study, which suggests that media coverage was beneficial in raising awareness of the need for government funding to help the destination recover following devastating bushfires. Additionally, positive news stories can be a powerful way to help to address some of the negative images of a destination distributed post-disaster (Chacko & Marcell, 2008; Tsai & Chen, 2010). In Chapter 5, Wise presents a detailed example of how the travel media in particular can transform a destination in despair. However, in order to ensure positive publicity, destinations must actively work with the media and develop a media management plan.

Avraham (2013), drawing on earlier work by Avraham and Ketter (2008), points to the importance of having an image restoration plan. They highlight the need to focus on three types of communication – source strategies (destination marketers' attempts to influence the source of what they believe to be negative reports about their destination); audience strategies (where a destination focuses on appealing to the values, attitudes and beliefs of potential visitors); and message strategies (which are designed to contradict negative perceptions that are held about their destination). In the context of this study, the Middle East, Avraham (2015) found that those destinations using all three types of strategies in their marketing communications were most successful in overcoming stereotypes and negative images associated with the Middle East as a travel destination.

Naturally, not all crises occur at the level of a destination. Rather, organisations within the tourism industry, such as airlines and cruise companies, often have to deal with specific crises affecting solely their own operations and reputation. These may include accidents, technical breakdowns, personal injuries and organisational mismanagement among others (Coombs, 1999). It is important to match crisis and disaster response carefully with the type of event that has occurred. The Situational Crisis Communication Theory (SCCT) is "a strategic communicative response can best protect the reputational resource by assessing the crisis situation and selecting a crisis response strategy that fits the crisis situation" (Coombs & Holladay, 2002: 167). This requires identifying the type of crisis (which evaluates how responsibility for the crisis is likely to be attributed) as well as how much control an organisation has over the response to the crisis. Responding to the crisis will depend on how much potential there is for reputational damage. The stronger the likelihood of reputational damage, and the more an organisation is held responsible for a crisis, the more the response strategy needs to focus on those adversely affected (Coombs & Holladay, 2002). The application of this theory is demonstrated in

Lastres and Johnston's case (Chapter 11) that provides a critical account of the reputational management strategies of the cruise line industry.

Marketing communications

There are many approaches to communicating with consumers when attempting to mitigate negative perceptions that may or may not have been generated via the media. Marketing communications can take the form of traditional advertising campaigns, public relations (PR) activities or messages that are communicated to the public directly by a representative of the organisation/destination. The extent and nature of reputational damage may well determine the kind of marketing communications strategy that is likely to be most effective in mitigating negative perceptions.

According to Greyser (2009) there are two kinds of reputational issues: those that involve bad news and the bad news is true; and those that involve bad news and the bad news is false. Further, the nature of crisis on which the news is based also differs in that there are those that occur suddenly with little warning (e.g. natural disasters, random mass shootings and terrorism attacks) and those that are long standing (political instability, environmental crises and lack of aesthetic appeal). Miller and Howell present a unique contribution to this book in Chapter 8 that explores the reputational damage that can arise as a result of destinations failing to implement sustainable waste management strategies. In terms of those that occur with little warning yet are short lived, the key aim of marketing communications would be to focus on the recovery efforts, and more importantly the progress that is being made to restore the safety and security status of the destination. In the case of a terrorism attack, the key concerns among the market are going to be security and safety and reassurance that the likelihood of this happening again is minimal. Destination resilience to such instances is positioned as extremely important in Chapter 6, where Benjamin, Lapointe and Sarrasin discuss the determinants of destination resilience in the event of a terrorism attack. The challenge destination marketers face in this instance is getting the balance right by promoting the safety and security elements without drawing too much attention to what actually took place. The timing of the marketing communications should also be considered. Walters and Mair's (2012) study on the Black Saturday fires revealed that the tourism market would not be averse to subtle promotional activities that encourage visitation immediately following a crisis or disaster. However, further research by the authors on the Queensland flood event in 2011 revealed that destinations should avoid promoting destinations whose communities are not ready physically or psychologically to welcome visitors (Walters et al., 2015)

In the case of long standing image issues, there are destinations that are labelled by the general public as risky due to past political unrest or disastrous events from which the destination has failed to redeem its reputation. Such labels may continue to exist despite the fact that the premise (i.e. the bad news) on which these negative images exist is no longer relevant. In this situation, the role of marketing communications would be to convince the consumer that the event or events underlying their concerns no longer exist (Avraham, 2015; Avraham and Ketter, 2008). Greyser advises however that such messages must be credible and evidence-based to make an impact. For destinations or organisations that face enduring image issues due to things that cannot be changed – i.e. a lack of aesthetic appeal or ongoing political unrest – marketing messages are likely to gain more credibility if they acknowledge the flaws, yet are seen to be making an effort to limit their impact (Coombs, 2007; Avraham & Ketter, 2013; Benoit, 2014). When the bad news is false, the primary aim of the marketing communications would be to mitigate the unfounded concerns that are causing the reputational damage. In this case, fact-driven information is critical, as is the communication source.

As Mair et al. (2016) point out, marketing and promotions are key to assisting a tourist destination to recover after a crisis or disaster. Additionally, research suggests that specific marketing strategies are more effective in the post-disaster phase than broad or unfocussed communications (Peters & Pikkemaat, 2005). In particular, it appears that potential tourists respond differently to crises and disasters depending on how geographically distant the destination is, as well as how well they know the destination. Pearlman and Melnik (2008) found that the images of New Orleans post-Hurricane Katrina held by those living further away from the affected destination were more positive than those held by residents living nearby the city. Walters and Clulow (2010) also found that distance had an impact on perceptions of the Gippsland region of Australia following significant bushfires in 2009, but in their study, those living further away were more likely to choose not to travel to the area. This demonstrates that distance is an important factor in image formation. It may be related to the level of personal involvement that a potential tourist feels with a destination (Mair et al., 2016); alternatively it may relate to the fact that the further away a destination is, the less knowledge of the area potential tourists are likely to have. In summary the type of crises will determine the type of marketing communications strategy employed to mitigate the damage caused.

The role of branding in crisis recovery

At their most basic level, brands are markers for the offering of an organisation (Keller and Lehmann, 2006). The foundations on which a brand is built include: the product itself, the accompanying marketing activities, and the popularity or consumer uptake of the product. Brands are 'perceptual entities' (MacInnis and Price, 1987) and as such appeal to the consumer's senses, reason and emotions. In a tourism context, Kumar and Kaushik (2017) revealed that how tourists identify with a particular destination brand will depend on how congruent the personality of the destination is with their own and the level of trust they have towards the destination. The authors contend that should a tourist identify with a particular destination, they are likely to display both advocacy and loyalty towards the destination. To this end, it is important for destinations and organisations alike in the tourism and hospitality sector to understand the personalities of their target segments and deliver consistent messages that promote the experiences and the characteristics of the destination that are congruent with their needs.

Place branding is another common term used in the tourism literature to explain destination branding. Braun (2012: 43) defines place branding as "the coordinated use of marketing tools supported by a shared customer-orientated philosophy, for creating, communicating, delivering, and exchanging urban offerings that have value for the city's consumers and the city's community at large". Understanding the modifications that have occurred to a brand image as a result of a crisis or disaster is a crucial step in the recovery process for any destination or organisation hoping to redeem its reputation. Kaikoura, New Zealand presents an excellent example of the application of this notion and Fountain and Cradock-Henry provide details of this particular case in Chapter 3.

When attempting to reinvent or rebrand a destination that has endured long standing reputation issues, Amujo and Otubanjo (2012) argue that this is more of a political exercise than one of marketing communication. Again, however, it is imperative that managers of such destinations have a solid understanding of the associations tourists hold regarding the destination. Rebranding for places seeking to reinvent themselves as being a tourism destination of choice requires the creative blending of the symbolic, historical and functional elements of the very features that deter tourists, as in many cases these cannot be changed (Amujo and Otubanjo (2012). Community resonance and acceptance of the new brand is also a critical success factor and this is discussed in more detail in Chapter 7 where Po-Hsin Lai and Walters propose a place branding strategy for industrial destinations.

The nexus between resilience and image recovery

Business resilience is an overarching framework that can be used to understand how organisations deal with risk, uncertainty and organisational change, while the concept of destination resilience complements and extends that of business resilience by incorporating the economic, social, cultural and environmental dimensions of tourism-dependent communities. A failure among tourism organisations and destinations to develop resilience not only undermines the economic viability of those areas, but threatens the way of life of that community, including their social prosperity, their sense of community and their identity. Declining tourist numbers, for example, lead to financial stress, business closure and job loss among tourist operators which, in turn, generate a 'dynamics of decline' (Lawrence & William, 1989) in affected communities. To date, little is known in relation to the interdependency between the resilience efforts of tourism and hospitality sectors and the ability of these sectors to redeem their reputation following a significant crisis or disaster.

Investigating resilience at the organisational and destination level requires an understanding of the policy and governance frameworks in place. In the case of tourism-dependent communities, local and state government policy and planning are an intrinsic component of the socio-ecological system. Commitments to resilience and industry-specific forms of collaboration are now commonplace in Australian disaster management frameworks (COAG, 2011; Queensland State

Government, 2016). These commitments reflect the popularity of resilience generally as a means of integrating the social, the economic and the public-managerial into preparations for extreme events (Comfort et al., 2010). Public-sector agencies often struggle, for example, to acknowledge and integrate private-sector concerns into their disaster management instruments (Drennan et al., 2015) and successful examples of public-private coordination in the disaster management space remain scarce (Stark, 2014). Values that are intrinsic to government bureaucracy often appear, moreover, to be inimical to the concept of resilience (Stark, 2014) and efforts at promoting community resilience can be undone by the hierarchical nature of state-centric policy frameworks (Stark & Taylor, 2014). These issues alert us to the need to evaluate the ways in which tourism organisations and destinations incorporate the concept of resilience in their disaster planning and the relationship between perceived resilience, destination image and reputational recovery. The nexus between reputation and perceived resilience is explored in Chapters 9 and 5 in this book. Shipway and Miles (Chapter 9) investigate the importance of perceived resilience for developing countries with long-standing image issues when hoping to secure major sporting events. Chapter 6 on the other hand explores the determinants of destination resilience for countries whose reputations have been damaged as a result of terrorism events. Collectively these contributions agree that resilient destinations are better placed to counter long or short term reputational damage.

Service recovery

Service recovery involves those actions designed to resolve problems and alter negative attitudes with the main focus being customer retention (Miller et al., 2000). Where a crisis takes place and who is deemed responsible will determine the need for a service recovery strategy that may in turn salvage the reputation of the tourism entity. The immediate response actioned by the service provider will either solve or worsen the situation, hence it is imperative that the actions taken are given careful consideration prior to being implemented. More often than not, however, an ineffective knee-jerk or 'quick-fix' response is given, which consequently causes more damage than good to an organisation's reputation (Demeter et al., 2019).

There are multiple factors that come into play when considering how effective a service recovery strategy is likely to be. These include the type of service (Mattila and Ro, 2008); the response speed (Boshoff, 1997); the type of failure (McDougall and Levesque, 1999); and who was considered responsible (Mattila and Ro, 2008). The nature of the service failure and who is considered responsible are particularly relevant to image and reputation recovery, as research indicates that tourists are likely to be more forgiving and loyal when the incident behind the service failure was deemed beyond the control of the service provider. For example, in an experimental study in the context of a natural disaster, Demeter et al. (2019) demonstrated that in a scenario where hotel guests' holidays were interrupted by a hurricane, the blame for the service failure was attributed to forces beyond the hotel's control, and thus these guests were more likely to be satisfied by the hotel's service recovery attempts. The study also demonstrated that such guests were less likely to engage in reputation damaging behaviours such as negative word of mouth. This finding confirms that of Coombs and Holladay (2005) whose study showed that the conclusions customers make about responsibility in the aftermath of a disaster or crisis directly affect their behaviour and judgements towards an organisation.

Undoubtedly, being cleared of accountability is an optimal outcome for tourism organisations involved in crises that impede service delivery. However, one could argue that it is dangerous to make the assumption that consumers will accept the organisation isn't to blame, or even assume that their holiday has been ruined. An important goal of any service recovery attempt is to preserve the image of the organisation and/or the host destination to ensure repeat visitation and minimise the temptation among consumers to engage in retributory reputation-damaging actions. In essence, consumers need to walk away satisfied that they have been adequately compensated for the inconvenience they have encountered. Yet what makes for adequate compensation? How can organisations be certain that their service recovery strategy is likely to lead to appease consumers and should all crises and disasters be responded to in the same way? Many of these issues are addressed in the chapter on service recovery in the context of a hospitality operation (Chapter 13) by Hutzinger and Weitzl.

Conclusion

This chapter has examined a range of theories, processes and frameworks drawn from several disparate disciplinary fields, with the aim of understanding the formation, damage and repair of destination image and reputation. Consumer behaviour concepts, such as emotions and involvement, help shed light on how tourists act following a crisis or disaster, and help us to elucidate why visitors react the way they do. Risk perceptions are also demonstrated to be of key significance in the destination choice process, and although they may be unfounded, or exaggerated, can make the difference between visiting a destination and crossing it off the list. The chapter also discussed the formation of image in the first place and identifies the various agents that contribute to both short and long term perceptions of place. The media in its multiple formats was identified as a key image formation agent, and several media theories were explored, including both agenda setting and framing, which influence not only what we pay attention to, but how important we perceive an issue to be. The chapter then moved on to consider marketing communications and the role of branding in crisis recovery. Finally, the chapter has highlighted the nexus between image recovery and resilience, pointing out that there is a significant, but under-researched interdependency between resilience and the ability of the tourism and hospitality industry to recover their reputation following a crisis or disaster.

References

Al Riyami, H, Ritchie, B., Walters, G (2016) Examining the change in tourist's perceived risk pre and post their trip. Proceedings of the 27th Annual CAUTHE Conference, Dunedin, New Zealand, February 7-10

Amujo, O. C., & Otubanjo, O. (2012). Leveraging rebranding of 'unattractive'nation brands to stimulate post-disaster tourism. *Tourist Studies*, **12**(1), 87-105.

Armstrong, E. K., & Ritchie, B. W. (2008). The heart recovery marketing campaign: Destination recovery after a major bushfire in Australia's national capital. *Journal of Travel & Tourism Marketing*, **23**(2-4), 175-189.

Avraham, E. & Ketter, E. (2013). Marketing destinations with prolonged negative images: towards a theoretical model. *Tourism Geographies*, **15**, 145.

Avraham, E. (2013). Crisis communication, image restoration, and battling stereotypes of terror and wars: Media strategies for attracting tourism to Middle Eastern countries. *American Behavioral Scientist*, **57**(9), 1350-1367.

Avraham, E. (2015). Destination image repair during crisis: Attracting tourism during the Arab Spring uprisings. *Tourism Management*, **47**, 224-232.

Avraham, E. & Ketter, E. (2008). *Media Strategies for Marketing Places in Crises: Improving the image of cities, countries, and tourist destinations*. Oxford: Butterworth Heinemann.

Avraham, E. & Ketter, E.(2008). Will we be safe there? Analysing strategies for altering unsafe place images. *Place Branding and Public Diplomacy*, **4**(3), 196-204.

Beirman, D. (2006). Best Education Network Think Tank V keynote address: "Marketing Tourism Destinations from Crisis to Recovery." *Tourism Review International*, 10, 7–16.

Benoit, W. L. (2014). *Accounts, Excuses, and Apologies: Image repair theory and research*, Albany, State University of New York Press.

Birkland, T. A. (1997). *After Disaster: Agenda setting, public policy, and focusing events*. Washington, DC: Georgetown University Press

Bloch, P.H., (1981). An exploration into the scaling of consumers' involvement with a product class. *Advances in Consumer Research*, **8**, 61-65.

Boshoff, C., (1997). An experimental study of service recovery options. *International Journal of Service Industry Management*, **8**(2), 110-130.

Braun, E., (2012). Putting city branding into practice. *Journal of Brand Management*, **19**(4), 257-267.

Cai, L.A., Feng, R. & Breiter, D., (2004). Tourist purchase decision involvement and information preferences. *Journal of Vacation Marketing*, **10**(2), 138-148.

Celsi, R.L. & Olson, J.C., (1988). The role of involvement in attention and comprehension processes. *Journal of Consumer Research*, **15**(2), 210-224.

Chacko, H. & Marcell, M. (2008). Repositioning a tourism destination. *Journal of Travel & Tourism Marketing*, **23** (2-4), 223-235.

Ciocco, L., & Michael, E. (2007). Hazard or disaster: Tourism management for the inevitable in Northeast Victoria. *Tourism Management*, **28**, 1-11.

Comfort, L.K., Boin, A. & Demchack, C.C. (2010). *Designing Resilience: Preparing for extreme events*, Pittsburgh, PA: Pittsburgh University Press

Coombs, T. W. & Holladay, S.J., (2005). An exploratory study of stakeholder emotions: Affect and crises. In *The Effect of Affect in Organizational Settings* (pp. 263-280). Emerald Group Publishing Limited.

Coombs, W. T. (1999). *Ongoing Crisis Communication: Planning, managing and responding*. CA: Sage.

Coombs, W. T. (2007). *Ongoing Crisis Communication: Planning, managing, and responding.* Los Angeles: SAGE Publications.

Coombs, W. T. & Holladay, S. J. (2002). Helping crisis managers protect reputational assets: Initial tests of the situational crisis communication theory. *Management Communication Quarterly,* **16**(2), 165-186.

Council of Australian Governments [COAG] (2011). National Strategy for Disaster Resilience. Available at: https://www.ag.gov.au/Publications/Pages/COAGadoptsNationalDisasterResilienceStrategy.aspx accessed 11/03/2019

Demeter, C., Walters, G. & Mair, J. (2019). *The influence of service recovery strategies on tourist behaviour following a natural disaster.* Paper presented at the Centre of Australian University Tourism and Hospitality Education (CAUTHE) Conference, 11-14 February, Cairns, Australia

Dey, L., Haque, M., Khurdiya, A. & Shroff, G. (2011) Acquiring competitive intelligence from social media. In *Proceedings of the 2011 joint workshop on multilingual OCR and analytics for noisy unstructured text data,* p. 3. ACM,

Drennan, L., McConnell, A. & Stark, A. (2015). *Risk and Crisis Management in the Public Sector.* Abingdon: Routledge.

Etzioni, A. (1988). Normative-affective factors: Toward a new decision making model. *Journal of Economic Psychology,* **9**, 125-150.

Fodness, D. & Murray, B. (1997). Tourist information search. *Annals of Tourism Research,* **24**(3), 503-523.

Gartner, W.C., (1994). Image formation process. *Journal of Travel & Tourism Marketing,* **2**(2-3), 191-216.

Ghaderi, Z., Puad Mat Som, A. & Henderson, J. (2012). Tourism, crises, and island destinations: Experiences in Penang, Malaysia. *Tourism Management Perspectives,* **2-3**, 79-84.

Greyser, S.A. (2009). Corporate brand reputation and brand crisis management, *Management Decision,* **47**(4), 590-602,

Henderson, J.C. (2006). Communicating in a crisis: flight SQ 006. *Tourism Management* **24**(3), 279-287

Huang, Y., Tseng, Y. & Petrick, J. (2008). Crisis management planning to restore tourism after disasters. *Journal of Travel & Tourism Marketing,* **23** (2-4), 203-221.

Keller, K. L. & Lehmann, D. R. (2006). Brands and branding: Research findings and future priorities. *Marketing Science,* **25**(6), 740-759.

Kumar, V. & Kaushik, A. K. (2017). Achieving destination advocacy and destination loyalty through destination brand identification. *Journal of Travel & Tourism Marketing,* **34**(9), 1247-1260.

Lawrence, G. & Williams, C., (1990). The dynamics of decline: implications for social welfare delivery in rural Australia. In Cullen, T., Dunn, P. &

Lawrence, G. (eds), *Rural Health and Welfare in Australia*. Wagga Wagga, NSW: Charles Sturt University-Riverina, pp. 38-59

Lehto, X., Douglas, A. C. & Park, J. (2008). Mediating the effects of natural disasters on travel intention. *Journal of Travel & Tourism Marketing*, **23**(2), 29–43

Lepp, A., Gibson, H. & Lane, C. (2011). Image and perceived risk: A study of Uganda and its official tourism website. *Tourism management*, **32**(3), pp.675-684.

MacInnis, D.J. & Price, L.L., (1987). The role of imagery in information processing: Review and extensions. *Journal of Consumer Research*, **13**(4), pp.473-491.

Mair, J., Ritchie, B. W. & Walters, G. (2016). Towards a research agenda for post-disaster and post-crisis recovery strategies for tourist destinations: A narrative review. *Current Issues in Tourism*, **19**(1), 1-26.

Mattila, A. & Ro, H. (2008), Discrete negative emotions and customer dissatisfaction responses in a casual restaurant setting, *Journal of Hospitality & Tourism Research*, **32**(1), 89-107

McCombs, M. E. & Shaw, D. L. (1972). The agenda-setting function of mass media. *Public Opinion Quarterly*, **36**(2), 176-185.

McCombs, M. E., Llamas, J. P., Lopez-Excobar, E. & Rey, F. (1998). Candidate's images in Spanish elections: second-level agenda-setting effects. *Journalism & Mass Communication Quarterly*, **74**(4), 703-717.

McDougall, G.H. & Levesque, T.J., (1999). Waiting for service: the effectiveness of recovery strategies. *International Journal of Contemporary Hospitality Management*, **11**(1), 6-15.

Miller, J.L., Craighead, C.W. & Karwan, K.R., (2000). Service recovery: a framework and empirical investigation. *Journal of Operations Management*, **18**(4), 387-400.

Moors, A., Ellsworth, P.C., Scherer, K.R. & Frijda, N.H., (2013). Appraisal theories of emotion: State of the art and future development. *Emotion Review*, **5**(2), 119-124.

Nisbet, M. C. & Mooney, C. (2007). Framing science. *Science - New York and Washington*, **316**(5821), 56-69.

Pearlman, D. & Melnik, O. (2008). Hurricane Katrina's effect on the perceptions of New Orleans leisure tourists. *Journal of Travel & Tourism Marketing*, **25**(1), 58-67.

Peters, M. & Pikkemaat, B. (2005). Crisis management in Alpine Winter Sports Resorts – The 1999 Avalanche Disaster in Tyrol. *Journal of Travel & Tourism Marketing*, **19** (2-3), 9-20.

Queensland State Government (2016). Queensland State Government Disaster Management Plan. Available at http://www.disaster.qld.gov.au/Disaster-Resources/pages/PGF.aspx accessed 11/03/2019

Rittichainuwat, B. N. (2008). Responding to disaster: the case study of Phuket, Thailand. *Journal of Travel Research*, **46**(4), 422-432.

Schiffman, L. & Kanuk, L. (2010). *Consumer Behavior* 10th ed.,Boston, MA: Global; London: Pearson Prentice Hall.

Sharifpour, M., Walters, G., Ritchie, B.W. & Winter, C. (2014). Investigating the role of prior knowledge in tourist decision making: A structural equation model of risk perceptions and information search. *Journal of Travel Research*, **53**(3), 307-322.

Sönmez, S.F. & Graefe, A.R., (1998). Influence of terrorism risk on foreign tourism decisions. *Annals of Tourism Research*, **25**(1), 112-144.

Stark, A. & Taylor, M. (2014). Citizen participation, community resilience and crisis-management policy. *Australian Journal of Political Science.* **49**(2), 300-315.

Stark, A. (2014). Bureaucratic values and resilience: an exploration of crisis management adaptation. *Public Administration*, **92**(3), 692-706.

Tasci, A. D. A., Gartner, W. C. & Tamer, C. S. (2007). Conceptualization and operationalization of destination image. *Journal of Hospitality & Tourism Research*, **31**(2), 194-223.

Teare, R., Mazanec, J.A., Crawford-Welch, S. & Calver, S. (1994). *Marketing in Hospitality and Tourism: a consumer focus*. Cassell plc.

Tsai, C. H., & Chen, C. W. (2010). An earthquake disaster management mechanism based on risk assessment information for the tourism industry-a case study from the island of Taiwan. *Tourism Management*, **31**(4), 470-481.

van der Meer, T.G.L.A. & Verhoeven, J.W.M. (2014) Emotional crisis communication. *Public Relations Review*, **40**, 3 526-536.

Voorhees, C. C., Vick, J. & Perkins, D. D. (2007). 'Came hell and high water': the intersection of Hurricane Katrina, the news media, race and poverty. *Journal of Community & Applied Social Psychology*, **17**(6), 415-429.

Walters, G., Sparks, B. & Herington, C. (2008). Marketing: Shifting the focus from mainstream to upbeat. In Australia and New Zealand Marketing Academy Conference (pp. 1-7).

Walters, G. & Clulow, V. (2010). The tourism market's response to the 2009 Black Saturday bushfires: the case of Gippsland. *Journal of Travel & Tourism Marketing*, **27**(8), 844-857.

Walters, G. & Mair, J. (2012). The effectiveness of post-disaster recovery marketing messages—The case of the 2009 Australian bushfires. *Journal of Travel & Tourism Marketing*, **29**(1), 87-103.

Walters, G., Mair, J. & Ritchie, B., (2015). Understanding the tourist's response to natural disasters: The case of the 2011 Queensland floods. *Journal of Vacation Marketing*, **21**(1), 101-113.

Walters, G., Mair, J. & Lim, J., (2016). Sensationalist media reporting of disastrous events: Implications for tourism. *Journal of Hospitality and Tourism Management*, **28**, 3-10.

Walters, G., Wallin, A. & Hartley, N., (2018). The threat of terrorism and tourist choice behavior. *Journal of Travel Research*, **58**(3) /doi.org/10.1177/0047287518755503

Watson, L. & Spence, M.T., (2007). Causes and consequences of emotions on consumer behaviour: A review and integrative cognitive appraisal theory. *European Journal of Marketing*, **41**(5/6), 487-511.

Wright, E. R. (2003). Travel, tourism, and HIV risk among older adults. *Journal of Acquired Immune Deficiency Syndromes*, **33**, S233-7.

Wong, J.Y. & Yeh, C. (2009). Tourist hesitation in destination decision making. *Annals of Tourism Research*, **36**(1), 6-23.

2

3 The road to recovery: Reimagining Kaikōura after a natural disaster

Joanna Fountain and Nicholas Cradock-Henry

Introduction

It is widely recognized that tourist destinations are vulnerable to disruptions caused by natural disasters, and understanding tourism response and recovery to natural disasters is a critical topic of research internationally (Mair et al., 2016). Post-disaster recovery is defined as: "the development and implementation of strategies and actions to bring the destination back to a normal (pre-event) condition or an improved state" (Mair et al., 2016: 2). Recovery may commence immediately following a crisis or disaster, or can be delayed if a destination has been considerably damaged and residents and businesses profoundly affected. Scott et al. (2008) have suggested that the disaster recovery process contains three phases – recovery of damaged infrastructure, marketing responses (revolving around communication and recovery marketing), and adaptations to the new system. These phases may occur sequentially or simultaneously, with different stakeholder groups managing them (Mair et al., 2016).

While a destination's physical damage may be repaired relatively quickly, the process of restoring the image and reputation of a destination can be protracted, making recovery marketing and communication management critical to the process of re-establishing a destination's tourism industry in a post-disaster environment. The speed with which the mainstream and social media spread news (often sensationalized or factually incorrect) and visual images, potentially undermining recovery marketing campaigns, can make this task more challenging (Ritchie et al., 2004; Walters & Clulow, 2010; Walters et al., 2016). Recovery marketing and communication management is generally focused on two main goals: changing perceptions of the destination caused by media reporting or destination damage; and restoring visitor confidence in the destination (Ciocco & Michael, 2007; Scott et al., 2008; Walters & Mair, 2012; Mair et al., 2016). These goals may be achieved by reinforcing pre-existing destination images and correcting negative impressions, or creating entirely new propositions for destinations based on new markets or products (Mair et al., 2016).

Previous research highlighting successful recovery marketing campaigns stress the importance of clear leadership and coordination (Scott et al., 2008; Orchiston & Higham, 2016) and marketing strategies aimed at restoring market confidence at the destination level (Scott & Laws, 2005; Ciocco & Michael, 2007; Hystad & Keller, 2008; Becken & Hughey, 2013). This process is aided by the timely dissemination of consistent, well-considered, trustworthy and accurate information (Ritchie et al., 2004; Carlsen & Hughes, 2008; Walters & Mair, 2012; Mair et al., 2016; Orchiston & Higham, 2016). Relationship marketing, and building trust with the travel trade and key markets, particularly local visitor markets, is also critical to the destination recovery process (Walters & Clulow, 2010; Mair et al., 2016).

This chapter investigates the response of the Kaikōura tourism industry to the 2016 earthquake in the 18 months following the event. Data gathering for this chapter occurred in stages, and drew on existing networks and knowledge acquired through previous research in the region since the earthquake. Numerous visits to the town informed the researchers' understanding of the recovery process, as did the ten semi-structured in-depth interviews conducted with key stakeholders between April and July 2018. Respondents included council and emergency management staff in Kaikōura district, staff of Destination Kaikōura, senior representatives of key partners in the recovery process from the wider Canterbury region, and Kaikōura tourism operators central to recovery efforts.

The interviews, which lasted from 30 minutes to an hour, began with questions about the immediate impacts of the earthquake and initial responses, and the longer-term decision-making processes and activities involved in marketing recovery efforts in the months following the event. The interviews concluded by asking respondents to assess the current state of Kaikōura as a tourist destination, and to consider future directions for the district. All but one interview, which was conducted by telephone, was audio-recorded, and transcribed verbatim. Transcript data were coded by the authors using deductive and inductive methods (Babbie, 2012), with some themes identified in advance, informed by existing literature, and others emerging through the process of data analysis (Braun & Clarke, 2006). Documentary analysis included a review of local and regional policy and planning materials, news reports, promotional tourist material, including print and television advertisements and social media posts, and trade newsletters.

The case study

Kaikōura is located on the east coast of the South Island, Aotearoa-New Zealand. The surrounding district covers an area of approximately 2,000 km2, bounded by an inland range to the west, and the Pacific Ocean on the east (refer to Figure 3.1). At just over 2,000 square kilometres, it is the smallest district in New Zealand by area and rating base. The district had a resident population of 3,552, with two-thirds of the population residing in the township of Kaikōura at the time of the last Census in 2013. This Census revealed the significance of tourism to the district. At the time, the accommodation and food sector employed 25.5% of the district's population, followed by retail (15.3%) and agriculture, forestry and fishing sector (12.1%). In Kaikōura township approximately half of the workforce (50.4%) is directly employed in the tourism industry, with another 35% employed indirectly supporting the industry (Kaikōura District Council, 2017: 34).

The mainstay of tourism in the region is wildlife viewing and recreational opportunities. Commercial whale watching began in the 1980s and marine-based tourism has since expanded to include swimming with dolphins and seals, viewing marine birds, and diving and fishing charters. The popularity of the destination is due in part to its location on State Highway 1, halfway between Christchurch and Picton (where ferries depart for the North Island), and it is the most travelled route for tourists traversing the country. The region's tourism industry is highly seasonal; the months between December and April experience high visitation, but the winter months are quiet. At the time of the 2016 earthquake, tourist numbers and expenditure in the district were increasing year on year. There had been a 40% increase in annual spend between 2013 ($86m) and 2016 ($125m, year ending September, Destination Kaikōura, 2017), with guest arrivals numbering 195,664 in the year ending April, 2016 (MBIE, 2018). The increasing significance of tourism to the district saw Destination Kaikōura established as an independent RTO in 2014, one of only 30 in New Zealand and a fraction the size of any of the others.

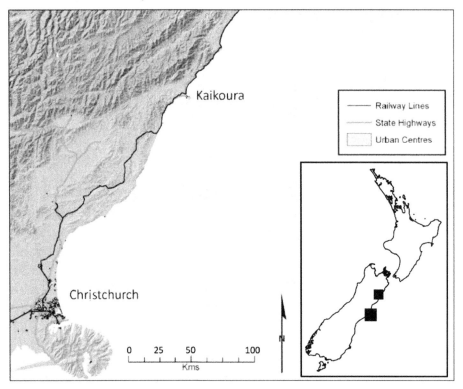

Figure 3.1: Kaikōura and surrounding area, South Island, Aotearoa-New Zealand. Source: created by the authors

The earthquake struck at the start of what was expected to be a bumper tourist season. With road access cut or open to emergency vehicles only, an estimated 1200 tourists were evacuated from the quake-stricken town in the first week (O'Connell, 2016; Stuff, 2016), leaving 300 rental vehicles stranded (Cropp, 2016). Tourism operations ground to a halt, as damage to infrastructure and limited road access impeded travel, and the whale watching vessels were idle for the large part of each day due to the raised seabed and damage to the marina. In a town where 80 percent of businesses cater directly to tourists (Kaikōura District Council, 2017), the immediate future looked bleak.

While the epicentre of seismic activity was 60km south-west of the town, the event was widely referred to as the 'Kaikōura Earthquake' due at least in part to the extensive media coverage of the damage caused to this important international and domestic tourist destination. Unlike the Christchurch earthquakes five years earlier, devastation to the landscape, rather than buildings, dominated media images emerging from the region. Despite Kaikōura's isolation by land, dramatic aerial footage of the many massive landslips and faultlines engulfing and decimating road and rail networks both north and south of the town was beamed around the world within hours. Images of the uplifted seabed around the coast made a lasting impression on viewers and raised questions about the survival of the marine life for which the region is renowned. In the days following the disaster the media used sensationalist and dramatic language to describe events, suggesting 'Kaikōura's tourism industry may need a miracle' (Dangerfield, 2016a) and asking 'Can Kaikōura survive?'(Dangerfield, 2016b). An article titled 'Quakes may be mortal blow for Kaikōura's tourism industry' states that "locals fear the tourism boom has come to a swift and violent end" and raises the suggestion that State Highway 1 "may never be rebuilt" (Mitchell & Redmond, 2016).

The earthquake on the 14 November, 2016 had profound and immediate impacts on the tourism industry in Kaikōura. With stranded tourists evacuated, the town cut off by land, and the majority of tourism businesses unable to operate, the future of the town was uncertain. An inland route (State Highway 70 [SH70]) became the main transportation link and opened within days, but was subject to frequent closures, considerable travel delays and limited opening hours for months following the event. Guest arrivals in the town plummeted from 10,877 in September, 2016 (the shoulder season), to 3,437 in December (the high season); an 85% decline on the previous December (Destination Kaikōura, 2017). The remainder of the high season reported significant decreases in visitor volume of between 43% and 70%. Guest arrivals in the town for the year ended September 2017 were down 51.1% over the previous year, and guest nights were down 40.2%; the latter figure being somewhat cushioned by the arrival of recovery workers tasked with repairing the severely damaged infrastructure (Destination Kaikōura, 2017). Not surprisingly, visitor spend in Kaikōura declined also, from a record high of $125m in 2016 (year ending September) to $63m the following year (Destination Kaikōura, 2017). The tourism industry of Kaikōura and the wider region did not sit back during this time, however, and the remainder of this chapter outlines the work going on behind the scenes after the earthquake to set Kaikōura on the road to recovery.

The earthquake aftermath: immediate response

The days immediately following the earthquake were described by respondents as chaotic. The manager of Destination Kaikōura explained: "Being an i-Site [information centre], people think we know everything, so even the day after the earthquake, everyone was on our doorstep trying to find out what was happening". He described the difficulty in accessing information, and of feeling powerless when basic infrastructure was severely disrupted:

> We couldn't contact members – we couldn't get into the building for a couple of weeks, and we didn't have power. When we did have power, we didn't have the internet. We couldn't do anything so it was pretty hard.

Despite this, staff of the i-Site set up a table outside the building and liaised with the Kaikōura District Council to provide a point of contact and information for visitors and other members of the community. Once their building was accessible, updating the database of tourism operators and providers, found to be incomplete and inaccurate, was a key priority (cf. Orchiston & Higham, 2016).

Within a week of the disaster, the government had announced a support package for businesses in the town (Fairfax Reporters, 2016), and additional support followed (MBIE, 2016). Support was on hand from the wider Canterbury tourism community also. For example, within a few days of the earthquake, representatives of Christchurch Canterbury Tourism (now ChristchurchNZ) and the Christchurch International Airport (CIAL) arrived by helicopter to offer moral support and share learnings from the ongoing recovery process of the Christchurch-Canterbury earthquakes (Orchiston & Higham, 2016). Tourism stakeholders in Kaikōura spoke appreciatively of the boost to morale this visit brought and the valuable advice received. A respondent who had been part of this Christchurch delegation spoke about the strong desire to share the lessons from Christchurch:

> We were able to deliver [our] message with real conviction because we had just had that experience. And it was one of the reasons to fly up, to say "we are here to support you; here's what we know. We don't have the roadmap through this, but here are the things you need to know".

Key messages shared at this meeting included "don't do things too quickly", and "you can't market your way out of this". This did not mean sitting back and waiting – clear, honest communication was critical – but suggesting that it was 'business as usual' for the destination was not appropriate, particularly in the age of social media. As a respondent explained based on Christchurch's experience:

> You can't say "Come to Christchurch 'cos everything's fine" because someone has just been there the day before and taken photographs of crumbling down buildings or nothing to do. You can't fool people anymore.

Kaikōura's tourism stakeholders were advised also to use the enforced 'down time' during their period of isolation to reassess the destination, its markets, and tourism offerings. This advice was summarised thus:

> Whatever you had before, you need to mark that position, and when you come out the other side of this you need to be stronger and better …. It is a forced opportunity to take stock.

Destination Kaikōura and the tourism community took these messages to heart in the months that followed. One of the first tasks was to establish a newsletter, and ten days after the earthquake the first 'Kaikōura Earthquake Update' was published by Destination Kaikōura and sent to Tourism New Zealand's database of 4,000 agents and other industry stakeholders (Destination Kaikōura, 2016a). The Kaikōura Earthquake Update initially was sent out weekly, then fortnightly and monthly to key stakeholders with much needed information about the town and district. This first issue reported on the condition of the State Highways (closed) and the state of other essential services (variable). As in every update, a list of the tourist attractions and accommodation operators open for business was presented, and only four, of more than fifty, tourist attractions were operational. In the face of foreboding media reports and an uncertain future, this newsletter presented a very positive image of the town to the world. For example, above the heading 'Kaikōura still looking pretty as a postcard' are three photos of Kaikōura, featuring the sea and the mountains in the late spring sunshine, and three more photos of the smiling faces of local residents "enjoying the [farmers'] market and the sunshine". On the front page is a message from the General Manager of Destination Kaikōura under the heading 'Best news of the week.' He states: "Our marine life with whales, dolphins, seals and birdlife have not been affected by the events of 14 November, 2016. The community and tourism operators are thrilled Kaikōura will remain New Zealand's premier marine mecca."

This accurate, but relentlessly optimistic, messaging was apparent in every issue of the update. The mix between positivity and honesty is apparent in the reporting of the repair of the Kaikōura Marina, significant damage to which limited marine viewing activities for a year, as vessels could only operate at high tide. This could have been framed as highly problematic, but instead in the update of 23 December, the General Manager of Whale Watch Kaikōura was able to report:

> *This week it's been great to get the vessels out on the high tide and do Whale Watch trips (for locals only). We had full sailings and seeing our wonderful whales and dolphins is very uplifting. Repairs at South Bay Marina have commenced which is really encouraging.*

While the major marine mammal attractions – Dolphin Encounter and Whale Watch – remained effectively closed, by Christmas 2016, 79% of tourism operators, 68% of accommodation and 82% of retail premises were open, State Highway 70 was open for unrestricted travel, and there was limited access via SH1 to the south of the town (Destination Kaikōura, 2016b).

This focus on positivity was a deliberate strategy to get the audience onboard with the recovery process – "to come with us on our journey" – a message learnt in Christchurch (Orchiston & Higham, 2016; see also Walters & Clulow, 2010; Walters & Mair, 2012). All industry stakeholders were aware of the reputational risk for the destination and the South Island as a whole, hence the need for positivity, as the marketing manager for a large tourist operator explained:

> *Me and my boss we were both having to front the camera and we were both "It's just got to be positive, positive, positive", because there is going to be a lot of negative [stories] … but there are just so many positives every day: … "Actually, that's not how it is, we're actually very fortunate… people actually have been working really hard to get that road open"*

To maintain this positivity, no images of the damage, and in particular the state of the roads and marina, were shared with agents via these newsletters for six months after the disaster. As one stakeholder remarked: "If people really saw how bad the road was, they wouldn't think we would ever get it back."

The road to recovery

While the infrastructure and tourism industry of Kaikōura was slowly restored, a significant marker in the recovery effort occurred in February 2017, when the government, through the Ministry of Business, Innovation and Enterprise (MBIE), made available $650,000 to Kaikōura for a recovery marketing plan and strategy (Dangerfield, 2017). This fund represented a windfall for the RTO, which usually had very limited funding and resources, being based in such a small region, and enabled a continuation of existing activities (where appropriate) with existing funds, primarily maintaining a presence at international trade shows. The new fund employed a marketing executive to maintain the communication strategy and develop marketing campaigns for key target markets and pursue new opportunities, as a tourism operator explained:

> We've always struggled with our marketing budget, and it gave us the opportunity to do some really cool stuff that we would never have considered. We had to do that to recover our business. But I think it sets your focus in a different area, you know?

It is widely acknowledged that recovery marketing strategies are best if developed collaboratively at the destination and regional level, and focused on restoring destination image as it is collectively that confidence will return (Ciocco & Michael, 2007; Hystad & Keller, 2008; Mair et al., 2016). This collaboration was evident within the Kaikōura tourism community, and between Kaikōura and the wider region. Respondents from Kaikōura's tourism industry spoke of the way the community pulled together. Larger enterprises with the financial and human resources to absorb the impact of the earthquakes took a lead role in the recovery efforts, on behalf of the smaller operators.

At the same time, there was a new appreciation in the community about the significance of tourism to the whole town, as a respondent explained: "before the earthquake many of the hospitality and retail businesses did not consider themselves part of tourism – now they know they are part of tourism, and realise how important the industry is". While the need to pull together during the recovery enhanced this camaraderie, there was a sense that the nature of the tourism industry in the town strengthened these ties: "We work really closely with everybody. We did already beforehand…. we're all *whanau* [family], sort of…. we all grew up here, so we all know each other". Regional tourism industry representatives also commented on the success of the collaborative efforts:

You saw Kaikōura flying in formation, absolutely... there were no dissenting voices. There were in the early phases, naturally, you know – "What are you going to do for me? My business is in trouble". And then it all started to move: "here's our plan; here is what we are planning to do."

Another key feature of this recovery process was the strengthening of relationships between the Kaikōura tourism industry and the wider Canterbury region, due to their shared experiences of adversity. As one tourism stakeholder explained: "everyone seems to have a connection now that is like a neighbour... You are all going through the same process at the same time". Respondents spoke of the way North Canterbury's dispersed townships and communities came together in the weeks and months following the earthquake. The reliance on State Highway 70 (the inland road) was critical to strengthening relationships and networks between tourism businesses in Hanmer Springs and Kaikōura. There was acknowledgement also of the economic strength that comes from working together with regional partners: "we are such a small rating base ... so we need to build really good relationships with our regional neighbours to share some of the resources that they can so readily tap into" (cf. Ciocco & Michael, 2007; Hystad & Keller, 2008; Becken & Hughey, 2013).

A legacy of this greater collaboration is the Alpine Pacific Touring Route (APTR), a re-imagining of a pre-existing trail that had 'fizzled out' due to lack of coordination and focus. This 450km route takes in Hanmer Springs, Kaikōura and Christchurch and the many rural communities of North Canterbury. This initiative was funded from the $350,000 earthquake recovery fund provided to Hurunui Tourism in December 2016, and with considerable support from Christchurch International Airport Ltd and ChristchurchNZ. It had its soft launch in April 2018, with an initial focus on untapped domestic markets, but with potential for the international travel trade (see Fountain et al., in press).

As acknowledged in the literature, regular visitors, and markets in close proximity, are often the first to return to a destination after a disaster (Mair et al., 2016). Targeting the domestic market was a focus when the marketing campaigns rolled out in May 2017, with 60-70% of the MBIE funding directed at advertising to the domestic market, particularly in Christchurch and Canterbury. As the General Manager of Destination Kaikōura explained:

We've been kept top of mind too; been kept in people's faces. We've done a lot of advertising through magazines… the internet and so forth… and I think the goodwill from people out there towards us... [the Christchurch people] … have empathy with us and they want to get back.

The fact that the people of Christchurch and Canterbury had their own recent experiences of earthquake devastation undoubtedly strengthened the resolve to support their neighbours through this difficult time.

As had been encouraged by the tourism stakeholders from Christchurch in the days following the disaster, the tourism industry in Kaikōura used the time, and funds, made available in the post-earthquake period to take stock of their tourism proposition, and to consider future directions for the town. Some funding was spent on establishing a new image and video library and building a stronger web presence for Destination Kaikōura, which at the time of the earthquake had no website or social media presence. Thoughts were given also to new tourism products which might bring the community together and reduce the marked seasonality of the region. For example, there is ongoing discussion about greater utilisation of the region's food produce, and particularly seafood, in tourism experiences, which would not only diversify the tourism product, but strengthen networks and spread the benefits of tourism to the primary sector (see Cradock-Henry et al., 2018). Other suggestions for product diversification include developing experiences based on the new interest in the geology and marine biology of the region, and developing cycle tourism alongside the newly upgraded state highway north of the town.

Kaikōura reimagined

A year to the day after the earthquake, the new marina precinct was opened in Kaikōura. A month later, State Highway 1 reopened along the length of the South Island. To coincide with this event, a series of light hearted television advertisements were released, highlighting the fact that 'Kaikōura is back'. Accompanying the key message "Kia ora from Kaikōura" were iconic images of local wildlife, accompanied by pun-laden slogans: "We're dolphinately open", "We're open; we've got the seal of approval"; and "Come, have a whale of a time". Over the Christmas/New Year period, another television advertisement was broadcast saying "Thank you New Zealand, for all your support", featuring Kaikōura's mayor and other local residents and acknowledging the support of the whole country on their recovery journey.

Eighteen months after the earthquake and there is little doubt that tourism in Kaikōura is recovering. The ambitious aim of the Kaikōura Recovery Marketing Plan 2017-2018 – "To achieve pre-earthquake annual visitor spend of $120 million within two years" (Destination Kaikōura, 2018: 3) – was on track. The goal at the end of the first year of recovery was to have regained 50% of lost visitor spend and visitors ($24m and 36,000 guests). This was close to being achieved; 147,268 guests arrived in the year ending April 2018 (a rebound of 33,048 guests), and annual visitor spend was $93m ($3m short of target; Destination Kaikōura, 2018). On a sunny April day, carparks in Kaikōura are full with private cars and camper vans, the boats are out on the water whale- and dolphin-watching, and the streets are humming with activity. It seems that the road reopened and the "tourist tap was turned back on". As a Christchurch respondent framed this: "We knew instinctively that once that road reopened it was going to recover, just like that, and it has." The new facilities in the town, including the new State Highway 1, and the new marina precinct have added to the tourism experience in the region, and the tourism industry has a new-found energy and enthusiasm.

While literature suggests that disasters frequently result in long-term reputational damage (Mair et al., 2016), there is general agreement both within the town and further afield that the earthquake has not damaged Kaikōura's destination image. In fact, a number of Christchurch-based tourism stakeholders believed the opposite was the case. As one respondent concluded: "I think the reputation has been strengthened … We can absolutely hand-on-heart say that Kaikōura has come out of this stronger and better." A local tourism operator concurred:

> We've proven that we can actually survive this, we've learnt a lot of stuff about ourselves, about each other, and about the community. And the cool think is the wildlife is still here – the tourism product is still here – and the people are still coming! We feel very, very blessed really.

Somewhat ironically, the relative isolation of Kaikōura for many months may have been a blessing in disguise. The road closure ensured there were no dissenting voices wanting to hasten recovery efforts; there was little to do but wait it out. This isolation meant also that the tourism industry was better able to manage the images shared of the town in a way that may not have been possible if there had been tourists in Kaikōura posting photos of damage, and stories of bad experiences, on social media.

As a note of caution, while the informants in Kaikōura generally supported the notion that the town had come out of this very well, there was also acknowledgement of the ongoing emotional toll that the recovery process has had on the community. It should be acknowledged that many residents will continue to suffer psychological distress even after a tourism destination's economy recovers (Ritchie, 2009), and face a sense of loss for the town as it was (Beirman, 2003).

3

Key lessons

The disaster recovery process for tourist destinations is often framed as a 'return to normal', but this is not always a possible, or even a desirable, outcome (Ritchie et al., 2004; Carlsen & Hughes, 2008; Scott et al., 2008). While disasters have undeniably negative impacts, they may act as a stimulus for innovation, offer an opportunity to identify new markets and products, and facilitate the building of new, or strengthen existing, networks and information flows (Faulkner, 2001; Ritchie, 2008; Scott et al., 2008; Mair et al., 2016; Brundiers & Eakin, 2018). Thus, a successful disaster response and recovery programme will contain within it the seeds of a resilient tourism future for a destination (Calgaro et al., 2014; Lew, 2014). Overall, there are signs that Kaikōura will emerge from the disaster recovery process as a more resilient destination, better prepared for future disasters or crises.

However, every destination, and disaster, is unique. Disasters occur on different scales, and in places with diverse social and ecological systems (Ritchie et al., 2004; Mair et al., 2016). Acknowledging these differences, this chapter offers a number of insights into successful tourism response and recovery to crises and disasters and the implications of these for practice conclude this chapter.

Recommendations for practice

- Collaborate to ensure you present a consistent marketing strategy. A strength of the Kaikōura recovery effort was the commitment of the tourism community to work together to maintain a united front to stay 'on message.'

- Maintain frequent, honest, and positive communication. An important lesson learnt from the Christchurch recovery process, the tourism reputation of Kaikōura was preserved at least in part due to a relentless positivity of messaging, while maintaining accuracy of information.

- Take advantage of the down time and review tourism product and positioning. Kaikōura's tourism community has spent considerable time and energy considering key markets, which has included renewed recognition of the value of the domestic market, and collaborated locally and regionally on new tourism products, including the Alpine Pacific Touring Route.

References

Babbie, E.R. (2012) *The Practice of Social Research*, 13th ed, Belmont, CA: Wadsworth Publishing.

Becken, S. & Hughey, K.F.D. (2013) Linking tourism into emergency management structures to enhance disaster risk reduction, *Tourism Management*, **36**, 77-85.

Beirman, D. (2003) *Restoring Tourism Destinations in Crisis*, Wallingford: CABI.

Braun, V. & Clarke, V. (2006) Using thematic analysis in psychology, *Qualitative Research in Psychology*, **3**, 77–101.

Brundiers, K. & Eakin, H.C. (2018) Leveraging post-disaster windows of opportunities for change towards sustainability: A framework, *Sustainability*, **10**, 1390. https://doi.org/10.3390/su10051390

Calgaro E., Lloyd, K. & Dominey-Howes, D. (2014) From vulnerability to transformation: a framework for assessing the vulnerability and resilience of tourism destinations, *Journal of Sustainable Tourism*, **22** (3), 341–360.

Carlsen, J. & Hughes, M. (2008) Tourism market recovery in the Maldives after the 2004 Indian Ocean Tsunami, *Journal of Travel & Tourism Marketing*, **23**(2-4), 139-149.

Ciocco, L. & Michael, E. (2007) Hazard or disaster: Tourism management for the inevitable in Northeast Victoria, *Tourism Management*, **28**, 1–11.

Cradock-Henry, N., Fountain, J. & Buelow, F. (2018) Transformations for resilient rural futures: The case of Kaikōura, Aotearoa-New Zealand, *Sustainability*, **10**, 1952. https://doi.org/10.3390/su10061952

Cropp, A. (2016) Kaikoura earthquake a logistical nightmare for rental car companies, *Stuff*, 24 November. https://www.stuff.co.nz/business/86840192/kaikoura-logistical-nightmare-for-rental-car-companies

Dangerfield, E. (2016a) Kaikōura's tourism industry may need a miracle', *Stuff*. 18 November. https://www.stuff.co.nz/national/nz-earthquake/86622009/kaikouras-tourism-industry-may-need-a-miracle?rm=m

Dangerfield, E. (2016b) Can Kaikōura survive?, *The Press*, 19 November. https://www.pressreader.com/new-zealand/the-press/20161119/281505045807943

Dangerfield, E. (2017) Tourism package to help promote quake-stricken Kaikōura, *Marlborough Express*, 1 March. www.stuff.co.nz/marlborough-express/news/89850805/tourism-package-to-help-promote-quakestricken-kaikoura

Destination Kaikōura (2016a) Kaikōura Earthquake Update #1 – 26 November

Destination Kaikōura (2016b) Kaikōura Earthquake Update #6 – 23 December

Destination Kaikōura (2017) Kaikōura Earthquake Update #19 – 14 November.

Destination Kaikōura (2018) Kaikōura Update #24 – 26 June, Winter Update.

Fairfax Reporters (2016) Kaikoura businesses welcome Govt's 7-5m relief package but some will miss out, *Stuff*, 17 November. https://www.stuff.co.nz/business/86570328/Kaikoura-businesses-welcome-Govts-7-5m-relief-package-but-some-will-miss-out

Faulkner, B. (2001) Towards a framework for tourism disaster management, *Tourism Management*, **22** (2), 135 –147.

Fountain, J., Cradock-Henry, N., Buelow, F. & Rennie, H. (in press) Agri-food tourism, rural resilience and recovery in a post-disaster context: insights and evidence from Kaikōura-Hurunui, New Zealand, *Tourism Analysis*.

Hystad, P.W. & Keller, P.C. (2008) Towards a destination tourism disaster management framework: Long-term lessons from a forest fire disaster, *Tourism Management*, **29**, 151-162.

Kaikōura District Council (2017) Reimagine Kaikōura: A sustainable future for the Kaikōura District, Kaikōura, NZ: Kaikōura District Council. https://www.kaikoura.govt.nz/assets/Recovery/Reimagine-Kaikoura-Kaikoura-Recovery-Plan-WEB.pdf

Lew, A.A. (2014) Scale, change and resilience in community tourism planning, *Tourism Geographies*, **16** (1), 14-22.

Mair, J., Ritchie, B.W. & Walters, G. (2016) Towards a research agenda for post-disaster and post-crisis recovery strategies for tourist destinations: A narrative review, *Current Issues in Tourism*, **19** (1), 1-26.

MBIE (2016) Support package for Kaikoura businesses extended, 9 December. Available: https://www.mbie.govt.nz/about/whats-happening/news/2016/support-package-for-kaikoura-businesses-extended

MBIE (2018) Kaikōura visitor statistics year-end-April 2018, Wellington, NZ: Ministry of Business, Innovation and Employment.

Mitchell C. & Redmond, A. (2016) Quake may be mortal blow for the tourism industry, *Stuff*. 17 November. www.stuff.co.nz/travel/destinations/nz/86518555/quakes-may-be-mortal-blow-for-kaikouras-tourism-industry?rm=m

O'Connell, B. (2016) Hospitality NZ & TIA: NZ open for business, *Tourism Ticker*, 15 November. https://www.tourismticker.com/2016/11/15/nz-tourism-open-for-business-despite-north-canterbury-no-go/

Orchiston, C. & Higham, J.E.S. (2016) Knowledge management and tourism recovery (de)marketing: the Christchurch earthquakes 2010–2011, *Current Issues in Tourism*, **19**, 64-84.

Ritchie, B. W., Dorrell, H., Miller, D. & Miller, G. A. (2004) Crisis communication and recovery for the tourism industry, *Journal of Travel and Tourism Marketing*, **15** (2-3), 199-216.

Ritchie, B. (2008) Tourism disaster planning and management: from response and recovery to reduction and readiness, *Current Issues in Tourism*, **11** (4), 315-348.

Ritchie, B. W. (2009) *Crisis and Disaster Management for Tourism*, Clevedon: Channel View.

Scott, N & Laws, E. (2005) Tourism crises and disasters: Enhancing understanding of system effects, *Journal of Travel and Tourism Marketing*, **19** (2-3), 149-158.

Scott, N., Laws, E. & Prideaux, B (2008) Tourism crises and marketing recovery strategies, *Journal of Travel and Tourism Marketing*, **23** (2-4), 1-13

Stuff (2016) Stranded Kaikoura tourists overwhelmed by generosity as helicopters fly evacuees out. *Stuff*, 15 November. https://www.stuff.co.nz/national/86460484/Stranded-Kaikoura-tourists-overwhelmed-by-generosity-as-helicopters-fly-evacuees-out

Walters, G., & Clulow, V. (2010) The tourism market's response to the 2009 Black Saturday bushfires: The case of Gippsland, *Journal of Travel and Tourism Marketing*, **27** (8), 844-857

Walters, G., & Mair, J. (2012) The effectiveness of post-disaster recovery marketing messages – the case of the Australian 2009 bushfires, *Journal of Travel and Tourism Marketing*, 29 (1), 87-103.

Walters, G., Mair, J. & Lim, J. (2016) Sensationalist media reporting of disastrous events: Implications for tourism, *Journal of Hospitality and Tourism Management*, **28**, 3-10.

4 Reputation and image recovery from the Great East Japan Earthquake: A long journey with high hopes

Kaede Sano

Introduction

Tourism is considered one of the more important industries in the world, contributing economically to many countries' development (Huang et al., 2008). The Japanese government has actively promoted inbound tourism since the launch of the 'Visit Japan' campaign in 2003, by implementing various policies, such as relaxing tourist visas, building a tourist-friendly environment, implementing a tax-free policy and so on. As a result, 28,691,073 international tourists visited Japan in 2017, compared to 5,211,725 in 2003 (JNTO, 2018a, 2018b). Undoubtedly, the booming tourism market brought a significant economic impact to Japan. According to data from the Japan Tourism Agency (JTA, 2017), the economic impact of tourism in 2015 amounted to 25.5 trillion Japanese yen (approximately USD 234 billion), and tourism accounted for four million jobs or 6.7% of nationwide employment (JTA, 2017).

However, the tourism industry is also more fragmented and vulnerable to crises and disasters (Faulkner, 2001; Ritchie, 2004), and the industry often finds it difficult to rebound quickly from crises and disasters that have damaged the image of a destination (Cassedy, 1992).

Although the number of international tourists to Japan has continually increased since 2003, the industry was greatly affected by the world-wide financial crisis in 2009 and the Great East Japan Earthquake (also called the 3.11 Earthquake and Tohoku Earthquake) in 2011 (see Figure 4.1).

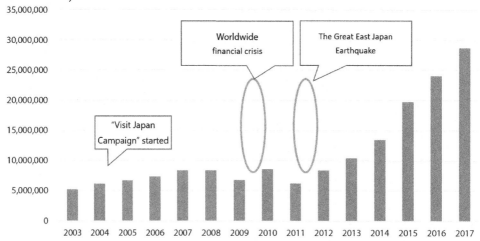

Figure 4.1: Changes in international tourist arrivals since the beginning of the 'Visit Japan' campaign. Source: JNTO, 2018b.

Tourism is difficult to develop in places that are perceived as danger-ous (Huang et al., 2008), because destination image plays a critical role in tourists' decision-making process and destination selection (Rittichainuwat, 2011). It is unlikely that tourists will visit places they believe are unsafe. Destination image is defined as "the perception of a person or a group of people regarding a place" (Baloglu et al., 2014: 1058), and it is formed by an individual's beliefs, ideas and general impressions about a given destination (Crompton, 1979; Baloglu et al., 2014). Destination image can be negatively affected by the mass media's exaggerated news reports after a disaster, which often furthers the belief that the entire destination has been damaged (Henderson, 1999; Huang and Min, 2002; Rittichainuwat, 2011). Japan, especially the Miyagi, Iwate and Fukushima prefectures, which were severely affected by the Great East Japan Earthquake, suffered because of the perception that the country was at a high risk of natural disasters and because of rumours regarding uncontrolled nuclear accidents. However, seven years after the annus horribilis, the tourism industry in Japan has completely rebounded, and local tourism—even in the disaster areas—has been greatly restored after the recent catastrophe.

Using data from white papers published by the Japan Tourism Agency (JTA) and from official websites, this chapter describes the Japanese government's efforts to effect image and reputation recovery in the tourism industry, as well as the reconstruction of Tohoku after the Great East Japan Earthquake. In contrast with efforts in response to other disasters and crises in the world—for example, the outbreak of hand-foot-and-mouth disease in southwest England, the September 11 terror attacks in New York City, the Sumatra-Andaman earthquake in the Indian Ocean and the Wenchuan earthquake in southwest China)—the Japanese government aimed to develop its own 'road' to reconstructing the tourism market (JTA, 2012a). In Japan, the relationship between 'tourism' and 'reconstruction' is inseparable, because tourism, to some extent, is believed one of the more effective methods of reconstruction (JTA, 2012a). This chapter first reviews the key strategies employed in the tourism market to attract both domestic and international tourists after the earthquake, and it then discusses Japanese-style tourism recovery with a specific focus on the relationship between tourism and reconstruction. Lastly, the chapter considers the implications of Japan's strategies for image and reputation recovery after the Great East Japan Earthquake.

Background: Sequence of events of the earthquake in Japan

The Great East Japan Earthquake occurred at 14:46 Japan Standard Time (JST) on 11 March 2011. The earthquake triggered giant tsunami waves and caused extensive and severe structural damage in northeastern Japan. The magnitude 9.0 earthquake and powerful tsunami resulted in the deaths of 15,894 people, while 6152 people were injured and 2558 people were listed as missing (Reconstruction Agency, nd). Moreover, the tsunami also caused nuclear accidents, primarily the level-seven meltdowns at the three reactors of the Fukushima Daiichi nuclear power plant. The total economic loss was estimated at over 16 trillion Japanese yen (approximately USD 160 billion) (Cabinet Office, 2011). The earthquake and the subsequent harmful rumours devastated the tourism industry in Japan, especially in the Tohoku area, including Miyagi Prefecture, Iwate Prefecture and Fukushima Prefecture (see Figure 4.2).

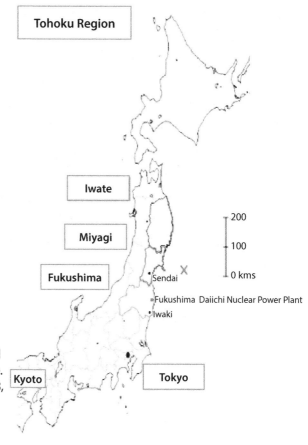

Figure 4.2: The areas most affected by the Great East Japan Earthquake. Source: Reconstruction Japan, 2018, http://www.reconstruction.go.jp/english/topics/GEJE, used with permission.

Impacts on the tourism industry

The earthquake greatly depressed the tourism industry, which experienced a harsh winter one year after the disaster. It was reported that in 2011, the total number of international tourists dropped to 72.2%, and the number of domestic tourists dropped to 95.9% compared with the previous year (JTA, 2012a). In the period soon after the earthquake, it was reported that the total number of international tourists declined by 51.3%, and the number of domestic tourists declined by 26.8% compared with the same period in the previous year. This negative impact on the tourism industry can be explained by two main causes. First, the nation voluntarily refrained from promoting tourism after the earthquake. Many businesses pulled their advertisements from TV, and because of the catastrophe, entertainment TV programmes were not shown. This action effectively stopped domestic tourism, as people believed it was not good to travel right after the national disaster. Second, exaggerated news reports, media sensationalism and misinformation about nuclear accidents painted Japan as a dangerous country in which to travel. As Frisby (2002) pointed out, mass media try to find a story that captures public interest, which results in sensationalism. This sensationalism greatly hurt the image of Japan as a tourism destination, and the rumours engendered by the earthquake and tsunami may be considered secondary damage of the disaster.

A journey towards reviving the tourism industry

4

To revive the tourism industry, the Japanese government implemented actively and promptly various policies immediately after the Great East Japan Earthquake, planning several steps for short- and long-term strategies. The basic objective of the strategies and efforts was to:

> First get the number of tourists in the Tohoku region and nationwide back to pre-disaster level, then continue to keep the number above that level and finally create an affordable and enjoyable traveling environment for sustainable development in the future. (JTA, 2012a: 27)

However, it was a long journey to recover from the secondary damage of the disaster. In this situation, the Japanese government made efforts to revive the tourism industry through various campaigns, tourism products and other related activities in both the domestic and international tourism markets. Promoting tourism was believed to be one of the more effective methods of reconstructing the disaster area in both the short and long terms.

Domestic tourism market recovery

The main cause of depression in the domestic tourism market was not the destruction of infrastructure and transportation. Except in some of the severe disaster areas, the transportation system (including roads, railways, airports and sea routes) was restored quickly after the earthquake (JTA, 2012a). However, as mentioned above, the voluntary national cessation of tourism promotion prevented the resumption of tourism and intentions to travel. To revive the domestic tourism market and end the voluntary embargo, JTA stated that efforts to promote tourism were also a type of reconstruction and encouraged related organisations, including local governments, travel agencies and so on, to cooperate on tourism-promotion activities.

The first campaign

The first official campaign, the Domestic Travel Reviving Campaign, was started in April 2011, less than one month after the earthquake. This campaign was conducted in the public and private sectors, and it aimed to end the voluntary embargo and address the harmful rumours caused by the earthquake and nuclear accidents, with the hope of stimulating demand for domestic tourism. It encouraged people to travel not only to the affected areas but also nationwide. A standard logo, *Ganbaro, Nippon!* (Try our best, Japan!), was used in various media, such as posters, newspapers, journals and the like, to disseminate information about recovery from the disaster. As such, the Domestic Travel Reviving Campaign created many opportunities in the domestic tourism market, including attractive tourism commodities that greatly stimulated tourism demand in Japan (JTA, 2012a).

New tourism-product creation: Tohoku Tourist Expo

Because the Tohoku region especially suffered a sharp decline in tourism, the public and private sectors conducted a campaign from March 2012 to March 2013 dubbed the 'Tohoku Tourist Expo', promoting the entire Tohoku region as an expo venue. This campaign promoted exchanges between local residents and tourists that represented a new tourism style at the time. In this campaign, the Tohoku region was divided into 28 major areas that were considered core tourism zones. Local residents served as tour guides to show visitors their hometown attractions, and travel salons were set up where such guides welcomed tourists. Moreover, 'Tohoku passports' were created to encourage encounters and exchanges between local residents and tourists, to whom the passport offered various discounts. Tourists could also use the passport to collect a series of stamps at tourist spots. To support this campaign, a portal website was set up to provide integrated tourist information (JTA, 2012a). The framework of the Tohoku Tourist Expo is shown in Figure 4.3. This campaign operated for 13 months and brought 84 billion yen (approximately USD 768 million) of economic gains to the Tohoku region. In total, 25.7 million tourists visited Tohoku, an increase of 3.1 million visitors compared with the same period in the previous year (JTA, 2013a).

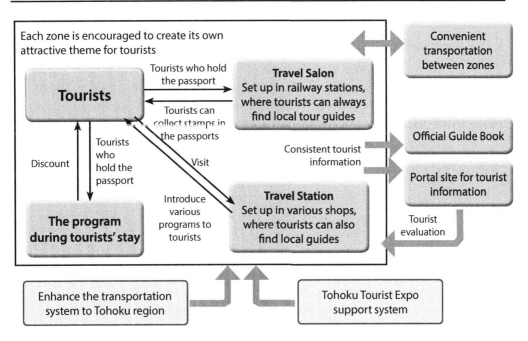

Figure 4.3: The framework of the Tohoku Tourist Expo. Source: JTA, 2012a: 22, translated and modified by the author.

Green Reconstruction Project

To attract more visitors to Tohoku, dispel harmful rumours and revive tourism in the area, the Ministry of the Environment created a project called the 'Michinoku Coastal Trail' (http://tohoku.env.go.jp/mct/english/), a 700-km walking trail following the Pacific coast from Hachinohe City in Aomori Prefecture to Soma City in Fukushima Prefecture. The construction of this project began in 2013, and the official opening of the full trail is scheduled for the end of March 2019. Michinoku is the ancient name of the Tohoku area, and it is still familiar as a nickname. This trail winds through a number of national parks in Tohoku, aiming to attract tourists with its breath-taking views of the Pacific, beautiful coastline scenery and other natural wonders. The trail is divided into 22 sections corresponding to Tohoku regions, with various walking distances and diverse themes to attract hikers. Tourists can select the section they want to visit or choose a model course recommended on Michinoku's official homepage. All of the sections and model courses include detailed information, including trail guides, appealing tourist spots, maps and useful information to promote Tohoku's natural beauty and attractions to tourists (JTA, 2014a, 2015a).

Accurate information provision

The Reconstruction Agency (RA) opened its official Facebook page (www.facebook.com/Fukkocho.JAPAN/) on 11 November 2016 to introduce the recovery process and the various efforts for Tohoku's reconstruction. The use of social media may be considered an innovation compared to the traditional promotional strategy of the government, because the Facebook page was used not only to introduce government policies, but also to highlight the attractiveness of local areas and promote reconstruction-related events and efforts in both the public and private sectors. Moreover, the various RA teams used their true names rather than the agency's name in all posts on the page, which served to make the Facebook page more accountable and approachable. Posts fall into seven main topics, including business, events, tourism, disaster victim assistance, contest information, employment and newsletters. The page has 41,786 followers (as of 5 May 2018), the average number of readers for each post is 5000 and the average number of 'likes' for each post is 700. Visitors to the Facebook page can discover many new things about Tohoku while reading posts that deliver an accurate account of the 'true current Tohoku', helping the area to recover from its negative image and reputation. There is no panacea for the recovery of an area's image and reputation, but efforts such as RA's Facebook page, which provides accurate information about earthquake-affected areas, seem effective in reconstruction.

Inbound tourism market recovery

The sharp decline in the number of international tourists after the Great East Japan Earthquake was attributed to rumours about the nuclear accidents at the Fukushima Daiichi nuclear power plant and to the fear of earthquakes and tsunamis. Exaggerated news reports, Internet-based information about the disaster and bulletins issued by other countries urging their citizens to refrain from traveling to Japan depressed the inbound tourism market. To revive the market and relieve international tourists' anxiety, the Japanese government issued accurate information to foreign countries, launched various campaigns, engaged in numerous projects and appealed to the governments of major countries. Those immediate and subsequent efforts revived Japan's inbound market, which welcomed 8.37 million international tourists in 2012, an increase of 34.6% from the previous year.

Accurate information to foreign countries

In addition to providing a domestic transportation operation status and radiation-level information, the Japan National Tourism Organisation (JNTO) created videos in various languages to show that life was ongoing in Japan and to send the message that things had returned to normal after the earthquake and reconstruction. Information about the process of recovery and the status of reconstruction was difficult to find overseas, so these videos, by providing accurate information, reduced international tourists' anxiety about traveling to Japan. Relieving their uncertainties seemed the most critical task.

Moreover, Hiroshi Mizohata, the commissioner of JTA in 2011, officially visited the commissioner of China's National Tourism Administration on 10–11 April 2011 and the commissioner of the Ministry of Culture, Sports and Tourism of South Korea on 22–23 April 2011 to convey accurate information about the nuclear accidents and promote travel to Japan.

At the same time, JNTO published the results of monitoring research that compared radiation levels in the main cities of Japan (including Tokyo, Osaka, Nagoya, Sendai, Sapporo, Fukuoka and others) to the radiation levels of other prominent cities in the world (for example, New York City, Paris, Berlin, Beijing and Seoul). Additionally, JNTO published live radioactivity monitoring figures for the main areas of Fukushima Prefecture, where the nuclear accidents occurred. These data reflected real daily life in Japan and made it possible to evaluate from an objective perspective the situation after the disaster.

Furthermore, from April 2011 to March 2012, the Japanese government conducted more than 100 overseas information sessions for local media, travel agencies and public organisations to disseminate accurate information about post-disaster Japan. The government also invited about 1000 representatives from approximately 800 foreign travel agencies to Japan for inspections. These efforts were made to correct misinformation about travel to Japan, to encourage accurate coverage of the situation in Japan and to promote the creation and sale of Japanese tourism products.

In addition to fear and misinformation about radiation, the other big barrier to inbound tourism were provisions enacted by foreign governments concerning travel to Japan. To counter these measures, the Japanese government asked the governments of the main source countries of inbound tourism to revise their policies based on objective scientific information. As a result, such measures regarding tourism to Japan were sequentially relaxed (JTA, 2012a).

Main campaigns

The 'Visit Japan' campaign was launched in 2003 with the aim of attracting more tourists from international regions and promoting the inbound tourism market in Japan. To attract international tourists back to Japan after the disaster and promote the inbound market, Visit Japan launched a half-year-long (September 2011–March 2012) campaign called 'Visit Japan Omotenashi'. *Omotenashi* means 'Japanese hospitality' and derives from the Japanese *sado* (tea ceremony). In this campaign, 4432 tourism-related facilities supported the Omotenashi system, and 330,000 'Visit Japan' cards (coupons that could be used in retail establishments, restaurants, lodging facilities and the tourism sector) were distributed to international visitors. Moreover, a custom smartphone application was developed to help international tourists search for a variety of special information during their stay in Japan. The campaign began in September 2011, half a year after the earthquake. Safety information and the latest travel information were updated on the campaign website in eight languages, including English, simplified Chinese, traditional Chinese, French, German, Russian and Thai.

In February 2012, just one year after the earthquake, JTA and JNTO cooperated with other organisations in the public and private sectors to conduct the 'Japan. Thank You' campaign with the purpose of expressing Japan's gratitude to the world for its support after the disaster. During this campaign, the traditional tourism campaign message of 'Japan. Endless Discovery' was replaced by a special logo, 'Japan. Thank You', which appeared in international airports, on shopping-street banners and on buses, taxis and hotel flags in the main cities of Japan, as well as in New York City. Additionally, a special poster with the message 'Japan, Rising Again' was created to accompany the 'Japan. Thank You' campaign. Its message, 'Gateway to Success' (which comes from the proverb 'Toryumon,' about a carp that swam up a waterfall and became a dragon), was intended to convey the spirit of overcoming any difficulties. Various activities supported this campaign. For example, on 21 February 2012, the government and Mitsubishi Estate launched a 'Thank You, Senbazuru' campaign in Marunouchi, Tokyo, which encouraged people near Marunouchi to fold paper cranes. The finished cranes were given as gifts to international tourists who visited the JNTO tourist information centre beginning 11 March 2012. Tourists who showed the paper cranes at a Marunouchi café from 11 March to 6 April 2012 were given a free cup of coffee (JTA, 2012a).

From 1 September 2012 to 15 February 2013, JTA conducted the 'Share Your WOW! Japan Photo Contest' using a social networking service (SNS). The campaign encouraged international tourists to post photos taken during their visit to Japan on the campaign's official website. The website linked with the campaign's Facebook page and Sina Weibo (a popular Chinese SNS), making it possible to share the photos with friends via SNSs. The campaign aimed to show daily life in Japan and promote safety, recovery, as well as the charm of Japan through electronic word of mouth (e-WOM). In total, 17,070 international tourists from over 100 countries and regions took part in the campaign, posting 38,817 photos. The campaign's Facebook page had about 250,000 followers. The photo contest included six themes, headed 'Cool!', 'Delicious!', 'Happy!', 'Beautiful!', 'Funny!' and 'Miracle!', and one image in each theme was selected by JTA as the best photo (JTA, 2013b).

Creation of new tourism product

Since the depression of the inbound tourism market following the Great East Japan Earthquake, the total number of international tourists has rebounded, and the over 10 million international tourists recorded in 2013 represented an increase in the number recorded before the disaster (JNTO, 2018b). However, although the figures for the Tohoku region, especially the three most severely affected prefectures (Miyagi, Iwate and Fukushima), have shown signs of recovery since 2012, these figures still lag well behind the numbers of the nationwide inbound tourism boom.

To attract international tourists to the Tohoku region, the Japanese government created a Tohoku tourism product by highlighting that tourists could enjoy the cherry blossoms (*sakura*) and snow, at the same time as the World Conference on Disaster Risk Reduction being held at Sendai in March 2015. This tourism product was dubbed the 'Corridor of Sakura and Snow', and it featured four recommended travel courses. Its main targets were tourists from Southeast Asia, where there is no snow. To promote this product, media companies from Southeast Asia and bloggers from Hong Kong were invited to join the tour and provide information about the beautiful natural resources, as well as the cultural experiences of Tohoku (JTA, 2016a).

Another tourism product, 'Explore to the Deep North of Japan', proposed by the Tohoku Tourism Promotion Organisation (TTPO), has also attracted numerous international tourists since June 2015. This product's website shows Tohoku's areas through various lenses, such as famous tourist spots, world heritage sites in Tohoku and things to do or attractions to visit in different seasons. The website suggests six model tours, including Seasonal Highlights of the Tohoku Region, Scenic Beauty of the Japan Sea Shoreline and others. Tourists can also design their own trip using the 'Deep North of Japan Concierge'. Visitors easily design their travel plan by adding places that they would like to see, after which the system automatically provides the most efficient itinerary for visiting the places, including routes and time required, in a tailored day plan. TTPO conducted marketing research in the target markets of Taiwan, Hong Kong, China, ASEAN countries, Europe, North America and Australia. In addition to providing various languages on the 'Explore the Deep North of Japan' website, TTPO works to improve the tourist environment in local areas.

Lessons learned from the tourism recovery after the Great East Japan Earthquake

As mentioned above, the entire tourism industry in Japan was sharply depressed by the Great East Japan Earthquake and the rumours surrounding the nuclear accidents in 2011. The tourism industry had a difficult recovery in the year immediately following the catastrophe, even though the infrastructure quickly returned to normal. The two main causes of this depression were the voluntary embargo on tourism promotion and anxieties about the safety of traveling to Japan, especially the Tohoku region, which was severely affected by the earthquake. After identifying the problems that prevented the recovery of tourism in both the domestic and inbound markets, the Japanese government implemented promptly various recovery strategies, including both traditional approaches and Japanese-style recovery strategies that were innovative in the literature of tourism disaster and crisis recovery. The entire tourism industry rebounded in 2012, and the number of international tourists in 2013 exceeded the number recorded from the year before the disaster in the inbound tourism market. Although the inbound tourism market's growth rate in the Tohoku region was relatively low compared to the nationwide rate, significant recovery was still evident (see Figure 4.4). The speed of tourism crisis and disaster recovery is considered below.

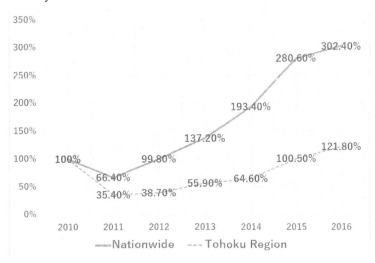

Figure 4.4:. Total number of guest nights of foreign visitors at tourist-oriented accommodations
Note 1: Change in index with numbers for 2010 represented as 100.
Note 2: All data were calculated by the author based on Lodging and travel statistical research: International tourists for tourism only.
Source: JTA, 2010, 2011, 2012b, 2013c, 2014b, 2015b, 2016b.

Year	Nationwide	Tohoku Region
2010	13,582,880 (100%)	305,570 (100%)
2011	9,022,620 (66.40%)	108,220 (35.40%)
2012	13,553,940 (99.80%)	118,310 (38.70%)
2013	18,636,550 (137.20%)	170,800 (55.90%)
2014	26,268,970 (193.40%)	197,420 (64.60%)
2015	38,118,400 (280.60%)	307,060 (100.50%)
2016	41,070,390 (302.40%)	372,290 (121.80%)

The first important lesson of the recovery from the Great East Japan Earthquake is the necessity to control and dispatch accurate information immediately after the disaster. Tourists shape a destination image in their mind through the synthesis and analysis of information combined over a period (Lehto et al., 2008), and they make travel decisions based on the destination image formed in their mind (Echtner and Ritchie, 1991; Santana, 2003). Tourists only visit places they believe are safe (Huang et al., 2008). However, after an unexpected and unavoidable disaster, chaos brings misinformation that sometimes exaggerates and distorts the real situation of the disaster (Rittichainuwat, 2011). As numerous previous studies have shown (for example, Ritchie et al., 2004; Huang and Min, 2002; Rittichainuwat, 2011), providing correct and consistent information about the destination to the public is a critical task in the initial period after the disaster.

Japan's prompt responses after the earthquake—the video in various languages describing the nation's recovery, the official visit of the JTA commissioner to China and South Korea, the publishing of monitoring research comparing radiation levels in Japan to those of various cities in the world, the more than 100 information sessions conducted overseas and efforts to relax provisions established by foreign governments concerning travel to Japan—seem to have controlled effectively the spread of misinformation and conveyed a positive image of a return to normalcy. Moreover, these quick responses to the negative impact on the tourism industry greatly minimised the secondary damage brought about by rumours.

The consequences of the Great East Japan Earthquake, including the reconstruction of infrastructure, have been longer lasting than those of other major natural disasters (for example, the Sumatra-Andaman earthquake in the Indian Ocean or the Wenchuan earthquake in China) because past earthquakes and tsunamis did not result in radiation problems. Even now, some areas in Tohoku still suffer from rumours about radiation. Thus, the reconstruction of image (the software aspect) seems to require more time than the reconstruction of infrastructure (the hardware aspect). In this case, as a number of researchers have pointed out, the continual publication of correct information and deepening the understanding of the reconstruction process are effective methods (Faulkner, 2001; Huang and Min, 2002; Carlsen and Hughes, 2008; Rittichainuwat, 2011). For this purpose, JTA launched its official Facebook page to publish, in signed posts, the progress of Tohoku's reconstruction. Building a strong relationship and trust between the public and private sectors was also essential to Tohoku's reconstruction.

Second, numerous campaigns enhanced effectively the image of Japan and Tohoku, and they played a significant role in accelerating recovery after the earthquake. Such campaigns are believed to be among the more efficient ways of facilitating image and reputation recovery (Ritchie, 2004; Rittichainuwat, 2011; Yang et al., 2011; Walters and Mair, 2012), especially in foreign markets (Frisby, 2002). Detailed communication strategies and marketing communication plans are required to identify the audience, develop goals and create impressive and positive messages (Walters and Mair, 2012; Tham et al., 2013), such as the strong message 'Ganbaro! Nippon' in the Domestic Travel Reviving Campaign and 'Japan, Rising Again', used in the Japan. Thank You campaign.

The most innovative campaign involved tourist-led marketing communication. In Japan, the commodification of SNS started in 2011, and it was a still a new tool of marketing communication at the time. Facebook, a representative social media platform, was employed in the 'Share Your Wow! Japan Photo Contest', a campaign launched by JAT but expanded by tourists themselves. Instead of promoting the attractiveness of Japan through the Japanese government and Japanese travel agencies, JAT encouraged international tourists to find things that evoked a 'Wow' from them. This campaign transformed traditional marketing communication by pioneering a new kind of tourist-led marketing communication, intelligently utilising social media to expand the 'Wow' of Japan through tourists themselves.

Lastly, the case of the Great East Japan Earthquake has shown that creating new tourism products to enhance local tourism is an efficient method of reviving the industry. According to a JTA white paper published in 2012, the disaster should be seen as a trigger of the better understanding and development of Tohoku's attractions. To increase tourism demand in Tohoku, especially in the earthquake-affected areas, it was necessary to practice various methods. In this regard, the close relationship between tourism and reconstruction is highlighted. In past decades, it was widely believed that destinations must be completely recovered before it would be possible to attract tourists again, but in recent years, tourism is more likely to be treated as one of the more efficient methods of reconstruction. This is because not only can tourism bring many economic benefits, including employment and tax income, but it can also add a vibrancy that helps disaster-affected places to restore themselves. As the JTA stated:

> The Great East Japan Earthquake was an unfortunate event; however, if all of us have the common goal of 'Reconstruction' and strongly work together, we can find the new charms of local places and create new tourism resources that bring new opportunities (JTA, 2012a: 27).

New tourism products produced by the public and private sectors assist in reconstruction by reviving the local tourism industry. The 'Michinoku Coastal Trail' and 'Explore the Deep North of Japan' are good examples. Both brands attracted not only domestic tourists but also international tourists. The understanding of tourism product brands is low compared to the branding of products in the manufacturing market. If we suppose that a destination is something like a company and the recommended tours are the company's products, then it follows that awareness of the company can be increased by building strong brands. The 'Michinoku Coastal Trail' and 'Explore the Deep North of Japan' are the two tourism product brands of Tohoku. The marketing principles of product branding can also be practiced in the tourism industry, especially in image and reputation recovery.

Recommendations for practice

- The lessons of reputation and image recovery from the Great East Japan Earthquake show the importance of disseminating accurate information, launching various campaigns and creating new tourism products. Providing accurate information and launching campaigns are vital actions immediately after a disaster and are believed the more effective short-term strategies, while creating new tourism products that support the sustainable development of disaster-affected areas is more important in the long term.

- Publishing accurate information decreases tourists' perceptions of risk and counters the misinformation and rumours that destroy the destination's image and cause the secondary damage from the natural disaster, while various campaigns stimulate short-term demand in the tourism market after a disaster. Such campaigns as the 'Share Your Wow! Japan Photo Contest' pioneered a new method of tourist-led marketing communication by encouraging tourists to share their own experiences during their travel in Japan. Compared to traditional campaigns led by the public sector, the use of SNS suggests a new business model for restoring the destination image. This tourist-led campaign provided a good example of the power of SNS and e-WOM. With the development of social media, the tourism industry entered a new era called 'Tourism 2.0' (Parra-López et al., 2011), in which tourists use social media to search for information related to their travel and tend to be more influenced by information from SNSs. Indeed, information provided by tourists seems more reliable (Parra-López et al., 2011). Thus, both the public and private sectors should understand the role that social media plays in image and reputation recovery and know how to promote tourist-led marketing communication.

■ Creating various new and attractive tourism products seems essential to long-term recovery. The disaster of the Great East Japan Earthquake was characterised not only by damage from the earthquake and tsunami but also by the nuclear accidents, which prolonged the recovery process. The tourism products introduced in this case (for example, 'Explore the Deep North of Japan') are known as *chakuchi*-type regional tourism products, and they are mainly proposed and conducted by local organisations, such as the Destination Management Organisation (DMO), rather than by nationwide travel agencies. New products stimulate demand in the tourism markets of disaster-affected areas and play a critical role in reconstruction. The examples of tourism products introduced in this case suggest that building a tourism product brand can attract tourists successfully and change the negative image brought about by disasters. Moreover, through building new tourism products, many new charms and attractions can be discovered.

The Great East Japan Earthquake is a distressing page in Japanese history that will never be forgotten. Even though infrastructure quickly recovered after the disaster (except in some areas severely affected by the earthquake), the rumours and negative image of Tohoku persisted for a long time. However, countless efforts have been made in tourism destination recovery, which led to new business models and increased expertise. Although the image and reputation recovery from the Great East Japan Earthquake was a long journey, these new business models and the knowledge created in the tourism industry after the catastrophe brought great hope to Japan.

References

Baloglu, S., Henthorne, T. L. & Sahin, S. (2014) Destination image and brand personality of Jamaica: A model of tourist behavior, *Journal of Travel & Tourism Marketing*, **31** (8), 1057-1070.

Cabinet Office, Government of Japan (2011) Higashinihondaishinsai ni okeru higaigaku no suitei ni tsuite, 2011 (Estimation of the amount of damage of the Great East Japan Earthquake, 2011) [Press release]. http://www.bousai.go.jp/2011daishinsai/pdf/110624-1kisya.pdf (Accessed: 14 May 2018).

Carlsen, J. C. & Hughes, M. (2008) Tourism market recovery in the Maldives after the 2004 Indian Ocean tsunami, *Journal of Travel & Tourism Marketing*, **23** (2-4), 139-149.

Cassedy, K. (1992) Preparedness in the face of crisis: An examination of crisis management planning in the trav el and tourism industry, *World Travel and Tourism Review*, **2**, 169-174.

Crompton, I. (1979) Motivations for pleasure vacation, *Annals of Tourism Research*, **6**, 408-424.

Echtner, C. & Ritchie, J. R. B. (1991) The meaning and measurement of destination image, *Journal of Tourism Studies*, **2** (2), 2-12.

Faulkner, B. (2001) Towards a framework for tourism disaster management, *Tourism Management*, **22** (2), 135-147.

Frisby, E. (2002) Communicating in a crisis: The British tourist authority's responses to the foot-and-mouth outbreak and 11th September, 2001, *Journal of Vacation Marketing*, **9** (1), 89-100.

Henderson, J. C. (1999) Managing the Asian financial crisis: Tourist attractions in Singapore, *Journal of Travel Research*, **38**, 177-181.

Huang, J. H. & Min, J. C. H. (2002) Earthquake devastation and recovery in tourism: The Taiwan case, *Tourism Management*, **23**, 145-154.

Huang, Y.-C., Tseng, Y.-P. & Petrick, J. F. (2008) Crisis management planning to restore tourism after disasters, *Journal of Travel & Tourism Marketing*, **23** (2-4), 203-221.

JNTO (Japan National Tourism Organisation) (2018a) Heisei 30 nen honichi gaikyakusu syukkoku nihonjinsu (2018 visitor arrivals and Japanese overseas travellers) [Press release]. https://www.jnto.go.jp/jpn/statistics/data_info_listing/pdf/180418_monthly.pdf (Accessed: 14 May 2018).

JNTO (2018b) Kokuseki/tsukibetsu honichi gaikyakusu, 2003–2018 (Nationality/month of the number of international tourists to Japan, 2003–2018) [Press release]. https://www.jnto.go.jp/jpn/statistics/visitor_trends/index.html (Accessed: 14 May 2018).

JTA (Japan Tourism Agency) (2010) Shukuhaku ryoko tokei chosa, Heisei 22 nen 1gatsu–12 gatsu bun, nen no kakuteichi (Confirmed data of lodging and travel statistical research, January to December 2010). www.mlit.go.jp/kankocho/siryou/toukei/shukuhakutoukei.html (Accessed: 26 May 2018).

JTA (2011) Shukuhaku ryoko tokei chosa, Heisei 23 nen 1gatsu–12 gatsu bun, nen no kakuteichi (Confirmed data of lodging and travel statistical research, January to December 2011). http://www.mlit.go.jp/kankocho/siryou/toukei/shukuhakutoukei.html (Accessed: 26 May 2018).

JTA (2012a) Heisei 24 nen ban kanko hakusyo (White paper on tourism in Japan, 2012). Tokyo: Nikkei insatsu kabushikigaisha.

JTA (2012b) Shukuhaku ryoko tokei chosa, Heisei 24 nen 1gatsu–12 gatsu bun, nen no kakuteichi (Confirmed data of lodging and travel statistical research, January to December 2012). http://www.mlit.go.jp/kankocho/siryou/toukei/shukuhakutoukei.html (Accessed: 26 May 2018).

JTA (2013a) Heisei 25 nen ban kanko hakusyo (White paper on tourism in Japan, 2013). Tokyo: Showa jyoho purosesu kabushikigaisha.

JTA (2013b) Honichi sokushin SNS kyanpen 'Share Your WOW! Japan Photo Contest' no jushosha kettei (The winners of the 'Visit Japan SNS' campaign 'Share Your WOW! Japan Photo Contest') [Press release]. http://www.mlit. go.jp/kankocho/news08_000164.html (Accessed: 14 May 2018).

JTA (2013c) Shukuhaku ryoko tokei chosa, Heisei 25 nen 1gatsu–12 gatsu bun, nen no kakuteichi (Confirmed data of lodging and travel statistical research, January to December 2013). http://www.mlit.go.jp/kankocho/siryou/toukei/ shukuhakutoukei.html (Accessed: 26 May 2018).

JTA (2014a) Heisei 26 nen ban kanko hakusyo (White paper on tourism in Japan, 2014). Tokyo: Showa jyoho purosesu kabushikigaisha.

JTA (2014b) Shukuhaku ryoko tokei chosa, Heisei 26 nen 1gatsu–12 gatsu bun, nen no kakuteichi (Confirmed data of lodging and travel statistical research, January to December 2014). http://www.mlit.go.jp/kankocho/siryou/toukei/ shukuhakutoukei.html (Accessed: 26 May 2018).

JTA (2015a) Heisei 27 nen ban kanko hakusyo (White paper on tourism in Japan, 2015). Tokyo: Nikkei insatsu kabushikigaisha.

JTA (2015b) Shukuhaku ryoko tokei chosa, Heisei 27 nen 1gatsu–12 gatsu bun, nen no kakuteichi (Confirmed data of lodging and travel statistical research, January to December 2015). http://www.mlit.go.jp/kankocho/siryou/toukei/ shukuhakutoukei.html (Accessed: 26 May 2018).

JTA (2016a) Heisei 28 nen ban kanko hakusyo (White paper on tourism in Japan, 2016). Tokyo: Showa jyoho purosesu kabushikigaisha.

JTA (2016b) Shukuhaku ryoko tokei chosa, Heisei 28 nen 1gatsu–12 gatsu bun, nen no kakuteichi (Confirmed data of lodging and travel statistical research, January to December 2016). http://www.mlit.go.jp/kankocho/siryou/toukei/ shukuhakutoukei.html (Accessed: 26 May 2018).

JTA (2017) Keizai hakyu koka (The economic impact). http://www.mlit.go.jp/ kankocho/siryou/toukei/kouka.html (Accessed: 14 May 2018).

Lehto, X., Douglas, A. C. & Park, J. (2008) Mediating the effects of natural disasters on travel intention, *Journal of Travel & Tourism Marketing*, **23** (2-4), 29-43.

Parra-López, E., Bulchand-Gidumal, J., Gutiérrez-Taño, D. & Díaz-Armas, R. (2011) Intentions to use social media in organizing and taking vacation trips, *Computers in Human Behavior*, **27** (2), 640-654.

Reconstruction Agency (nd) Great East Japan Earthquake. http://www. reconstruction.go.jp/english/topics/GEJE/index.html (Accessed: 14 May 2018).

Ritchie, B. W. (2004) Chaos, crises and disasters: A strategic approach to crisis management in the tourism industry, *Tourism Management*, **25** (6), 669-683.

Ritchie, B. W., Dorrell, H., Miller, D. & Miller, G. A. (2004) Crisis communication and recovery for the tourism industry, *Journal of Travel & Tourism Marketing*, **15** (2-3), 199-216.

Rittichainuwat, B. (2011) Ghosts, *Annals of Tourism Research*, **38** (2), 437-459.

Santana, G. (2003) Crisis management and tourism: Beyond the rhetoric, *Journal of Travel & Tourism Marketing*, **15** (4), 299-321.

Tham, A., Croy, G. & Mair, J. (2013) Social media in destination choice: Distinctive electronic word-of-mouth dimensions, *Journal of Travel & Tourism Marketing*, **30** (1-2), 144-155.

Walters, G. & Mair, J. (2012) The effectiveness of post-disaster recovery marketing messages: The case of the 2009 Australian bushfires, *Journal of Travel & Tourism Marketing*, **29** (1), 87-103.

Yang, W., Wang, D. & Chen, G. (2011) Reconstruction strategies after the Wenchuan earthquake in Sichuan, China, *Tourism Management*, **32** (4), 949-956.

5   Hope for Haiti: How media narratives can transform a destination in despair

Nicholas Wise

Introduction

Haiti has been beset by a series of natural disasters over the past decade, notably the 2010 7.0 magnitude Haiti Earthquake and Hurricane Matthew in 2016, which caused catastrophic flooding. However, in addition to the natural disasters, Haiti is the poorest economy in the western hemisphere and has a history of politically turbulent events, each of which have contributed to despair and a negative destination image (Séraphin, 2018; Séraphin et al., 2017). This is a troubling combination for a tourist destination. Haiti, as a destination in the Caribbean, has a strategic advantage with its expansive coast and natural attractions, but the underdevelopment of tourism in Haiti is linked to shadows of natural disasters, economic dependence on foreign aid and political uncertainty (see Séraphin et al., 2017; Wise and Díaz-Garayúa, 2015). The power of nature has placed much media attention on Haiti, and it has gained much negative attention in recent years in the media, but the images of a 'beautiful destination' is now changing the narrative to a destination on the rise (Caribbean News Now, 2017a; The World Bank, 2018). However, tourism in a developing country comes with numerous obstacles, as extensive investments are needed to allow tourism to thrive in the increasingly competitive Caribbean market. This is where the media plays a crucial role in transforming how a destination is portrayed. This chapter will assess narratives sourced from newspaper travel articles published in 2017 to understand how presentations of tourism in Haiti are constructing a new image of the country as an emerging tourism destination—an attempt to overcome the range of negative connotations. However, while the chapter focuses on image recovery in relation to the recent natural disasters in Haiti, it must also be noted that Haiti is also a destination with longstanding image issues given the extent of poverty, violence and political corruption (Séraphin, 2018).

This chapter begins with a review of the literature on tourism and destination image. Then the method of data collection and analysis is presented to discuss the content assessed from the academic search engine *Nexis Uni*. The subsequent analysis section addresses the importance of qualitative content analysis and presents the case of Haiti as a destination in despair looking to transform and see its tourism image recover. The analysis is organized into three sections from the newspaper content: positive stories, stories of concern and stories of future development. The conclusion offers some recommendations going forward concerning challenges and potential for tourism in Haiti that may be relevant to other developing destinations.

Tourism and destination image

In October 2016, Hurricane Matthew devastated Haiti as the country unfortunately sat right in the path of the storm. In 2017, Hurricane Maria devastated Puerto Rico and Dominica, and these destinations are seeking ways to reinvigorate their tourism economies (Peltier, 2018). Natural disasters and hazards can leave destinations in a state of despair and this has attracted much attention in academic research on tourism (see, for example, Gotham, 2017; Guo et al., 2017; Khazai et al., 2018; Mika, 2018; Ritchie, 2009). Earthquakes and hurricanes have had a major impact on destinations across the Caribbean (Morakabati, 2017), and while many of these small islands are dependent on the tourism industry, it can take months and sometimes years for tourism to recover and restore this sector of the economy (see Guo et al., 2017). The economic situation is further impacted by destinations failing to reach their economic potential, especially when they need to promote deals and discount packages to bring back tourists to show all has been recovered. Moreover, whilst destinations spend a lot to recover, there is always an imminent threat that another disaster could happen in the future.

Various perspectives and/or models have been devised by scholars, and such studies are often concerned with identifying measures to managing the recovery process (e.g. Khazai et al., 2018; Okuyama, 2018; Tsai & Chen, 2011). However, while building materials can be used to reduce damage, it is a challenge to completely hold back the full threat of nature, especially when succumbing to major earthquakes and Category 5 hurricanes. In the context of tourism, disasters and hazards, there is also the need to address destination image. Much of the research into tourism and natural disasters is concerned with seeking solutions to mitigate long-term declines in order to restore destinations, and one area that requires more attention is to show how the media has helped to re-create a destination's image. Jiang and Ritchie (2017: 70) note that "past experience and relationships can influence the development of collaboration after a disaster". This is further complicated in destinations that are not financially or politically stable. Therefore, consistent, adequate and informative communication is not only necessary to engage and motivate stakeholders in the rebuilding process, but also needs to appeal to potential visitors.

Leading into a focus on image, Khazai et al. (2018: 75) acknowledge that after a disaster, tourism declines because tourists cancel reservations or seek alternative destinations, and "a key part of managing recovery of tourism destinations is restoring the destination image and reputation which can be affected by negative or inaccurate media coverage". Therefore, what is needed is an emphasis on safety, physical recovery and business recovery so that tourists are assured and informed (Khazai et al., 2018). Hennessey et al. (2010: 218-219) note, "given the ever-expanding number of tourism destinations and the increased supply of products and services, the competition for visitors is intense and bound to become more so in the future". Because of the increased competition, national tourism organizations are faced with increased pressures to present what is most unique about their country and its attractions to catch the attention of those planning future travel—but headlines of a natural disaster can greatly burden efforts.

In marketing a destination's image, the strategy is to highlight significant developments, attractions and tourism resources in a destination (Govers et al., 2007), which links with how we come to recognize a place (Baloglu & McCleary, 1999; Nelson, 2013; Wise & Mulec, 2015). Baloglu and McCleary (1999) assess how destination images are formed when people have not experienced a destination. This is related to the focus of this chapter, which is to show how images are forged through media content to tell a story of progress opposed to persistent decline. Wise and Mulec (2012) highlight that for a destination to be successful, tourists must have some general destination knowledge/awareness, which helps shape an expected image, and such insight may be positive or negative. Destination image is important to understand because this concept refers to how people perceive a place, and this will influence whether people will travel to a destination. Looking at destination image holistically, Beerli and Martín (2004) present nine dimensions pertinent to how destination images are perceived: natural resources, tourist leisure/recreation, natural environment, general infrastructure, culture/history/art, social environment, hotel/self-catering, political/economic factors and place atmosphere. Arguably, natural environments play a key role in the development of image perceptions (Kim & Perdue, 2011). National tourism organizations and managers also must consider psychological factors, split between personal (values, age, motivation) and stimulus (information sources, previous experiences) factors (Baloglu & McCleary, 1999). Stimulus factors can evoke cognitive memories—linked to the past associations people might have of a place—such as the images of destruction across Haiti after the earthquake and hurricane left havoc across the country. We read about stories of disaster, and these can persist as people remember the wrath of destruction caused by natural hazards. This said, destination images are also constructed (and re-created) through tourism textual narratives that describe or capture unique destination attributes and can be used to replace a negative association (see Wise, 2011; Wise et al., 2015; Wise & Mulec, 2012, 2015).

Method and content data

There has been recent literature acknowledging the role of the media as a powerful intermediary and how it shapes place and destination images post-disaster (e.g. Ali, 2013; Avraham, 2016; McQuail, 2010; Sharpley & Wright, 2018; Walters et al., 2016; Wise, 2011; Wise and Mulec, 2015). Media texts, whether print or online, are thus important sources of information that create, or re-create, a destination image and can produce a particular awareness (Lai & Vinh, 2013). According to Castelltort and Mäder (2010) media coverage has always been a concern among those involved in tourism management, marketing and destination planning (see also Muhoho-Minni & Lubbe, 2017; Wang et al., 2015; Wise, 2017). This is especially important in places such as Haiti that are recovering from natural disasters, because such disasters have resulted in a negative destination image.

For this chapter, newspaper articles that provide a full narrative based on travel journalistic reporting in Haiti were analyzed. *Nexis Uni* was used to extract archived full-text newspaper articles published in the English language from around the world. This search engine assists with analyzing a range of perspectives to look for trends in presentation, narration and representation across newspaper texts. Articles presented below were based on the search terms 'Haiti', then a search within results for 'tourism'. Only content from articles published in 2017 were used to collect the data – 2017 articles were selected because this year is mentioned as a transition year aimed at reviving Haiti's image (The New York Times, 2017), so it is important to assess if and how this is occurring. Articles were only included if they told the story of 'Haiti' and 'tourism', thus many articles were excluded from the review of data if they only had a brief mention of Haiti with no real depth in the development of a narrative of tourism in the country. From the search terms, *Nexis Uni* yielded 1,442 results, with 150 of these being newspaper sources. In all, 91 articles offered in-depth insight.

Journalists prepare travel articles using primary information providing personal or experiential insight from their own reflections, and/ or by bringing in perspectives from interviews in the field. Academics use media content analysis to conceptualize reactions and responses concerning past, present and future destination images, which ultimately influence consumer choice. The media can present an image of place through their communication (Muhoho-Minni & Lubbe, 2017), and analysis of textual content has been shown to be useful in tourism research (Wise & Mulec, 2015). According to Hammett (2014), images produced through the media can be a form of *place-scripting*. This is about creating imaginations of places so that the reader can imagine experiences based on the narrative, insight or journey presented (see Chatterji, 2016). Moreover, texts are sources of information, or what Baloglu and McCleary (1999) refer to as stimulus factors, that create (or re-create) awareness, discussed above. This chapter will consider how content and the wider narratives displayed in newspaper travel articles on Haiti present the destination following the recent natural disasters in 2010 and 2016 that devastated the country's tourism industry.

Transforming a destination in despair

The narratives from the newspaper content assessed in this study were grouped into three subsections: positive stories, stories of concern and stories of future development (as inductively derived from the content). Initial observations demonstrate how the content portrays positive images of Haiti, thus, it could be suggested that newspaper narratives help transform the image of the destination going forward. However, there are points of concern (and critique) as well, and prospective developments that are needed to ensure future sustainability. Haiti is a vulnerable destination that is susceptible to natural disasters, such as high-magnitude earthquakes and storms such as Hurricane Matthew in 2016. These are issues that also impact proximate island countries in the Greater and Lesser Antilles in the Caribbean that sit on geologic fault lines or hurricanes paths. The important thing is the media is reporting on Haiti and its progress to restore the destination to its tourism potential. Here, the media is an intermediary to clarify change, reporting on past problems affecting a destination and framing the current situation to display recovery and future developments. As noted, the media is powerful in helping to re-create perception initially; however only actual consumer experiences will assist with developing a new narrative of the destination, and more importantly a new image. As noted in The *New York Times* (2017): "it has been several generations since Haiti was a major tourist destination, but it may become one again. International hotel chains have arrived, and the number of flights to the country has increased substantially". The same article notes that several airlines are also transporting passengers to Haiti. Finally, Jean Cyril Pressoir (a travel operator and tour guide from Haiti), speaking to the *London Evening Standard* (2017), suggested that visitors come see and enjoy Haiti to make their own impression, stating: "if you ask, 'how can you help Haiti?', come as a tourist. Help us break from away from this pre-conceived idea, this prejudice that has us defined as a place where you come to help". Experience here is a key element, and encouraging travelers to visit Haiti and gain from their own personal experiences can help mitigate concern – and this can be used to help display a positive outlook of Haiti.

Positive stories

The media has the power to change and influence perceptions. Positive stories of Haiti give the destination hope as narratives display a destination in recovery (and with much potential). A unanimous thread across the articles was the emphasis on encouraging people to experience Haiti and see the destination for themselves. The travel journalists whose articles were used as data for this study positioned themselves in the destination as a way of presenting the good in what may sometimes seem challenging (as will be discussed further in the next section) in a country with a difficult past. Such stories offer a new narrative of their experience in the destination, which is a form of place-scripting.

In encouraging a positive outlook on Haiti, the *London Evening Standard* (2017) suggests to: "look beyond the rubble and find its rich history and natural beauty; beyond Haiti's turbulent recent history, outsiders are now discovering its natural beauty and rich culture". Adding further emphasis, the same article encourages potential visitors to ask, "Why come to Haiti? Because it is overwhelming. It's out of your comfort zone. Because it will shake you. That's why you should come" (speaking with Jean Cyril Pressoir) (London Evening Standard, 2017). By framing a more positive image and encouraging visitors to go to a relatively unknown place, the reference to the point that the destination will shake you refers to what people might not expect to explore and experience in Haiti. This also attempts to present Haiti as a diverse destination, beyond perceptions of sea, sand and sun. *Caribbean News Now* (2017a) discusses "the extraordinary tourism potential of Haiti's cultural calendar", outlining the impact of events across the island throughout the year, and *The Daily Telegraph* (2017) on cruising the Caribbean highlights "Royal Caribbean's private beach resort of Labadee in Haiti, likely to be the favourite port of call for families". Elements of heritage tourism are also discussed, with the *London Evening Standard* (2017) mentioning "You come because Haiti is unique" and "Haiti's culture is so rich", further adding:

> *The first and only nation in the world born of a slave revolt (in 1804), Haiti's African and European roots imprinted on its Creole culture in still living and breathing ways. Vodou – a fusion of African religions, Roman Catholicism and other influences, such as Freemasonry – is a vivid example. Widely practiced across Haiti, temples become easy to spot, while ornate sequin flags bearing symbols seem omnipresent.*

This narrative offers insight into local life, with positive insight portrayed as an attempt to highlight Haiti's potential. Travel journalists writing about a destination seeking to recover from a negative image, a tragic past, or seeking to rebuild its image, try to frame a clear picture of 'now', referring to the present time at writing so the discourse is altered in people's mind, and a new image emerges (see Wise & Mulec, 2012). Thus, positive stories are a way of explaining to the reader what has previously happened, so that readers are clear that the destination is recovering. Baloglu and McCleary (1999) refer to stimulus factors, that create (or re-create) an awareness of a destination, which is a psychological factor in image formation. *Travel Pulse* (2017) mentioned that Haiti was once a popular Caribbean destination (in decades past); nowadays, as an underexplored destination, this is helping arouse interest once again in the destination. Such insight was present in the articles, for example:

> *Haiti may be little discussed as a tourism destination today, but it wasn't always this way [...]. In the 1950s and 60s, Port-au-Prince's intoxicating mix of music, gingerbread architecture, and colourful art, inspired Hollywood greats, artists, and bohemians to flock here. Many of the capital's many great historic mansions remain earthquake bruised, but they're no less beautiful for it [...] In the South, you'll swim in pristine bright blue waterfalls like Bassin-Bleu, near arts capital Jacmel. Recent tourism investments have added bright mosaics to the streets. And tours are now returning to the hurricane hit south, injecting much needed cash into the ocean-front communities*
> (London Evening Standard, 2017).

The emphasis on then and now is clear, and the stories of what is happening showcase a destination attempting to overcome the impacts of natural disasters and build a reputation as a destination again. Another point of emphasis was that Haiti is not burdened by mass- or over-tourism like so many other Caribbean countries:

> *looking purely from a visitor's point of view, there is already much to lure travellers, especially those looking to experience that rarest of things; a non-commercialised destination. But being one of just a handful of tourists at each staggering place that you visit also serves to underline Haiti's huge tourism potential. The question is, where does it go from here?*
> (Independent, 2017).

Stories of concern

However, while there is much hope for Haiti going forward, we must still be critical of the overwhelmingly positive insight displayed, as there are still points of concern. While it was a series of natural hazards in 2016 that devastated Haiti, there are still lingering concerns relating to its political stability. An example of this is in the article from the *New York Times* (2017), which offers a narrative of Haiti under the headline: "tracing a paradise lost". Despite this positive positioning, points of concern around uncertainty are present in the travel stories presented by journalists; while Haiti is "ideal for tourism: perfect sand, warm water, and a massive, mysterious fort evoking pirates and buried treasure... Its future is uncertain". Haiti's political history is deeply contested and from a socio-economic standpoint, the country is the poorest country in the western hemisphere (Wise and Díaz-Garayúa, 2015). With political issues and an unstable socio-economic situation impacting the country's residents, travelers are warned of serious safety risks in the country (The New York Times, 2017). However, the travel media articles present stories of residents who strive to welcome people so that they can build and sustain local tourism businesses. Although people live in extreme poverty across Haiti, tourism represents a chance for local people to find service-sector employment directly in tourism to supply visitor demand (or indirectly as part of the supply chain). Many places have attempted to restore their image by offering discounted options to attract visitors again (Wise, 2011), but in Haiti this is a challenge due to how much the tourism industry relies on imported goods. On top of this, "Haiti isn't cheap. While a good hotel is upwards of £100 per night, budget around £20 per meal" (London Evening Standard, 2017).

Underdevelopment and a lack of people with necessary skills is a major concern for development, and tourism development in Haiti (Caribbean News Now, 2017b). Despite an overwhelming emphasis on bringing forward a positive image of tourism in Haiti, there are major concerns of widespread displacement and the widening wealth-gap in the country. The *London Evening Standard* (2017) notes that from the airport to the city center, a visitor is presented with:

> *a small section of the city's slums. Goats and pigs pick at piles of burning rubbish. Teens poised at red lights wait to wash the windows of halted traffic. My first hotel meanwhile, has a lush tropical pool and armed guards.*

A main concern beyond the armed guards is the wealth gap, and this was mentioned in a few stories where journalists describe the hotel situation and the conditions outside the perimeters of (luxury) hotels. Whilst this is seen elsewhere in Latin America and the Caribbean, it can be discomforting for visitors who may not want to leave the hotel grounds. Remaining in a hotel because one feels safe there does not spread the impact of tourism to local residents in the community, especially as there are efforts to promote entrepreneurism and new businesses to add to the tourism offering.

There is also the question of stability and investment. "The U.N. says the country is now stable, and tourism is growing. But the former vacation paradise still has a faded beauty" (The New York Times, 2017), again suggesting uncertainty given there are numerous attractions with potential that are not currently thriving. The same article in the *New York Times* (2017) presented a narrative of a destination with potential, but only if much-needed development progresses. The struggles that Haiti faces are widespread given the social conditions and extreme poverty. *The Boston Globe* (2017) compares an environmental disaster in US with the situation in Haiti using the headline: "Houston will recover. Haiti might not". The article goes on to point to several concerns regarding how business and government funds are not enough to repair devastated infrastructures, with much reliance on international aid. Another concern noted by *The Boston Globe* (2017) is the dependence local residents have on tourism, emphasizing how a disaster involving earthquake destruction and/or flooding from tropical storms/hurricanes can restrict people's ability to earn income. Haiti thus suffers from a double disadvantage, where ensuring survival and getting back to everyday life are difficult enough, without taking into account the difficulties of investing in tourism in a country with one of the lowest average incomes per capita.

Natural resources are also not always protected either. According to the Impact Travel Media Network (2017), environmental (as well as cultural and heritage) preservation is something tourism ministers need to prioritize. For instance, Haiti struggles with deforestation, and this has consequences on tourism development, especially along coastal areas with abundant natural beauty. However, as noted in numerous articles, Haiti just does not have the infrastructure to fully diversify their tourism product. The *London Evening Standard* (2017) highlights the range of tourism opportunities, such as sea/sun, hiking to remote waterfalls, cultural tourism in remote villages and historical structures such as Citadelle Laferrière, but it is difficult to fully develop adequate infrastructure to allow for tourist mobility, and this is exacerbated as people are skeptical given the chances of natural disasters.

Stories of future development

Arguably, elements of this section could be considered as positive stories, but this section focusses on what is needed, as opposed to stories of what is happening. From a policy and development standpoint, the *London Evening Standard* (2017) reports that "increasing tourism is a key pledge of the new Haitian government" to restore vital infrastructure and help stabilize the economy by showcasing the country's wealth of culture and natural attractions. In Haiti there is a desire to rebuild in a way that will benefit not only tourism but the residents so that they can live more sustainable (and rewarding) lives. The *Miami Hurricane* (2017) reported that a new cathedral is being planned for Haiti and one aim is to make it hurricane- and earthquake-proof. There are also plans to increase education about the environment so to enhance eco-tourism, with the *Comox Valley Record* (2017) discussing the "Haiti Ocean Project to educate the youth and fishermen of Haiti to ensure the long-term survival of their marine environment". Other articles also mentioned that "giving communities ownership of projects and the direct ability to have a financial stake in them will, of course, be crucial if the country is serious about using tourism" (Independent, 2017). It is hoped that this will improve local living conditions, job opportunities, housing and the environment (Caribbean News Now, 2017a). Perhaps this relates to the wider message that is presented in the *London Evening Standard* (2017) that: "life is moving on. And Haitians want you here to see it£. The article was written by a journalist that went along on a G Adventures tour of the country, and speaking with representatives of the company, highlights: '"one of the reasons we wanted to start a tour was to put it on the radar. To help Haiti rebuild its image," says Kelly Galaski, from adventure travel company, G Adventures (London Evening Standard, 2017). Perhaps without the support of travel operators, initially people may be reluctant to go and explore the country beyond the safe sanctuaries of the resorts (with armed guards). Other articles stressed that developing new events may be a way to "promote tourism development in the country" (Weekly Trust, 2017). This was a finding by Wise et al. (2015) on how events helped transform the image of Serbia after war battered the country.

When it comes to prospective developments, a focus on sustainability is essential. Hertiage tourism too offers potential. Additionally, there is the need for efforts to be spread geographically. In many instances, development may be limited to capital cities or the prime coastal tourism areas, but limiting tourism can be an issue, as explained in the *New York Times* (2017):

> *with recently paved streets and some new construction, the camps for earthquake victims, which used to cover every open space, were gone. Despite these improvements, though, it was clear that Port-au-Prince was not going to be a tourism hot spot for a long time to come. It is too difficult to move around, and security concerns dominate. If tourism ever returns to Haiti in a meaningful way, it will likely happen first in the provinces.*

With the range of positive stories, stories of concern and stories of future development, there is hope for Haiti as a destination, but it will not be an instant fix or success as there is much work to do going forward as the destination's image is re-created.

Conclusions and recommendations going forward to restore hope for Haiti

This chapter examined how the media reported on post-disaster Haiti, and based on the quotes, narratives and analysis presented in this chapter, the findings reinforce the power of the media to showcase a place (as a destination) in transition and recovery to an international audience. Further research into the role of the media as a powerful intermediary for portraying the image of a destination going through transaction and recovery would be highly valuable.

Destination marketers and managers need to tell their story using the media. Thus, stakeholders involved in the tourism industry need to seek ways to engage with travel journalists so that they can promote local businesses and the destination holistically through travel (journalistic) narratives. In the case of Haiti, there is a strong desire to promote growth and development, and this needs to be fueled by tourists who can help revive the destination and tourism economy in Haiti. Media narratives that tell the story of the past, yet articulate the positives in the present, can reassure travelers that the destination is open for business, reinforcing nascent positive perceptions of Haiti.

Infrastructure improvements are needed, although they will be difficult given the lack of funds, but key considerations going forward to attract visitors include reassuring potential tourists that Haiti is safe, focusing on the natural and cultural attractions of the island and developing event tourism.

Recommendations for practice

Based on this case study on Haiti, the authors recommend that destinations that face similar issues consider the following:

- Destination stakeholders need to be able to differentiate between the news media and travel journalists – this will allow the destination to properly tailor the messages and information that is released to the media.

- Destination stakeholders need to work closely with travel journalists not just to promote the destination broadly, but also to showcase the experiences of traveling in the destination. This will allow potential travelers to learn about the destination in a different, arguably more personal way and may help to overcome some of the more negative images that people hold about the destination.

- Following on from the point above, destination managers, planners and policy makers need to focus more on encouraging local and everyday experiences for visitors in the destination, as opposed to only focusing on infrastructural improvements, so that these are available to be reported on by travel journalists.

- When working with the media reporting on tourist destinations affected by disaster, it is important for destination managers to make clear that the destination is recovering. For example, travel journalists could be encouraged to emphasize the rich history and culture of a place, or its natural attractions, rather than focusing on the past disaster.

- Travel journalists can be encouraged to place their emphasis on how tourism is being consumed and developed, which will help to attract attention away from what has happened in the past and will help shape a more socially and economically sustainable future for countries such as Haiti that are recovering from natural disasters.

References

Ali, Z. (2013) Media myths and realities in natural disasters, *European Journal of Business and Social Sciences*, **2** (1), 125-133.

Avraham, E. (2016) Destination marketing and image repair during tourism crises: The case of Egypt, *Journal of Tourism and Hospitality Management*, **28**, 41-48.

Baloglu, S. & McCleary, K. (1999) A model of destination image formation, *Annals of Tourism Research*, **26** (4), 868-897.

Beerli, A. & Martín, J.D. (2004) 'Factors influencing destination image'. *Annals of Tourism Research*, **31** (3), 657-681.

Boston Globe (2017) Houston will recover. Haiti might not, *Boston Globe*, 6 September.

Caribbean News Now (2017a) OPINION: The extraordinary tourism potential of Haiti's cultural calenda', *Caribbean News Now*, 25 February.

Caribbean News Now (2017b) Digicel and the entrepreneurial spirit in Haiti, *Caribbean News Now*, 26 December.

Castelltort, M. & Mäder, G. (2010) Press media coverage effects on destinations – A Monetary Public Value (MPV) analysis, *Tourism Management*, **31**,724-738.

Chatterji, R. (2016) Scripting the folk: history, folklore, and the imagination of place in Bengal, *Annual Review of Anthropology*, **45**, 377-94.

Comox Valley Record (2017) Haiti: Supporting a sustainable Haiti, *Comox Valley Record*, 9 June.

Daily Telegraph (2017) 50 Great ocean cruises; Holidays on the crest of a wave, *The Daily Telegraph*, 25 February.

Gotham, K.F. (2017) Touristic disaster: Spectacle and recovery in Post-Katrina New Orleans, *Geoforum*, **86**, 127-135.

Govers, R., Go, F.M. & Kumar, K. (2007) Promoting tourism destination image, *Journal of Travel Research*, **46** (1), 15-23.

Guo, Z., Robinson, D. & Hite, D. (2017) Economic impact of Mississippi and Alabama Gulf Coast tourism on the regional economy, *Ocean & Coastal Management*, **145**, 52-61.

Hammett, D. (2014) Tourism images and British media representations of South Africa, *Tourism Geographies*, **16** (2), 221-236.

Hennessey, S. M., Yun, D., MacDonald, R. & MacEachern, M. (2010) The effects of advertising awareness and media form on travel intensions, *Journal of Hospitality Marketing and Management*, **19** (3), 217-243.

Impact Travel Media Network (2017) Why Haiti needs sustainable tourism more than ever before, *Impact Travel Media Network*, 25 May.

Independent (2017) Haiti tourism: How this beautiful Caribbean country aims to attract more travellers, *Independent*, 8 May.

Jiang, Y. & Ritchie, B.W. (2017) Disaster collaboration in tourism: Motives, impediments and success factors, *Journal of Hospitality and Tourism Management*, **31**, 70-82.

Khazai, B., Mahdavian, F. & Platt, S. (2018) Tourism Recovery Scorecard (TOURS) – Benchmarking and monitoring progress on disaster recovery in tourism destinations', *International Journal of Disaster Risk Reduction*, **27**, 75-84.

Kim, D. & Perdue, R.R. (2011) The influence of image on destination attractiveness, *Journal of Travel and Tourism Marketing*, **28** (3), 225-239.

Lai, W-H. & Vinh, N. (2013) Online promotion and its influence on destination awareness and loyalty in the tourism industry, *Advances in Management and Applied Economics*, **3** (3), 15-30.

London Evening Standard (2017) Haiti: look beyond the rubble to find its rich history and natural beauty; Beyond Haiti's turbulent recent history, outsiders are now discovering its natural beauty and rich culture, *London Evening Standard*, 5 May.

McQuail, D. (2010) *Mass Communication Theory*. London: Sage.

Miami Hurricane (2017) Architecture students inspire reconstruction of Haiti, *The Miami Hurricane: University of Miami*, 25 January.

Mika, K. (2018) *Disasters, Vulnerability, and Narratives: Writing Haiti's Futures*, London: Routledge.

Morakabati, Y. (2017) It's important to keep tourism afloat in areas that experience natural disasters, *The Conversation*, 26 September, https://theconversation.com/its-important-to-keep-tourism-afloat-in-areas-that-experience-natural-disasters-84461 [accessed 12 July 2018].

Muhoho-Minni, P. & Lubbe, B.A. (2017) The role of the media in constructing a destination image: the Kenya experience, *Communication*, **43** (1), 58-79.

Nelson, V. (2013) Place image during transition: the case of Rijeka, Croatia, *Journal of Travel and Tourism Research (Online)*, **13** (1/2), 116-131.

New York Times (2017) In Haiti, tracing a paradise lost, *The New York Times*, 4 December.

Okuyama, T. (2018) Analysis of optimal timing of tourism demand recovery policies from natural disaster using the contingent behavior method, *Tourism Management*, **64**, 37-54.

Peltier, D. (2018) Puerto Rico emerges from Hurricane Maria with a plan and new hope for tourism, *Skift*, 12 July, https://skift.com/2018/07/12/puerto-rico-emerges-from-hurricane-maria-with-a-plan-and-new-hope-for-tourism/ [accessed 12 July 2018].

5

Ritchie, B.W. (2009) *Crisis and Disaster Management for Tourism*, Bristol: Channel View Publications.

Séraphin, H. (2018) The past, present and future of Haiti as a post-colonial, post-conflict and post-disaster destination, *Journal of Tourism Futures*, **4** (3), 249-264.

Séraphin, H., Butcher, J. & Korstanje, M. (2017) Challenging the negative images of Haiti at a pre-visit stage using visual online learning materials, *Journal of Policy Research in Tourism, Leisure and Events*, **9** (2), 169-181.

Séraphin, H., Yallop, A.C., Capatîna, A. & Gowreesunkar, V.G. (2018) Heritage in tourism organisations' branding strategy: the case of a post-colonial, post-conflict and post-disaster destination, *International Journal of Culture, Tourism and Hospitality Research*, **12** (1), 89-105

Sharpley R. & Wright D. (2018) Disasters and disaster tourism: The role of the media, in P. Stone, R. Hartmann, T. Seaton, R. Sharpley & L. White (eds.), *The Palgrave Handbook of Dark Tourism Studies*. London: Palgrave Macmillan, pp. 335-354.

Travel Pulse (2017) Haiti poised for huge tourism bounce back, *Travel Pulse*, 15 March.

Tsai, C-H. & Chen, C-W. (2011) The establishment of a rapid natural disaster risk assessment model for the tourism industry, *Tourism Management*, **32** (1), 158-171.

Weekly Trust (2017) Dancing to beats at 2017 African Drums Festival, *Weekly Trust*, 6 May.

Walters, G., Mair, J. & Lim, J. (2016) Sensationalist media reporting of disastrous events: Implications for tourism, *Journal of Hospitality and Tourism Management*, **28**, 3-10

Wang, D., Chan, H. & Pan, S. (2015), The impacts of mass media on organic destination image: A case study of Singapore, *Asia Pacific Journal of Tourism Research*, **20** (8), 860–874.

Wise, N.A. (2011) Post-War tourism and the imaginative geographies of Bosnia and Herzegovina, and Croatia, *European Journal of Tourism Research*, **4** (1), 5-24.

Wise, N. & Díaz-Garayúa, J. (2015) The island of Hispaniola: Disputed/ contested territorial histories and cultural identities between the Dominican Republic and Haiti, in E. Brunet-Jailly (ed.), *Border Disputes: A Global Encyclopedia*, Westport, CT: ABC-Clio.

Wise, N., Flinn, J. & Mulec, I. (2015) Exit Festival: Contesting political pasts, impacts on youth culture and regenerating the image of Serbia and Novi Sad, in T. Pernecky and O. Moufakkir (eds.), *Ideological, Social and Cultural Aspects of Events*, Wallingford, UK: CABI, pp. 60-73.

Wise, N. (2017) Interpreting media content post-conflict: Communications of 'travel' and 'Bosnia and Herzegovina in U.S. newspapers, 20 years post-Dayton', *Društvena Istraživanja*, **26** (3), 363–383.

Wise, N.A. & Mulec, I. (2012) Headlining Dubrovnik's tourism image: Transitioning representations/narratives of war and heritage preservation, 1991–2010, *Tourism Recreation Research*, **37** (1), 57-69.

Wise, N. & Mulec, I. (2015) Aesthetic awareness and spectacle: communicated images of Novi Sad, the Exit Festival and the Event Venue Petrovaradin Fortress, *Tourism Review International*, **19** (4), 193-205.

World Bank (2018) What is next for Haiti's tourism? Improving resilience and creating a new destination in the Caribbean, World Bank, https://www.worldbank.org/en/news/feature/2018/04/03/what-is-next-for-haitis-tourism [accessed 1 October 2018].

5

6 Tourism and terrorism: The determinants of destination resilience and the implications for destination image

Cassiopée Benjamin, Dominic Lapointe, Bruno Sarrasin,

Introduction

Safety is essential in order for a destination to maintain and increase tourism activities (Gupta et al., 2010; Hall et al., 2004). In comparison, terrorist attacks are more likely to have negative effects on tourism than natural disasters (Sönmez et al., 1999). During the last decades, several terrorist acts have been committed in touristic cities of the North and South (including Boston, Istanbul, Manchester, New Delhi, New York, Paris, and Tunis). Security concerns and the threat of violence perpetrated by certain groups with radical political and religious demands do not only affect a destination's image and reputation and individual decisions about whether to visit a given destination. They also influence the political and economic balance, which in turn affects the environment in which the tourism industry operates (Hall et al., 2004). While some destinations appear to be suffering the long-term consequences of terrorist attacks on their tourism industry (Liu and Pratt, 2017), others are successfully keeping their industry afloat and avoiding significant economic downturns (Gurtner, 2007; Putra and Hitchcock, 2006). We are therefore seeking to understand the reasons why some destinations manage to maintain their image and remain attractive to tourists despite terrorist acts and others struggle to overcome the consequences of such acts on their industry, even years after the fact.

To date, some case study-based research has documented recovery strategies for tourism destinations following one or more attacks (Mansfeld, 1999; Thapa, 2003; Fletcher & Morakabati, 2008; Jallat & Shultz, 2011). Research has also addressed the link between political instability and difficulties in tourism destination recovery (Sönmez, 1998; Saha & Yap, 2014; Bhattarai et al., 2005) and the ways in which risk perception influences how tourists plan their itineraries (Gupta et al., 2010; Rittichainuwat & Chakraborty, 2009). The literature shows that, following one or more crises, factors such as risk perception and political instability affect variations in tourist flows to destinations. It also demonstrates that vulnerabilities such as political and economic inequalities (Calgaro et al., 2014) impact a destination's image and reputation, revealing an interplay between power, resource distribution and resilience. Calgaro et al. (2014) also proposed a link between destination vulnerability and resilience, clarifying how some vulnerability factors influence the resilience process following shocks or stressors.

Inspired by this existing framework, this chapter addresses the link between vulnerability factors and internal/external determinants, that, in the context of a terrorist attack, support or undermine the resilience of tourist destinations in southern countries. In this approach, we want to identify, from a documentary corpus on the subject, the determinants of resilience for a tourist destination and the vulnerability factors (weaknesses) that influence them. We therefore propose considering the tourist destination as a complex, dynamic political entity where past, present and expected transformations are interacting with internal and external elements.

Terrorism represents a rupture in tourism development, making more linear understandings of destination evolution, like Butler's (1980) tourism area life-cycle analysis, harder to apply. In the aftermath of terror, a different frame of analysis based on resilience may be more fitting, as it invites an investigation into how vulnerability factors take form, and why they become obstacles to resilience for some destinations and not others. Based on an exploratory approach, we will first present the main concepts of our analysis and build on the cases of Bali and Nepal, which are among the best-documented from the Global South. These will allow us to better understand the relationship between vulnerability factors and the determinants of destination resilience in post-terrorism and ongoing conflict contexts and examine how a destination's image is transformed within this process.

Tourism: a political risk factor

Although travellers are not systematically targeted by terrorism, the perception of potential risk is sufficient to influence whether they will visit a destination. Agnew (2010) describes terrorism as "the commission of criminal acts, usually violent, that targets civilians or violates conventions of war when targeting military personnel; and that are committed at least partially for social, political, or religious ends."The fear of travelling to so-called high-risk destinations (those with active advisories and alerts) is fuelled by the fact that some radical groups target tourism, which to them, represents Western hegemonic power and a predominantly liberal version of its modernity (La Branche, 2004).

Terrorism directly affects tourism demand (Liu & Pratt, 2017; Sarrasin, 2004). These effects have an influence on a destination's image and tend to dissuade travellers, who will choose a destination with similar characteristics without risk factors. According to Liu and Pratt (2017), effective post-attack crisis management and quickly-applied image restoration can minimize the effects of terrorism on tourism. Thus, isolated terrorist attacks that do not result from recurring political conflicts have a negligible influence on destination choice (Mansfeld & Pizam, 2006). The cases of Bali and Nepal confirm this hypothesis and reveal different variations of vulnerability.

From vulnerability to destination vulnerability

The notion of vulnerability is closely linked to that of social resilience and corresponds to components that are likely to weaken a community's ability to adapt to change (Maguire & Cartwright, 2008). Traditionally associated with the field of geography, in relation to natural disasters and poverty and, more recently, climate change and adaptation, vulnerability is largely determined by the lack of opportunity inherited from the inequitable distribution of land, power and resources (Maguire & Cartwright, 2008, Calgaro et al., 2014).

As shown in Figure 6.1, vulnerability factors – elements with the potential to weaken resilience – can be in place prior to a shock (terrorist attacks and conflicts, in this case). They can also arise later on, depending on the destination's political, economic and social situation. Thus, a destination's vulnerability is constantly changing as the disruptive shocks that shape it change over space and time. A destination's capacity to cope with such shocks is also in constant flux (Calgaro et al., 2014). In this context, vulnerability is closely linked to the notion of resilience.

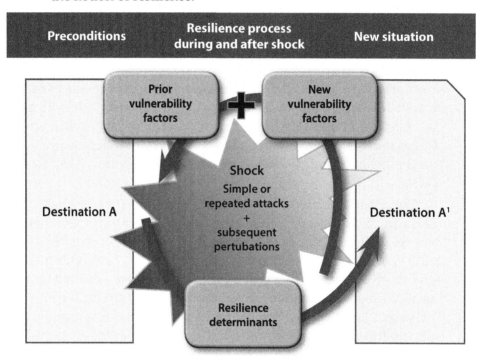

Figure 6.1: Vulnerability factors and resilience determinants. Source: Authors compilation.

Figure 6.1 explains how understanding prior vulnerability factors can help to better address the new ones that arise post-attack. It also allows for improved resilience management strategy design, so that the destination can return to pre-shock state, and even evolve towards an adaptive state.

From social resilience to destination resilience

Social resilience is the ability of a community to cope with disruptions or changes and to maintain adaptive behaviour. The Resilience Alliance Research Consortium defines resilience as "the capacity of an ecosystem to tolerate disturbance without collapsing into a qualitatively different state of affairs". (Brozovi & Schlenker, 2007). Recent interpretations of this notion consider social resilience as the possibility to evolve into a new sustainable state, which is more in line with the new environment created by the disruption (Maguire & Cartwright, 2008). Resilience is particularly well-suited to the study of tourism (Becken, 2013; Biggs et al., 2012; Dahles & Susilowati, 2015; Lew, 2014; Orchiston et al., 2016). In a context of trade expansion, the tourism industry is facing increasingly complex transformations and accelerated environmental, social and economic changes that require adaptation initiatives (Luthe & Wyss, 2014). In this way, tourism stakeholders are led to assess, plan and manage resilience.

A study by Liu and Pratt (2017) quantifying the relationship between tourism and terrorism using international tourism demand models concluded that only nine of the 95 countries surveyed have experienced any real, long-term consequences of terrorism on tourism. In total, 25 of the 95 countries experienced short-term impacts, according to the time series model. International tourism therefore appears to be more resilient to terrorism.

In the following sections we will show that the resilience of destinations is influenced by internal and external determinants. In other words, the resilience of destinations following a terrorist attack depends on determinants defined by actions taken (initiatives of the leaders and managers and/or those of the citizens), and determinants that rely on criteria that influence the decisions of travellers, such as the perception of risk in the country of origin, etc. (Sönmez, 1998). Two case studies, Bali and Nepal, based on articles published between 2001 and 2017, identify certain vulnerability factors and their potential links to the determinants of resilience for a destination and its image and reputation.

Case studies and how we built them

To complete our analysis, we conducted a comprehensive search on the Google Scholar database, in English and in French, with the following key words: resilience AND tourism AND terrorism, tourism AND terrorism, adaptability AND tourism AND terrorism, vulnerability AND tourism AND terrorism. French research was completed using the same process. The corpus of research-based texts, while fruitful in terms of content, excluded frequently one of the three aspects of our research. Studies looking at vulnerability and tourism, such as Calgaro et al. (2012), do not delve into any details about terrorism in non-western countries. Several texts look at resilience (Becken, 2013; Luthe et al., 2012; Lapointe & Sarrasin, 2017) or tourism vulnerabilities in the face of climate change and/or disruption (Moreno & Becken, 2009). Others assess the effects of terrorism on tourism (Tarlow, 2006; Mukesh & Pradhan, 2014; Korstanje & Clayton, 2012) and strategies to prevent and cope with the risks and effects of terrorism in tourist destinations from a managerial point of view (Paraskevas & Arendell, 2006). Ultimately, vulnerability, resilience, terrorism and tourism are rarely addressed all together. As a result, few studies specify which elements and practices could help or hinder a destination's resilience to terrorism, based on the observation of specific cases, and presenting the characteristics that distinguish non-western countries.

In order to summarize the data to list and categorize them, we favoured the terms 'determinants' and 'factors.' When referring to determinants of destination resilience, we mean any actions or elements that favour resilience. These can be internal or external, depending on whether the actions that lead to resilience come from initiatives intrinsic to the destination, be they at the legislative, local, or community level; or initiated outside the destination, as with the involvement of foreign heads of state, international media coverage and other outside interventions. Similarly, for our current purposes, when we refer to vulnerabilities, we mean elements that contribute to or interfere with a destination's resilience following one or more terrorist attacks; as with determinants of resilience, they too can be internal or external.

A review of articles published between 1998 and 2017 allowed us to highlight certain characteristics that favour or threaten the stability of tourism in destinations following terrorist attacks. The corpus made it possible to retrace, through the chosen literature, different vulnerability factors and resilience determinants that influence resilience—either positively or negatively. This exercise directed our search towards an analysis grid that could be used to explore cases of interest. Post-attack risk management planning considered vulnerabilities that emerged during the resilience process, such as an unfair media coverage (Fletcher & Morakabati, 2008; Malenfant, 2004; Pizam & Smith, 2000; Rittichainuwat & Chakraborty, 2008; Manfield, 1999; Jallat & Shultz, 2011), the recurrence of the attacks (Fletcher & Morakabati, 2008; Pizam & Smith, 2000; Liu & Pratt, 2017) and perceived violation of human rights or political stability (Fletcher & Morakabati, 2008; Liu & Pratt, 2017; Thapa, 2003; Bhattarai et al., 2005; Sönmez, 1998). It also took into account the ways in which post-shock vulnerability is correlated to the scale of the event (Fletcher & Morakabati, 2008; Liu & Pratt, 2017).

The vulnerabilities described in the texts (see Appendix 1), although very relevant, were rarely combined or connected to pre-existing vulnerabilities specific to certain southern countries. These pre-existing vulnerabilities were considered when discussing a destination's historical context but not when developing its resilience strategies. Nevertheless, the literature review gave us a better understanding of the internal and external influences of vulnerability factors and resilience determinants, and helped us highlight some distinctions that may explain the variations in the cases of Nepal and Bali.

Bali

6

The island of Bali is one of the thousands of islands that make up the archipelago of Indonesia (Baker & Coulter, 2007: 251). Between 1999 and 2002, the annual number of tourists visiting Bali ranged from 1,335,779 to 1,412,849 (Baker & Coulter, 2007:253). Bali is predominantly Hindu and Buddhist, while the rest of Indonesia is predominantly Muslim (Baker & Coulter, 2007:251). This pre-attack context already raised fears of possible inter-ethnic tensions and open conflict. In addition to this pre-attack vulnerability, the area was and is highly dependent on tourism. The tourism industry has been growing, particularly since 1968, when the local airport began receiving international flights (Vickers,1989:184-191 in Gurtner, 2016:13). From then on, tourism has been a significant economic sector, one that has attracted locals and off-island migrants. One of the major components of Bali's tourism image is a romantic projection of cultural uniqueness. This aspect is so important that Picard (2008) claimed that culture and tourism are intertwined to such an extent that a large part of the population considers cultural tourism as proof of cultural authenticity.

On October 12, 2002, two bombs exploded consecutively in the compound and periphery of a nightclub in Bali. A third bomb went off seconds later, close to the US consulate. A total of 202 people were killed, including more than 100 tourists (Baker & Coulter, 2007; Suryani et al., 2008). Subsequently, Bali underwent a severe tourism slowdown, causing a significant impact on the island's economy. Many tourists left Bali immediately after the attacks and daily arrivals dropped from 4,650 to 2,800 in the days following the explosions (Jakarta Post, 2002, in Henderson, 2004:21). In addition to these terrorist attacks, the SARS crisis and the war in Iraq had an impact on international tourism, Bali included (Darma Putra & Hitchcock, 2006: 157). As a result, in 2003, international arrivals in Bali declined by more than half compared to the previous two years (Hitchcock & Darma Putra, 2005:67). However, by 2004, despite another attack in Jakarta, the country's capital, the situation had improved considerably. In some months, international arrivals even exceeded pre-attack volumes (Hitchcock & Darma Putra, 2005:67). On October 1, 2005, more bomb attacks took place in the resorts of Jimbaran and Kuta, killing 25 people, including the terrorists who orchestrated the attacks (Baker & Coulter, 2007:263). As a result, tourist arrivals to Bali in October 2005 were down 37% from the previous year (Baker & Coulter, 2007:263). This marked decrease, however, was less pronounced than the drop that followed the 2002 attacks (Baker & Coulter, 2007:263; see Figure 6.2). Overall, arrivals to Bali increased by more than 100% between 2002 and 2015.

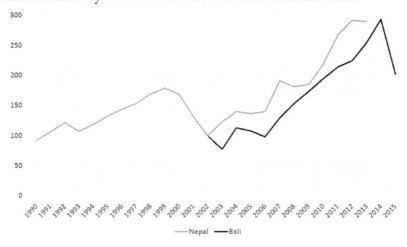

Figure 6.2: Fluctuations in tourist arrivals to Bali and Nepal: A Comparison. Index evolution (100 = 2002) of tourist arrivals to Bali (2002-2015) and to Nepal (1990-2013)

Sources: Authors' compilation from Ministry of Culture, Tourism and Civil Aviation, Government of Bali and Bali Hotel Association

Suryani et al. (2009:1317) observed an increase in suicide rates that they link, in part, to the socio-economic effects of the decline in tourism that followed the first attack in 2002. In their research, Baker and Coulter (2007:262) conclude that after the 2002 attacks, the beach vendors were "struggling to survive and unable to sustain earlier improvements to livelihoods built on tourism" and that "without the development of any form of 'safety net', informal sector workers in tourism remain extremely vulnerable, as do others whose livelihoods have come to depend on this sector."

New vulnerability factors were added to those present before the attacks, presenting a potential for a weakened resilience process (Table 6.1). The existing literature has allowed us to identify some of these new factors. First of all, in the weeks after the 2002 attacks, major tour operators withdrew their Bali vacations travel and hotel offers in Indonesia just before the high season for tourists from the northern hemisphere (Baker & Coulter, 2007:253). As a result, the occupancy level of Bali hotels dropped from 75% to 14% for a comparable season (WTO, 2002 in Baker & Coulter, 2007:253). Added to this vulnerability factor were the repeated attacks targeting the islands of Indonesia: Jakarta in 2003, Bali in 2005 and Jakarta in 2017 (Putra & Hitchcock, 2005, 2006; Coulter, 2007:263). What's more, as of 2003, one year after the 2002 attack, visas on arrival were introduced, which inevitable affected tourism revenues (Hitchcock & Darma Putra, 2005, 2006). Until then, Indonesia had had an open-door policy for more than 20 years (Hitchcock & Darma Putra, 2005, 2006). The 2002 bombing didn't generate any major backlash against minority groups, due to the widespread recognition the importance of tourism in Bali (Hitchcock & Darma Putra, 2005). The terrorist attacks did raise some ethnic tensions between Muslims and Hindus, however. Those tensions were expressed through violent acts, such as the burning of the Seririt Market in 2003 (Baker & Coulter, 2007).

Table 6.1: Vulnerability factors for Bali

Prior vulnerability factors	
Inter-ethnic tensions	Fear of possible inter-ethnic tensions and open conflict (Hitchcock & Darma Putra, 2006).
Dependence to the tourism industry	More than 50% of Bali's official income (CGI 2003 in Guntner, 2007:13).
Cumulative vulnerability factors following the attack	
Repeated attacks	Attacks in Bali (2002) and Jakarta (2003)
Inter-ethnic tensions	The Seririt market is burned (Baker & Coulter, 2007: 257).
Withdrawal of travel offers from some operators	Withdrawal from tour operators offers and hotels in Indonesia just before the high season for tourists from the northern hemisphere (Baker & Coulter, 2007: 253).
Weakening of the informal sector workforce	Significant economic struggle for workers of the tourism industry

Source: Authors' compilation

Several elements contributed to the recovery of tourism in Bali. Attempts to recover from the attacks were initiated internally (government initiatives, citizens, etc.) and externally (international support, etc.). We have traced some of these determinants of resilience in the existing literature. First, the resolution of the 1999 crisis in East Timor and its subsequent 2002 declaration of independence, along with the election of a new president of Indonesia appear to have contributed to a political context favouring a certain degree of stability (Hitchcock & Darma Putra, 2005, 2006). In addition, leaders in Bali and Indonesia attempted to set up stabilization strategies quickly (Hitchcock & Darma Putra, 2006; 2008). An increased visibility of representatives of the order became a strategy for maintaining an image of security. The number of intelligence officers tripled, and they were expected to position themselves at all points of entry of the island, and a 'Baywatch'-type 'Tourist Police' beach patrol was inaugurated to recreate an image familiar to tourists from the United States and Australia (Hitchcock & Darma Putra, 2005:71). Nationals from those two countries participated in training these officers in the use of English, American and Australian protocol (Hitchcock & Darma Putra, 2005:71).

In order to increase the feeling of security for tourists and islanders, a series of events, including collective prayers and purification rituals, were also organized to promote interreligious harmony. These events were widely publicized in the international media as symbols of peace and were entirely in phase with the importance of culture and religion in Bali's tourism image. Some political leaders supported these ceremonies by taking part in them (Hitchcock & Darma Putra, 2005:72). A significant budget was allotted to a range of conferences and receptions on the island, including the 2003 Association of Southeast Asian Nations Summit (ASEAN), attended by leaders from participating countries (Hitchcock & Darma Putra, 2006:164).

The support of the Australian Prime Minister and his presence at the first commemoration service for the bombings, as well as the visit of the US president in 2003, also potentially enhanced the destination's international image (Hitchcock & Darma Putra, 2006:164). International companies with access to marketing resources that promoted the island of Bali internationally also contributed to the reestablishment of the destination's reputation.

The presence of foreign investment in Bali's tourism system, which is sometimes seen as a threat to Balinese people's ability to control their industry (Picard, 2008), could have been another factor affecting image and reputation recovery. Indeed, foreign investors continually relay the discourse of security and peace on the island, while securing new niches that are less influenced by western perceptions of local tension. For Bali, these niches tend to be on the Asian market, especially in China (Picard, 2008). Furthermore, in order to promote internal displacement and to prevent a drop in international tourist arrivals, the President of the Republic of Indonesia granted additional holidays to Indonesian citizens. Finally, Balinese culture itself potentially helped avert a socio-political crisis following the attacks (Hitchcock & Darma Putra, 2005, 2006) and played a role in destination image recovery, as Balinese culture is the main product sold to the international tourism market. Artistic performances have taken on new forms, and references to shelling, tourism and the hope of harmony have been integrated into Bali's well-known dance-drama and shadow theatre performances.

With respect to external determinants that potentially contributed to the destination's resilience, it should first be noted that the Bali bombings crisis was managed on several scales. This multi-level management included the addition of practical security measures to cultural strategies designed to prevent inter-communal conflict (Hitchcock & Putra, 2008:74) and the combination of international, governmental and local measures that helped restore the image and perceived trustworthiness of tourism services and products in Bali (Putra & Hitchcock, 2006:164). The information gleaned from the two papers by Hitchcock and Putra (2005, 2006) presented in Tables 6.1 and 6.2, supports the hypothesis that some pre- and post-attack vulnerability factors may influence the internal determinants of resilience. Putra and Hitchcock (2006:164) conclude, however, that Bali was already well-engaged in a functional tourist dynamic before the attacks. If the destination had been at a less advanced stage of development, the effects could have been greater and the recovery process longer and more laborious, if not impossible (Putra & Hitchcock, 2006:164). This Balinese case study demonstrates that destination reputation and image, and tourism stability are determinants of resilience that can help minimize the negative effects of isolated attacks and favour a faster return to the initial state.

The next section applies the same analytical framework to a case study in Nepal, and reveals some key variations in how vulnerabilities and determinants can play out in destinations in the Global South.

Nepal

In Nepal, post-terrorism tourism recovery does not unfold in the same ways as does in Bali. This small Himalayan country, home to a rich and diverse culture and many unique attractions, including Mount Everest, has been the geographical centre of a politically charged area for more than 50 years. From the Chinese invasion of Tibet in 1950, to the three Indo-Pakistani wars of 1947-48, 1965 and 1971, and more recently, the Afghan conflict, Nepal has been long been surrounded by various conflicts. Despite this politically tense regional context, Nepal sustained tourism growth from 1960 to 1999. However, the intensification of the Maoist rebellion in the late 1990s dealt a serious blow to the local tourism industry, and the country's economy on the whole. A steady recovery began in 2003, after three years of decline, but it took another four years to return to 1999 levels (Figure 6.2). Vulnerability factors prior to the 'trouble' and those that emerged during the Maoist conflict are shown in Table 6.2.

Between 1960 and 1999, Nepal saw a sharp increase in the number of incoming tourists (Thapa, 2003:119, Upadhayaya et al., 2011:22). The government has been consistently committed to promoting tourism to attract more visitors and promote longer stays. Earnings growth and the proliferation of local operators in a context of favourable trade terms for tourism have made the Nepalese economy dependent on this sector.

Nepal enjoys a reputation as a quiet and peaceful place (Thapa, 2003). In 1989, neighbouring India reduced transit and trade access points, and Nepal's economy has suffered considerably ever since. This upheaval seriously penalized the tourism industry by limiting the resources of host communities. The following years were marked by armed conflicts that resulted in a drop in tourist arrivals (Thapa, 2003:125). In 1996, a movement of Maoist rebels emerged, waging a guerrilla war that intensified until 2002, at which point movement leaders advised tourists travelling to the region to be careful, but informed them that they were not targeted (Thapa, 2003; Upadhayaya et al., 2011). Many Western countries then issued warnings to travellers and labelled the country as high-risk, noting that recent threats against US tourists indicated a lack of security. The Maoist attacks were compounded by the hijacking of a plane in 1999 and the massacre of the queen and king in 2001.

Table 6.2: Vulnerability factors for Nepal

Prior vulnerability factors	
Infrastructures	Access to information, precarious transport options and security (Thapa, 2003: 118).
Uneven tourism structure	Concentration in some privileged cities (Upadhayay et al., 2014: 25).
Monopoly of control and concentration of foreign capital	Economic development is hampered by a concentration of foreign capital and accessibility to employment in touristic geographic areas (Bhattarai et al., 2005:686; Upadhayay et al., 2014:25).
Random tourist demands	Particularly affected by unpredictable demand for tourism based on internal and external influences (Hall & O'Sullivan, 1996; Richter, 1992, cited in Thapa, 2003:118).
Instability	Frequent change of governments (Upadhayay et al., 2014:26) and the 'People's War' claims several thousand victims (Thapa, 2003:119).
Tourism-dependent economy	Economy dependent on tourism in Nepal (Thapa, 2003:120).
Economic crisis	Reduction of transit access points (1989) and trade that impeded imports and the tourism industry (Thapa, 2003:123).
Proximity of countries in conflicts and wars	Proximity to other areas in conflict (Thapa, 2003:131).
Cumulative vulnerability factors following the attack	
Difficulties of coopera-tion	Stakeholders are pessimistic about the future of Nepal's tourism industry and do not seem to be inspired by the Nepal Tourism Board's initiatives. (Thapa, 2003:134).
Withdrawal of an impor-tant tourist niche	Withdrawal of American tourists following Maoist threats (Upadhayay et al., 2014:26).
Travel advisory	In 2001-2002, foreign countries advise tourists to not travel to Nepal (Thapa, 2003:119); The United States is the only country that, even after the conflict period, has continued to issue non-trip notices. For Upadhayay et al. (2014:31), these unrealistic negative opinions are associated with power relations and the use of tourism as a political tool.
Persistent threat	Government declare the Maoist as terrorists and impose a state of emergency in 2001-2002 (Thapa, 2003:119).
Image / Media	Images and discourses about neighbouring countries affected by war and conflict (Afghanistan, India, etc.) have a negative effect on Nepal (Thapa, 2003:118) Incidents unrelated to tourist safety were quickly exaggerated by the media, portraying the destination as dangerous for tourists (Upadhayay et al., 2014:30).

Source: Authors' compilation

6

These elements contributed to negative media coverage and were a part of a general trend of war- and conflict-related danger in the region (Afghanistan/India and Pakistan Border) (Thapa, 2003). The destination lost control of its image abroad as the foreign press applied a geopolitical generalization to the area. As a result, tourists tended to look for alternative destinations offering the same type of experience but without any perceived security risk (Bhattarai, 2005:686). Since the 2000s, despite its impressive attractions, its rich and diversified culture, and its attempted revivals, Nepal is still struggling to regain its former tourism levels. Table 6.2 suggests that the vulnerability factors observed in Nepal prior to attacks and exacerbated by local and peripheral armed conflicts (in neighbouring countries) take precedence over the determinants of resilience.

Following the decline of the industry and the political instability created by the Maoist guerrillas, new vulnerability factors emerged. Between 2000 and 2001, the NTB (Nepal Tourism Board) was allocated $1.6 million US, of which 62% went towards international promotion and destination marketing with the goal of rebranding the destination (Thapa, 2003). Despite this notable effort, stakeholders were pessimistic about the future of Nepal's tourism industry and did not seem to be inspired by the Nepal Tourism Board's initiatives (Thapa, 2003). In fact, at the same time, the Nepalese government declared the Maoists to be terrorists and, in 2001-2002 imposed a state of emergency (Thapa, 2003:119). This resulted in a ban on travel to Nepal from several foreign countries (Thapa, 2003; Upadhayaya et al., 2011). In the case of US travellers, the situation has had lasting effects: travel bans went up in 2002-2003, and the United States continued to issue travel advisories, even after the conflict period. For Upadhayaya et al. (2011:31), these unrealistic negative opinions are associated with power relations and the use of tourism as a political tool. In addition, images and discourses about neighbouring countries affected by war and conflict (Afghanistan, India etc.) have had a lasting negative effect on Nepal (Thapa, 2003:1). Incidents that were not related to the safety of tourists were quickly exaggerated by the media and the destination was portrayed as dangerous for tourists (Upadhayaya et al., 2011: 30). These political vulnerabilities were exacerbated by Nepal's Maoist crisis, which amplified the vulnerabilities associated with the very structure of the tourism industry, and was especially harmful to the destination's image as a safe place to travel. Thus, two fundamental challenges act as important vulnerabilities: the monopoly of control and geographical favouring (Bhattarai et al., 2005:686). In a circuit of dependence on foreign capital, the industry often operates under the monopoly of control by the ruling elite and the merchant classes. Economic development is hampered by a concentration of foreign capital and accessibility to employment in tourist geographic areas (Bhattarai et al., 2005:686).

Facing decline, the destination took initiative and began promoting itself in new and outward-looking ways. In addition to the NTB investing heavily in promoting the destination abroad, it also began communicating information about the political situation. In fact, following the imposition of the first declaration of emergency in 2001, the authorities published an update stipulating, among other things, that given the violence perpetrated in certain areas of the country, security would be significantly strengthened. The update also stated that, despite the common perception of the notion of 'emergency,' visitors to Nepal could expect a near-normal situation, since the state of emergency, in that context, referred to a temporary suspension of political activities and was imposed more as a preventive measure (Board, 2001, in Thapa, 2003:134). Subsequently, the 'Destination Nepal Campaign 2002-2003' was created to generate tourism awareness locally and reposition Nepal as a safe destination (Nepal Tourism Board, 2001, cited in Thapa, 2003:134). The High Level Crisis Management Coordination Committee was also formed to address the growing crisis in the tourism industry generated by political unrest (Upadhayaya et al., 2011:32). A set of measures were implemented to make the destination more accessible and attractive. These measure included a reduction in entry fees to world heritage sites; the removal of visa fees for visitors under 3 days; the opening of 15 and 103 new mountains for climbing in 2002 and 2003, respectively; and the waiving of royalties for more than 70 peaks for 3 years (High Level Task Force, 2005; NTB, 2008, cited in Upadhayaya et al., 2011:32).

On top of these internal measures, external support was offered to assist in the destination's recovery. International development agencies contributed to the creation of a project called Rural Poverty Alleviation Program (Upadhayaya et al., 2011: 32-33), and in January 2002, a visit by Secretary of State Colin Powell (USA) coincided with the lifting of the travel advisory by the US government (Thapa, 2003). Finally, while covering conflicts, some international media described the wonders of Nepal at length (landscapes, culture, lifestyle, etc.), thereby encouraging the interest of potential travellers and contributing to the relatively rapid increase in tourist arrivals that occurred after 2006 (Upadhayaya et al., 2011:31). A BBC documentary went so far as to declare that Nepal is one of the destinations to see before dying (Thapa, 2003:135). In addition, freedom of movement in the mountains after payment of the Maoists' fee and the possibility of interacting with guerrilla fighters became an attraction promoted by word of mouth (Upadhayaya et al. 2011:32), paradoxically making tourism recovery possible through the very source of political risk that compromises the destination. Despite figures shown in figure 6.2 (+189% between 2002 and 2013), Liu and Pratt (2017:409) qualify that among a range of cases studied, Nepal remains among the destinations that continue to suffer from the long-term effects of conflict on tourism demand. Upadhayaya et al.'s 2011 article is more optimistic: it explores the adaptation strategies applied by the tourism sector since the conflicts occurring between 1996 and 2006, and suggests that the negotiations surrounding the conflicts have actually favoured industry development. As an example, the article discusses how Nepal, as a developing country in the Asia Pacific region, experiences the vulnerability of developing countries with few resources and mechanisms to mitigate impacts, but that that tourism, when operated under principles and practices of sustainability, can have a positive impact on reducing tensions between visitors and host communities (Upadhayaya et al., 2011: 22-24). This research and its findings are aligned with the Social Theory of Terrorism and Tourism (Peters, 2002), and show how even a destructive and deadly conflict can be a constructive social force and an instrument of social change in society (see Table of Determinants of Resilience Nepal).

Conclusion

Destination resilience appears to be influenced by internal and external determinants. Some determinants are defined by actions (initiatives taken by leaders and managers and/or those of citizens), and others rely on the different criteria that influence the decisions of travellers, such as perception of risk (Sönmez, 1998). Based on the literature for Bali and Nepal, the two cases examined, we were able to identify some vulnerability factors as well as several determinants of destination resilience in a post-terrorism or ongoing conflict context. The two destinations are obviously difficult to compare in terms of the differences in their socio-economics, politics, history, geography, attractiveness, services and so on. But despite these differences, the two cases allow us to consider which vulnerabilities help and which ones hinder the application of determinants that appear to promote resilience. They also reveal which barriers to resilience persist even in the presence of such determinants. The importance of political stability stands out as a key indicator for destination resilience. This data confirms observations made in several studies (Fletcher & Morakabati, 2008; Sönmez, 1998; Neumayer, 2000; Saha & Yap 2014; Bhattarai et al., 2005) which argue that while it is generally possible for a destination to recover from a terrorist attack, the main vulnerability factor that slows or prevents recovery, even more than the severity of the attack, is political instability. This factor, which is intrinsically linked to the permanence of conflicts and tourists' perception of instability, can influence the destination's image, beyond any and all marketing efforts. Our two cases illustrate the importance of this perception of instability: Bali was able to quickly communicate a return to stability, but Nepal was constrained by its vulnerabilities and had to cope with a perception of instability fuelled by external elements.

Since there are clear distinctions of pre- and post-attack vulnerabilities and conflicts from one destination to another, appropriate targeted resilience strategies must be able to take those vulnerabilities into account and consider the destination's economic and political reality. As seen in the case of Bali, the possible exacerbation of inter-ethnic conflicts led to government and citizen initiatives aiming to restore and promote inter-religious harmony and restore tourists' confidence in the destination's safety. Using an analytical framework that considers the ways in which vulnerabilities and resilience intersect can provide a better understanding of the brakes and accelerators affecting the return to normal, or even allow for the recovery process to result in improvements. In other words, to support resilience-building initiatives in post-terrorism contexts, frameworks should consider pre-existing vulnerabilities of destinations, especially those of the Global South. Indeed, more in-depth research is needed to address the issue of resilience in social and political risk contexts, including those related to terrorism attacks. Such research will need to open up our understanding of destinations to see them as a dense fabric of social and power relations with diverse interests and different vulnerabilities and resilie nce strategies. It will need to keep in mind that what makes a destination resilient in one area, may make it vulnerable in another. Such differences remain to be properly analysed, and more comprehensive research is necessary in order to go beyond the current conceptual limitations and more fully understand the complexities at work in destination vulnerabilities and resilience

Observation and lessons learned

From the outset, Nepal appears to have had more pre-conflict and more constraining vulnerability factors than Bali. In particular, a different level of tourism stability was in place. Bali had a functional tourism structure and popularity before the attacks (Putra & Hitchcock, 2006:164). As for Nepal, although already known as a peaceful place, destination tourism was perhaps not as well-developed (Thapa, 2003:118). Although Bali was hit several times by attacks, these attacks were not persistent and declared, as was the case in Nepal. The severity of the impact of terrorism on Nepal's tourism industry seems to have been exacerbated by media coverage and conflict and war in neighbouring countries (Thapa, 2003:131). In Bali, the destination's image is built on cultural elements and operates under relatively local control which provides it with a more solid foundation for recovery. Nepal, one the other hand has an image based more on its amazing natural wonders, and had infrastructure and accessibility issues prior to the shock. This prior vulnerability played an unfavourable role in Nepal's capacity to act efficiently in recovering its image.

Table 6.1, based on the Bali case, shows that some vulnerability factors were pre-existing and others arose during and after the conflict. These factors can negatively influence the internal determinants of a destination's resilience, as is the case with vulnerability factors that are difficult to overcome, but they can also have a positive impact and guide actions that to tend towards resilience. For example, the fear that the region, where citizens of different religious persuasions coexist, is grappling with inter-ethnic conflicts, seems to have prompted political leaders and the local press to react promptly and cautiously to attacks (Hitchcock & Darma Putra, 2005:63). On the other hand, as previously shown, the precarity of tourism employment in a post-attack context, has significant impacts on those who work in the industry. This reveals the ways in which economic dependency on tourism is conducive to instability and hardship, and invites us to consider it as a prior vulnerability that impacts the resilience process. It also raises the question of the relationship between system resilience and destination image.

In observing globally similar determinants of resilience in both destinations (strengthening security, social transformations in the face of tourism, external support and the deployment of marketing and communication strategies), we see that the return to the pre-crisis situation did not unfold in the same way. This can be explained in part by the destinations' different pre-terrorism shock vulnerabilities. Indeed, and this is the crux of our argument, those distinct and observable vulnerabilities lead to different resilience strategies.

Prior to the terrorism shock, the two destinations were in different positions and had different images. Politically, Bali was in a stabilizing process: it had a new president and the East Timor crisis had recently been resolved. Nepal, on the other hand, was experiencing ever-weakening internal political stability, which culminated in the assassination of the royal family. It was also up against external political setbacks with the war in Afghanistan and India's closure of entry points. Externally, foreign countries reacted differently, and Nepal had to deal with extensive travel warnings, especially those issued by the USA, for longer than Bali did. This situation stresses the importance of external political vulnerabilities and how hard they are to act upon from the destination's perspective, no matter what marketing and image strategies are deployed. It is important to stress the fact that those vulnerabilities are also geopolitics and therefore can be influenced by an agenda that goes well beyond the confines of tourism. These pre-terrorism differences seemed to create a different scope of action for resilience processes. An acknowledgement of tourism's importance opened an inter-ethnic and inter-confessional dialogue in Bali, therefore lowering vulnerabilities, whereas in Nepal, the political vulnerabilities heightened risk levels and created a pessimistic attitude within the tourism industry.

The other major difference is related to destinations' industry structures. From the literature, we were able to pinpoint that Nepal's industry is more geographically concentrated, less accessible and held by a monopoly of elites. On the other hand, Bali is more of a mass destination with a diversity of stakeholders, greater accessibility and a more-developed notion of how important tourism is. This could have been an important difference in the reactions and resilience processes of the two destinations. In Nepal, pessimism and criticism of government actions arose and slowed down the process of stabilizing the destination's image and reputation. Bali reacted with a very visible and efficient strategy to enhance security, promote the destination and even include crisis elements its cultural tourism offerings. Nepal did not remain idle and eventually marketing and communication investments were made abroad. At the same time, the industry also underwent a social transformation and Nepal targeted its long-neglected domestic market as a source of development and lowered the access fees to sites and summits. As a result, tourism workers gained increased negotiating power and were able to better their conditions. Although these improvements do not have an instant effect on image recovery, they can gradually impact industry structure and contribute to strengthening long-term resilience.

Recommendations for practice

Our results suggest that destination managers should consider the following:

■ The complexity of the social and political web in which the recovery process is embedded must be assessed and acknowledged.

■ An early recognition of the destination's vulnerabilities and anticipation of their potential backlash could accelerate the resilience process in case of terrorist event.

■ Stakeholders are not evenly impacted by the shock of terrorism events; a resilient recovery process should address international image issues but also take advantage of the occasion to strengthen the most fragile links in the chain. The Nepali case shows how crisis can create opportunities to reconsider industry structures and workforce roles.

■ The Bali case illustrates how to anchor the image recovery process within the locally valued part of a destination's image. Their use of culture and cultural tourism as a tool of recovery targeted both tourism issues and domestic concerns.

■ During the recovery process, it is beneficial to target new clienteles and niche markets (especially domestic ones) with fewer sensitivities and a closer understanding of the actual situation. This strategy can diversify the destination and strengthen its resilience in the face of international opinion, particularly in the context of a hard to lift travel ban from western countries.

References

Agnew, R. (2010) A general strain theory of terrorism, *Theoretical Criminology*, **14** (2), 131-153.

Baker, K. & Coulter, A. (2007) Terrorism and tourism: the vulnerability of beach vendors' livelihoods in Bali, *Journal of Sustainable Tourism*, **15** (3), 249-266.

Becken, S. (2013) Developing a framework for assessing resilience of tourism sub-systems to climatic factors, *Annals of Tourism Research*, **43**, 506-528.

Biggs, D., Hall, C. M. & Stoeckl, N. (2012) The resilience of formal and informal tourism enterprises to disasters: reef tourism in Phuket, Thailand, *Journal of Sustainable Tourism*, **20** (5), 645-665.

Bhattarai, K., Conway, D. & Shrestha, N. (2005) Tourism, terrorism and turmoil in Nepal. *Annals of Tourism Research*, **32**(3), 669-688.

Brozovic, N., & Schlenker, W. (2007). Resilience, uncertainty, and the role of economics in ecosystem management (No. 381-2016-22109), 2007 Annual Meeting, July 29-August 1, Portland, Oregon, American Agricultural Economics Association.

Butler, R.W. (1980) The concept of the tourist area life-cycle of evolution: implications for management of resources, *Canadian Geographer*, **24** (1), 5-12.

Calgaro, E., Lloyd, K. & Dominey-Howes, D. (2014) From vulnerability to transformation: a framework for assessing the vulnerability and resilience of tourism destinations, *Journal of Sustainable Tourism*, **22** (3), 341-360.

Dahles, H. & Susilowati, T. P. (2015) Business resilience in times of growth and crisis, *Annals of Tourism Research*, **51**, 34-50.

Darma Putra, I. N. & Hitchcock, M. (2006) The Bali bombs and the tourism development cycle, *Progress in Development Studies*, **6** (2), 157-166.

Fletcher, J. & Morakabati, Y. (2008) Tourism activity, terrorism and political instability within the commonwealth: The cases of Fiji and Kenya, *International Journal of Tourism Research*, **10** (6), 537-556.

Gurtner, Y. K. (2007) Crisis in Bali: lessons in tourism recovery, in E. Laws, B. Prideaux & K. Chon (eds.), *Managing Tourism Crises*, Abingdon: CABI, pp. 81-97.

Gupta, A., Gupta, D. R. & Arora, N. (2010) The relationship between perceived travel risk, travel safety, travel anxiety and intentions to travel: a path analysis study of domestic traveller in India, *International Journal of tourism and Travel*, **3** (1), 25-36.

Hall, C. M., & O'Sullivan, V. (1996). Tourism, political stability and violence. *Tourism, Crime and International Security Issues*, 105-121.

Hall, C. M., Timothy, D. J. & Duval, D. T. (2004) Security and tourism: towards a new understanding?, *Journal of Travel and Tourism Marketing*, **15** (2-3), 1-18.

6

Henderson, J. (2004) Managing the aftermath of terrorism: The Bali bombings, travel advisories and Singapore, *International journal of hospitality and tourism administration*, **4** (2), 17-31.

High Level Task Force. (2005). *Report of a high level task force to revitalize tourism industry*. Kathmandu: High Level Task Force/Ministry of Tourism and Civil Aviation.

Hitchcock, M. & Darma Putra, I. N. (2008a) Old tourists and new tourists: management challenges for Bali's tourism industry, in J. Cochrane (ed.), *Asian Tourism: Growth and Change*, Oxford: Elsevier, pp. 209-220.

Hitchcock, M. & Darma Putra, N. (2008b) The Bali bombings: Tourism Crisis Management and Conflict Avoidance, *Current Issues in Tourism*, **8** (1), 62-76.

Jakarta Post (2002) Bali bets on recovery as peak season draws close, 26 November in J. Henderson (2004) Managing the aftermath of terrorism: The Bali bombings, travel advisories and Singapore, *International journal of hospitality and tourism administration*, **4** (2), 17-31.

Jallat, F. & Shultz, C. J. (2011) Lebanon: From cataclysm to opportunity—Crisis management lessons for MNCs in the tourism sector of the Middle East, *Journal of World Business*, **46** (4), 476-486.

Korstanje, M. E., & Clayton, A. (2012) Tourism and terrorism: conflicts and commonalities. *Worldwide Hospitality and Tourism Themes*, **4** (1), 8-25.

La Branche, S. (2004) Tourisme, terrorisme et mondialisation, *Téoros. Revue de recherche en tourisme*, **23** (1), 5-11.

Lapointe, D. & Sarrasin, B. (2017) (Re)production of resilient tourism space in the context of climate change in coastal Québec, Canada, in A. A. Lew and J. M. Cheer (eds.) *Tourism Resilience and Adaptation to Environmental Change: Definitions and Frameworks*. Routledge, pp. 141-156.

Lew, A. A. (2014) Scale, change and resilience in community tourism planning, *Tourism Geographies*, **16** (1), 14-22.

Liu, A. & Pratt, S. (2017) Tourism's vulnerability and resilience to terrorism, *Tourism Management*, **60**, 404-417.

Luthe, T. & Wyss, R. (2014) Assessing and planning resilience in tourism, *Tourism Management*, **44**, 161-163.

Luthe, T., Wyss, R. & Schuckert, M. (2012) Network governance and regional resilience to climate change: empirical evidence from mountain tourism communities in the Swiss Gotthard region, *Regional Environmental Change*, **12** (4), 839-854.

Maguire, B. & Cartwright, S. (2008) Assessing a community's capacity to manage change: a resilience approach to social assessment, report prepared for Australian Government Bureau of Rural Sciences.

Malenfant, É. C. (2004). Suicide in Canada's immigrant population. *Health Reports*, **15**(2), 9-17.

Mansfeld, Y. (1999) Cycles of war, terror, and peace: Determinants and management of crisis and recovery of the Israeli tourism industry, *Journal of Travel Research*, **38** (1), 30-36.

Mansfeld, Y. & Pizam, A. (2006) Tourism, terrorism, and civil unrest issues, in Y. Mansfeld, and A. Pizam (eds.), *Tourism, Security and Safety: From Theory to Practice*. 1st edn, Oxford: Elsevier, pp. 29-31.

Moreno, A. & Becken, S. (2009) A climate change vulnerability assessment methodology for coastal tourism, *Journal of Sustainable Tourism*, **17** (4), 473-488.

Nepal Tourism Board. (2001) Press-Release on Emergency Declaration. Retrieved on November 27, 2001 from www.welcomenepal.com in Thapa, B. (2012) Tourism in Nepal: Shangri-La's troubled times, in M. Hall, D. Timothy & D. Duval (eds.) *Safety and Security in Tourism*, Routledge, pp. 117-138.

Neumayer, E. (2004). The impact of political violence on tourism. *Journal of Conflict Resolution*, **48**(2), 259- 281.

NTB. (2008). *Annual Operation Plan 2008/09*. Kathmandu: Nepal Tourism Board.

Orchiston, C., Prayag, G. & Brown, C. (2016) Organizational resilience in the tourism sector, *Annals of Tourism Research*, **56**, 145-148.

Paraskevas, A., & Arendell, B. (2007) A strategic framework for terrorism prevention and mitigation in tourism destinations, *Tourism Management*, **28** (6), 1560-1573.

Picard, M. (2008) Balinese identity as tourist attraction: From 'cultural tourism' (pariwisata budaya) to 'Bali erect' (ajeg Bali). *Tourist Studies*, **8** (2), 155–173.

Pizam, A., & Smith, G. (2000) Tourism and terrorism: A quantitative analysis of major terrorist acts and their impact on tourism destinations, *Tourism Economics*, **6** (2), 123-138.

Richter, L. (1992). Political instability and tourism in the third world. In D. Harrison (Ed.), *Tourism and the Less Developed Countries* (pp. 35-46). New York: Wiley.

Rittichainuwat, B. N. & Chakraborty, G. (2009) Perceived travel risks regarding terrorism and disease: The case of Thailand, *Tourism Management*, **30** (3), 410-418.

Saha, S., & Yap, G. (2014) The moderation effects of political instability and terrorism on tourism development: A cross-country panel analysis, *Journal of Travel Research*, **53** (4), 509-521.

Sarrasin, B. (2004) Risque politique et tourisme: Nouveautés et continuités, *Téoros. Revue de recherche en tourisme*, **23** (1), 12-22.

Sönmez, S. F., Apostolopoulos, Y. & Tarlow, P. (1999) Tourism in crisis: Managing the effects of terrorism, *Journal of Travel Research*, **38** (1), 13-18.

6

Suryani, L. K., Page, A., Lesmana, C. B. J., Jennaway, M., Basudewa, I. D. G. & Taylor, R. (2009) Suicide in paradise: aftermath of the Bali bombings, *Psychological Medicine*, **39** (8), 1317-1323.

Thapa, B. (2012) Tourism in Nepal: Shangri-La's troubled times, in M. Hall, D. Timothy and D. Duval (eds.) *Safety and Security in Tourism*, Routledge, pp. 117-138.

Tarlow, P. E. (2006) Terrorism and tourism, in J. Wilks, D. Pendergast and P. Leggat (eds.) *Tourism in turbulent times: Towards safe experiences for visitors (Advances in Tourism Research)*, Oxford: Elsevier, pp. 79-92.

Upadhayaya, P. K., Müller-Böker, U. & Sharma, S. R. (2011) Tourism amidst armed conflict: Consequences, copings, and creativity for peace-building through tourism in Nepal, *The Journal of Tourism and Peace Research*, **1** (2), 22-40.

Vickers, A. (1989) *Bali: A paradise created*. Penguin Books Australia.

World Tourism Organisation (WTO) (2002) News, 4th Quarter Issue 4. http://www.World-Tourism.org. Accessed April 2003.

7 When two worlds collide: Branding industrial destinations

Po-Hsin Lai and Gabby Walters

Introduction

Many parts of the world are increasingly faced with the pressure to accommodate activities of various, and at times, conflicting functions (Holmes, 2006; Lai et al., 2017; Woods 2012). Areas rich in natural resources are often not only conducive to the development of industrial activities, such as mining, energy development, and manufacturing. The natural and socio-economic landscapes they host may also be promoted as assets attractive to tourists seeking unique, authentic, and/or educational tourism experiences (Beer et al., 2017; de Sousa & Kastenholz, 2015; Frantál & Urbánková, 2017). Tourism has been commonly used as a tool to support economic development or regeneration in rural areas and industrial cities (Lane & Kastenholz, 2015; Petrzelka et al., 2006). When an area's industrial activities are in decline and/or fall short in supporting its economy, tourism can provide a supplementary or alternative model to the existing industrial-based economy.

The terms 'industry' and 'tourism' are, however, often viewed as incompatible, since industry – is often associated with pollution, noise, and environmental degradation – and tourism with quietness, relaxation, and more recently, environmental sustainability (Otgaar et al., 2010). Regional destinations that play host to the mining and resources sector may be disregarded by some tourists, despite the importance of tourism to the host region's economic diversification and long-term sustainability. A possible explanation for this aversion may be that activities undertaken by the mining and resources sector may tarnish the image of host destinations which, while needing to present themselves as a destination that supports such activities, struggle to position themselves as an equally viable and attractive tourism destination (Otgaar et al., 2010). To date, factors contributing to the successful co-existence of tourism and mining in regional communities have not been well understood (Frew, 2008). From a branding perspective, it is not known how two highly disparate economic sectors can work towards a unified destination image for their host region.

This chapter lays out the long-standing brand image challenges faced by industrial destinations, and presents a combined stakeholder- and community-driven solution as to how they can be overcome. First, we present some background literature on image formation and its relevance to industrial destinations. Following this, the concept of place is discussed to reinforce the complexities that surround the branding of destinations that host conflicting activities. The chapter concludes with the proposition of a participatory branding approach as a viable image management strategy. This strategy encourages a community to embrace their industrial image and outwardly promote a unified brand image that communicates pride and acceptance.

Image formation and industrial destinations

Conventional destination marketing places great emphasis on creating and reinforcing a positive destination image in the mind of tourists. While the definition of destination image is vast and varied, there is strong agreement within the literature that in a general sense, destination image represents the beliefs that people, particularly tourists, hold about a place (Crompton, 1979; Echtner & Ritchie, 1991; Gartner, 1996; Mackay & Fesenmaier, 1997; Therkelsen & Halkier, 2008; Walters & Mair, 2012). Avraham and Ketter (2013) divide destination image into two distinct categories: 'open images' that enable flexibility, and 'closed images' that are otherwise known as 'stereotypes' (Elizur, 1986), or simplified beliefs or attitudes about a place that are difficult to change. According to research by Stern and Krakover (1993), destination image is formed based on first, the information consumers are exposed to, and second, on their own personal characteristics, which subsequently influence the way that the obtained information is processed.

Information sources play a vital role in the formation of destination image. Individuals may be exposed to information regarding a destination through a variety of means. Gartner (1993) contends that image formation occurs in response to one's exposure to various image formation agents. Primary images are those that are formed as a result of visiting and experiencing the destination. On the other hand, secondary images according to Gartner, are likely to be induced by these information agents, without the destination having been visited:

■ **Overt induced** images: formed as a result of exposure to conventional marketing campaigns and deliberate communication attempts to attract attention to and create awareness of the destination.

■ **Covert induced** images: formed in response to celebrity endorsements of a destination, or mainstream media articles that feature the destination.

■ **Autonomous** images: formed as a result of exposure to mainstream media reports, television shows and/or films in which the destination is featured, though not necessarily for tourism purposes.

■ **Solicited or unsolicited organic** images: formed in response to information provided by family and friends about the destination, which may or may not be actively sought

The secondary image formation agents such as those listed above are of most relevance to destinations that simultaneously accommodate tourism and other resource-dependent sectors. These destinations represent a unique context in terms of the management of negative perceptions, because they are unable to commit to, change or diversify their industrial focus due to their economic dependency on inward investment. Additionally, besides contributing to economic growth and prosperity, many of the activities associated with the mining and resources sector are renowned for causing significant negative environmental and socio-cultural impacts (Otgaar et al., 2010), and are subject to media sensationalism.

According to McLennan et al. (2017), mining towns are likely to attract national-level media coverage because of the conflict that often occurs between the tourism and the mining and resources sectors. The subsequent media attention that arises from such conflicts is likely to result in autonomous image formation among the public. However, news media reports do not necessarily need to have a tourism angle to induce negative destination images. The Latrobe Valley, located in the

Australian region of Gippsland, has been the subject of significant media reporting on health implications of being surrounded by coal-fired power stations (see, for example: Brown, 2014). Gloucester, located in the Australian state of New South Wales, presents another example of media coverage on local concerns over mining proposals which were considered by some as incompatible with the attributes of the area to support the image of a rural idyll (Rubbo, 2017). Media coverage such as this can lead to the overtly induced destination images (that is, those generated by conventional marketing campaigns) becoming tainted by the adversarial media framing that often accompanies environmental concerns (McLennan et al., 2017). For destinations targeting first-time visitors who are yet to experience the destination first hand, perceptions are far more influential than reality (Pike & Page, 2014). Consequently, the mainstream media is likely to have significant power when it comes to public formation of the region's image.

Media sensationalism and environmental lobbying surrounding these activities can contribute to the demise of the host destination's image as a place attractive to tourists. Sensationalist reporting of negative events represents one of the biggest challenges to destination marketers attempting to restore negative perceptions (Ghaderiet al., 2012; Pearlman & Melnik, 2008; Peters & Pikkemaat, 2005), and this is particularly difficult for industrial destinations that tend to have a long-term negative image (Avraham & Ketter, 2013; Otgaar et al., 2010). However, communicating a uniform message about such destinations to both tourists and investors is difficult for regional destination marketing organizations (DMOs), because the differences in perceived interests are often viewed as too large to be meaningfully combined into a synchronized brand image (Therkelsen & Halkier, 2008). In the case of tourism destinations that host an abundance of industrial developments, the destinations' profiles can be skewed towards the industrial sector at the expense of the tourism industry.

The impact of industrial activity on a tourism destination's image remains unexplored in the destination image literature. It is therefore necessary to draw on existing image recovery strategies to identify a possible image management solution. These include: ignoring the crises or problems, and pretending nothing is wrong with the destination (Avraham & Ketter, 2008; Holcomb, 1994; Young & Lever, 1997); disassociation from the problematic location (Carter, 1998; Ketter & Avraham, 2010); celebrity endorsement (Walters & Mair, 2012); delivering a counter message to offset the common negative perceptions

(Armstrong & Ritchie, 2008); ridiculing the stereotype (Avraham & Ketter, 2008); and spinning the negative characteristics into positive attributes (Avraham & Ketter, 2008; Chacko & Marcell, 2008; Sanders et al., 2008).

Undoubtedly, the industrial sector provides an economic contribution to their host destinations. It is therefore highly unlikely that industrial activities would cease for purposes of image management. Such activities are also difficult to hide or dissociate from, given the indiscrete nature of the infrastructure. Counter-messages are generally more effective when attempting to mitigate unfounded perceptions, and ridiculing the stereotype of industrial destinations may cause offence to the local community. Therefore, in order to provide an image management solution that allows both the tourism and industrial sectors to co-exist, we explore the application of the final strategy: 'spinning the negative characteristics into positive attributes.' The negative characteristics in this case would be industrial activities; while the positive attributes could be the unique brand identity of the destination whose community embraces a united and co-dependent relationship between non-tourism and tourism sectors.

The image management field holds a consensus that typically, marketers will focus on the positive, as opposed to the negative, attributes of a product or destination when devising their marketing strategies and developing their desired brand image. This chapter challenges this norm by demonstrating how the development of a participatory place branding management strategy, if applied effectively, may facilitate the development of a positive brand image for tourism destinations with long-standing image issues due to their affiliation with industrial activities.

The complexity of place

According to Campelo et al. (2014), tourism destinations "are embedded in places; it is the place with all of its networks, relationships and shared experiences that determines the nature of the destination" (p. 155). Tourism destinations are not only visited by tourists to consume any available experience; they are also places filled with meanings, be they economic, environmental, social, cultural, and emotional. These are all valued in various ways by local residents and others who share a connection with the destinations (Kavaratzis, 2017).

Places are subjects of social representations produced through social construction, and appropriated and reconstructed by stakeholders via their cognitive systems to reflect not only group-based norms, values, and collective identity, but also their experiences and personal interests (Abric, 2001; Lai et al., 2013). Consequently, place stakeholders are likely to perceive place and represent its meanings differently. Places, their meanings, and associated beliefs are not static. They are constantly being made, because place stakeholders continuously engage in representing, constructing, appropriating, negotiating, and re-presenting place meanings through direct and indirect interactions with different aspects of place (Lai et al., 2013; Kavaratzis & Hatch, 2013). The prevalence of social media platforms (for example, Facebook, Twitter, Instagram) allows dialogues between place stakeholders to co-construct and co-create the meaning and identity of place (Kavaratzis, 2017). Places are forever evolving because their economic, social and natural environments continue to be shaped by various internal (for example, local government decisions to invest in a tourism or non-tourism sector, developments leading to improved or degraded environmental qualities), and external forces (for example, external investments, changing society and/or political values) (Buijs, et al., 2012; Lai et al., 2013). This further contributes to the complexity of place. How a destination is developed and then promoted can be perceived negatively or positively by place stakeholders, which may include tourists, local residents, and those who are responsible for its planning and promotion, or have a vested interest in the place for economic, social, environmental, and/or emotional reasons.

The complex nature of place demands a different branding approach from the one applied to traditional goods/services practiced by private entities, and one that focuses on static/positive destination image (Kavaratzis & Kalandides, 2015). Tourists do not simply draw on formal elements of destination brands, such as slogans or logos, to form their destination image (Ashworth & Kavaratzis, 2009; Munar, 2011). Consequently, destination branding needs to acknowledge the complexities of image formation and move away from a focus on simple slogans and logos to present their desired image and portray a meaningful sense of place.

Place branding

Place branding initially emerged from the place promotion literature, and has since been examined and further developed across disciplines such as geography, sociology, anthropology, regional economy, and tourism studies (Braun et al., 2014; Hankinson, 2010). It is broadly practiced in various contexts to promote a product to its target market, a nation to foreign investors or skilled workers, and a city's cultural and entertainment services to both residents and non-residents. It is also used to refer to a tourist destination focusing on developing a desirable destination image attractive to tourists (Braun et al., 2014; García et al, 2012; Kavaratzis, 2005, 2017; Papadopoulos, 2004; Zenker et al., 2017). The complexity of place as a perceptual and substantial entity, and the stakeholders' role in it are incorporated in the definition of place brand by Zenker and Braun (2010). According to these authors, a place brand comprises "a network of associations in the place consumer's mind based on the visual, verbal, and behavioural expression of a place, which is embodied through the aims, communication, values, and the general culture of the place's stakeholders and the overall place design" (Zenker & Braun, 2010:4, cited in Zenker et al., 2017).

Place branding, in general, involves the effort to promote a place brand to its target market(s). Kavaratzis and Kalandides (2015), citing Läpple (1991), identify four interconnected constituent elements of place that are integral to place making and contribute to the process of forming a place brand.

- The first is **materiality** or the physical and material structure of a place (for example, an open space, an aesthetic landscape, or their lack thereof) which circumscribes social space, facilitates or constraints social relations, and allows history and collective memory to evolve.

- The second element, **practices**, encompasses the production, consumption, and appropriation of the material aspect of place. For example, tourism as an economic sector often focuses on the aesthetic aspect of a place's physical structure to support its production and consumption of tourism experiences; while the mining sector relies on the extraction of minerals from the physical structure to support related production and consumption.

- **Institutions**, as the third place element, refers to the formal and informal normative system (for example, property rights, legal regulations, planning guidelines, power relations, social norms) which mediate "the material substrate of social space and the social practice of its production, appropriation and use" (Kavaratzis & Kalandides, 2015:1374).

- The fourth element, **representations**, refers to the signs, symbols, and images that convey the meaning of place. The mental associations that place stakeholders form with a place and its constituent elements leads to what a place is in their mind, and simultaneously contributes to how a place brand is perceived and evaluated.

In the meantime, place stakeholders also actively engage in constructing and shaping these place elements to achieve a desired goal. They work collectively or competitively to appropriate and utilize the material substrate of place, and engage in various consumptive and productive practices to meet diverse economic goals via tourism, resource extraction, energy development, and/or manufacturing. This, in turn, also shapes the material landscape of place, enables or disables certain social interactions, and contributes to shared place memory.

More recently, place branding has been suggested as an approach to "integrate, guide and focus place management" (Kavaratzis 2005:334), and address the need for coordinated efforts to engage stakeholders in defining and co-creating the shared identity of a place. A place, through its brand message, tells the story about the destination and its people (Ashworth & Kavaratzis, 2009; Hankinson, 2007; Kavaratzis, 2017). Place branding in a tourism context can be used to forge a shared sense of place among place stakeholders who collectively engage in consuming and co-creating place meanings and values derived from direct and indirect place-based experiences. It can also be used to facilitate the communication and coordination between and across government and other non-tourism sectors to ensure consistent brand messages and communications. The concept of participatory place branding recognizes the complexity of place branding and the need to incorporate how destinations are perceived and experienced from the perspectives of all key place stakeholders, (Kavaratzis & Kalandides, 2015; Kavaratzis, 2017; Zenker & Erfgen, 2014). The relevance of this concept to managing the brand image of industrial tourism destination is discussed below.

A participatory approach to branding the industrial destination

Stakeholder participation is increasingly emphasized to address the challenges of promoting places as complex entities that often do not have a single identity or image, nor one singular function and meaning (Kavaratzis & Kalandides, 2015; Line & Wang, 2017; Otgaar, 2012; Zenker & Erfgen, 2014). Destination branding that focuses on developing simplified slogans and memorable logos, and ignores or eschews associations with industrial activities that are assumed to 'contaminate' the destinations' image, may achieve limited success (Avraham & Ketter, 2008; Ketter & Avraham, 2010). The effectiveness of such an approach can be particularly questionable for places such as industrial destinations that have yet to establish a clear destination image among target audiences, and where tourism is only one of the economic sectors contributing to the overall brand identity and destination image (Pike & Page, 2014). The need for stakeholder participation also arises from the recognition of its utility for managing conflicting interests and power imbalances, as well as expanding opportunities and values through stakeholder collaboration (Hardy & Pearson, 2017; Kavaratzis, 2017).

Stakeholder engagement and partnership development are now viewed by both scholars and practitioners as integral parts of the planning and implementation process of place branding (Ashworth & Kavaratzis, 2009; Hankinson, 2010; Kavaratzis, 2017). Conventionally, tourism stakeholders and partners have often been identified as including operators, tourists, residents, and those in regulatory positions who have the right and an interest in participating in tourism (García et al., 2012; Hardy & Pearson, 2017). However, for this approach to succeed, non-tourism industries (for example, mining, energy development, manufacturing) also need to be considered as important destination stakeholders and partners, as they can substantially shape the four elements of place (that is, materiality, practices, institutions, representations) and affect how the place brand of a destination is perceived and represented.

Figure 7.1 shows a participatory place branding framework as a continuing process that takes into consideration the need to "simultaneously address the needs of different economic sectors, different stakeholder groups and different audiences" (Kavaratzis, 2017:102–103).

Figure 7.1: The participatory place branding process

The process starts with gathering detailed information about how a destination is currently and can potentially be perceived by its internal and external audiences. Resources encompass the elements of place (materiality, practices, institutions, representations) which can be used to communicate to and create values for the target audiences, and other resources available to support the participatory process. This is followed by deliberation, where those attempting to brand the destination (for example, local authorities, tourism officials, researchers/consultants, other directly involved sectors) engage in deliberating and drafting a strategic vision of the destination's future. Consultation is then implemented to engage in extensive discussions with the destination community to refine the vision and related strategies, identify and forge a common ground, and establish mutually beneficial partnerships with sectors and other destinations. Actions are then taken to create a supportive participatory process that seeks to improve the material aspect of place and garner community involvement in identifying, representing, co-creating, and endorsing the place identity and associated images arising from the process. Actions are followed by communications aiming to publicize the shared vision and corresponding branding strategies. A feedback mechanism is also needed, so that the process remains dynamic to respond to internal or external changes to the destination.

The above framework allows tourism and other interests to be expressed and negotiated to build a common ground, seek synergies and support for collaborative effort to promote and develop the destination. Tourism planning is viewed in this framework as part of the place branding process, because tourism represents one of the economic sectors and interests contributing to the identity and brand of a destination. The destination management organization (DMO) plays a vital role in facilitating stakeholder engagement and partnership development in place branding to establish a clear vision for the destination brand and a set of core brand values. DMOs also help to ensure that the same brand values are shared across departments and partner organizations, and these values are consistently conveyed to different target audiences (Hankinson, 2010). On the other hand, place branding organizations (PBOs) may be formed as an alternative to better represent the needs to those outside of the tourism sector. Below we provide several approaches for the implementation of participatory place branding in destinations that simultaneously accommodate tourism and industrial activities.

Through collaborative and coordinated efforts facilitated by DMOs or PBOs, consistent and shared place brands for industrial destinations can be developed through the identification of a common ground across both tourism and non-tourism sectors. The spinning of potentially negative characteristics (that is, industrial and or mining sites) into positive destination attributes (that is, industrial tourism attractions) may be one approach that provides for a unified place brand image which allows both the tourism and industrial sectors to present a consistent outward image. The development of tourism attractions that align with the destination's core industries also present a range of opportunities, such as: economic diversification (Otgaar et al., 2010; Canalejo et al., 2010); the redevelopment of redundant industrial sites (Frew, 2008); and enhanced competitiveness via the development of distinctive visitor experiences (Ying, 2010). Such efforts can also promote partnerships between tourism and non-tourism sectors for the purposes of creating complementary resources and activities that are both educational and stimulating.

Because place branding involves a continuing process to engage place stakeholders, an online platform could be established for tourists, other non-local target audiences and local place stakeholders to share experiences and perceptions, and co-create values derived from various forms of interactions with the destination through textual and visual content. This, in turn, can be used to inform place branding efforts to better reflect the evolving nature of place. It also provides a mechanism to engender a sense of ownership among participants and reinforce commitment to the co-created place brand (Kavaratzis, 2017).

Media support is also essential to the success of place branding, because sensationalist reporting of negative events or images associated with industrial destinations can have a substantial negative effect on public perceptions (Ghaderi et al., 2012; Pearlman & Melnik, 2008). A partnership between DMOs or PBOs and media may assist with the renewal of a long-standing image issue for industrial destinations. In particular, travel media can be engaged via familiarization tours; while mainstream media may be more sensitive to the impact of their negative reporting on non-tourism related issues, should they be treated as an important participatory stakeholder.

International and domestic trade missions should also feature an industrial destination's reinvented brand image. Non-tourism sectors need to be mindful of the multiple destination image formation agents when representing the destination to national and international audiences. It is essential that once a consensus is reached regarding the desired place brand, the messages that represent the community and its stakeholders are consistent across all channels. Internal marketing also plays a role in instilling this newly devised sense of place among local community members to enhance community pride and acceptance of their region and its people.

Conclusion

This chapter presents challenges faced by destinations that accommodate industrial activities (for example, mining, energy development, or manufacturing), while attempting to position and market themselves as an equally viable tourism destination. Tourism destinations are places supportive of various functions, and are imbued with meanings that are variously represented by relevant stakeholders and constantly evolving. DMOs that are reliant on simple slogans and logos to establish or reinforce an overt induced destination images in tourists may not always be successful, because tourists are constantly subject to exposure to other secondary image formation agents that are beyond DMOs' control. As such, conventional destination marketing that focuses on promoting a positive and static destination image and eschews any association with industrial activities is unlikely to gain a competitive advantage.

Recommendations for practice

A participatory place branding approach is presented to capture the complex and dynamic nature of destination places. It can also be used as a framework to facilitate focused and coordinated effort for managing and promoting destinations' economic sectors beyond tourism, and deliver compatible and consistent place branding message to target audiences. Such effort requires support and involvement of place stakeholders. We conclude with the following recommendations for industrial destinations seeking to overcome their long-standing image issues:

■ Consider the development of industrial tourism attractions that allow for a consistent brand image which will appeal to both investors and tourists.

■ Engage multiple community stakeholders in consultation around place branding decisions to understand the values and meanings stakeholders attribute to the destination, and enhance community support of a shared identity.

■ Establish an active social media presence, and encourage community members, tourists, and other key stakeholders to engage with the place brand through textual and visual content that represents the desired destination image.

■ Consider the media an important influencer in relation to the maintenance of the established destination brand image, and ensure they understand the implications of negative reporting to the community that hosts industrial destinations.

■ Create an internal marketing campaign to create a sense of pride among residents, and encourage ownership and endorsement of their destination's place brand.

References

Abric, J. C. (2001) A structural approach to social representation, in K. Deaux and G. Philogene (eds.), *Representations of the Social: Bridging theoretical traditions*, Malden, MA: Blackwell, pp. 42–47.

Armstrong, E.K. & Ritchie, B.W. (2008) The heart recovery marketing campaign: destination recovery after a major bushfire in Australia's National Capital, *Journal of Travel & Tourism Marketing*, **23**(2/4), 175–189.

Ashworth, G. & Kavaratzis, M. (2009) Beyond the logo: Brand management for cities, *Journal of Brand Management*, **16** (8), 520–531.

Avraham, E. & Ketter, E. (2008) *Media strategies for marketing places in crisis: Improving the image of Cities, Countries and Tourist Destinations*, Oxford: Butterworth Heinemann.

Avraham, E. & Ketter, E. (2013). Marketing destinations with prolonged negative images: Towards a theoretical model. *Tourism Geographies*, **15**(1), 145-164.

Beer, M., Rybár, R. & Kaľavský, M. (2017) Renewable energy sources as an attractive element of industrial tourism, *Current Issues in Tourism*, **21** (18), 2139–2151.

Braun, E., Kavaratzis, M. & Zenker, S. (2013) My city – my brand: The different roles of residents in place branding, *Journal of Place Management and Development*, **6** (1), 18–28.

Brown, R. (2014) Coal mine smoke drives primary school students out of classrooms, February 20, accessed July 2018 from http://www.abc.net.au/am/content/2013/s3948412.htm?site=gippsland

Buijs, A., Hovardas, T., Figari, H., Castro, P., Devine-Wright, P., Fischer, A. Mouro, C. & Selge, S. (2012) Understanding people's ideas on natural resource management: Research on social representations of nature, *Society & Natural Resources*, **25** (11), 1167–1181.

Campelo, A., Aitken, R., Thyne, M. & Gnoth, J. (2014) Sense of place: The importance for destination branding, *Journal of Travel Research*, **53** (2), 154–166.

Canalejo, A., Guzman, T & De la Torre, G. (2010). Industrial mining tourism as a development strategy in geographical areas in decline: A case study. *Tourism Perspectives*, **19** (3) 382–393.

Carter, S. (1998). Tourists' and travelers' social construction of Africa and Asia as risky locations, *Tourism Management*, **19** (4) 349–358.

Chacko, H. E. & Marcell, M. H. (2008) Repositioning a tourism destination: The case of New Orleans after Hurricane Katrina, *Journal of Travel & Tourism Marketing*, **23** (2), 223–235.

Crompton, L. (1979) Motivations for pleasure vacation, *Annals of Tourism Research*, **6** (4), 408–424.

de Sousa, A. J. G. & Kastenholz, E. (2015) Wind farms and the rural tourism experience – problem or possible productive integration? The views of visitors and residents of a Portuguese village, *Journal of Sustainable Tourism*, **23** (8/9), 1236–1256.

Elizur, J. (1986) *National Images*, Jerusalem: Hebrew University.

Etchner, C. & Ritchie, B. (1991). The meaning and measurement of destination image, *Journal of Tourism Studies*, **2** (2), 2–10.

Frantál, B. & Urbánková, R. (2017) Energy tourism: An emerging field of study, *Current Issues in Tourism*, **20** (13), 1395–1412.

Frew, E. (2008) Industrial tourism theory and implemented strategies, *Advances in Culture, Tourism and Hospitality Research*, **2** (27-42),

García, J. A., Gómez, M. & Molina, A. (2012) A destination-branding model: An empirical analysis based on stakeholders, *Tourism Management*, **33** (3), 646–661.

Gartner, W. C. (1993). Image formation process, in Uysal, M. & Fesenmaier, D. (eds.) *Communication and Channel Systems in Tourism Marketing*. New York: Haworth Press, pp. 191–215.

Gartner, W. C. (1996) *Tourism Development: Principles, Processes and Policies*. New York: Van Nostrand Reinhold.

Ghaderi, Z., Mat Som, A. P. & Henderson, J. C. (2012) Tourism crises and island destinations: Experiences in Penang, Malaysia, *Tourism Management Perspectives*, **2/3**, 79–84.

Hankinson, G. (2007) The management of destination brands: Five guiding principles based on recent developments in corporate branding theory, *Journal of Brand Management*, **14** (3), 240–254.

Hankinson, G. (2010) Place branding theory: A cross-domain literature review from a marketing perspective, in G. J. Ashworth & M. Kavaratzis (eds.), *Towards Effective Place Brand Management*, Cheltenham: Edward Elgar, pp. 15–35.

Hardy, A. & Pearson, L. J. (2018) Examining stakeholder group specificity: An innovative sustainable tourism approach, *Journal of Destination Marketing & Management*, **8**, 247–258.

Holcomb, B. (1994) City make-over: Marketing the post-industrial city, in J. R. Gold and S. V. Ward (eds), *Place Promotion: The use of publicity and marketing to sell towns and regions*, Chichester, UK: John Wiley and Sons, pp. 115–131.

Holmes, J. (2006) Impulses towards a multifunctional transition in rural Australia: Gaps in the research agenda, *Journal of Rural Studies*, **22** (2), 142–160.

7

Kavaratzis, M. (2005) Place branding: A review of trends and conceptual models, *Marketing Review*, **5** (4), 329–342.

Kavaratzis, M. (2017) The participatory place branding process for tourism: Linking visitors and residents through the city brand, in N. Bellini and C. Pasquinelli (eds.), *Tourism in the City: Towards an Integrative Agenda on Urban Tourism*, Cham: Springer International Publishing. pp. 93–107.

Kavaratzis, M. & Hatch, M. J. (2013) The dynamics of place brands: An identity-based approach to place branding theory, *Marketing Theory*, **13** (1), 69–86.

Kavaratzis, M. & Kalandides, A. (2015) Rethinking the place brand: The interactive formation of place brands and the role of participatory place branding, *Environment and Planning A: Economy and Space*, **47** (6), 1368–1382.

Ketter, E. & Avraham, E. (2010) How African countries promote themselves using the Internet, *International Journal on Tourism Policy*, **3** (4), 318–331.

Lai, P.-H., Hsu, Y.-C. & Nepal, S. (2013) Representing the landscape of Yushan National Park, *Annals of Tourism Research*, **43**, 37–57.

Lai, P.-H., Morrison-Saunders, A. & Grimstad, S. (2017) Operating small tourism firms in rural destinations: A social representations approach to examining how small tourism firms cope with non-tourism induced changes, *Tourism Management*, **58**, 164–174.

Lane, B. and Kastenholz, E. (2015) Rural tourism: The evolution of practice and research approaches: Towards a new generation concept?, *Journal of Sustainable Tourism*, **23** (8/9), 1133–1156.

Läpple, D. (1991) Essay über den Rau, in H. Häußermann, D. Ipsen, T. K. Badoni, D. Läpple, W. Siebel & M. Rodenstein (eds.), *Stadt und Raum: Für ein gesellschaftswissenschaftliches Raumkonzept*, Berlin: Pfaffenweiler. pp 157–207.

Line, N. D. & Wang, Y. (2017) A multi-stakeholder market oriented approach to destination marketing, *Journal of Destination Marketing & Management*, **6** (1), 84–93.

Mackay, K. J. & Fesenmaier, D. R. (1997) Pictorial elements of destination image formation, *Annals of Tourism Research*, **24** (3), 537–565.

McLennan, C.-l. J., Becken, S. &Moyle, B. D. (2017) Framing in a contested space: media reporting on tourism and mining in Australia, *Current Issues in Tourism*, **20**, 1–21.

Munar, A. M. (2011) Tourist-created content: rethinking destination branding, *International Journal of Culture, Tourism and Hospitality Research*, **5** (3), 291–305.

Otgaar, A. (2012) Towards a common agenda for the development of industrial tourism, *Tourism Management Perspectives*, **4**, 86–91.

Otgaar, A., van den Berg, L., Berger, C. & Feng, R. (2010) *Industrial Tourism: Opportunities for Cities and Enterprise*. Farnham: Ashgate Publishing Ltd.

Papadopoulos, N. (2004) Place branding: Evolution, meaning and implications, *Place Branding and Public Diplomacy*, **1** (1), 36–49.

Pearlman, D. & Melnik, O. (2008) Hurricane Katrina's effect on the perception of New Orleans leisure tourists, *Journal of Travel & Tourism Marketing*, **25** (1), 58–67.

Peters, M. & Pikkemaat, B. (2005) Crisis management in Alpine Winter Sports Resorts: The 1999 Avalanche Disaster in Tyrol, *Journal of Travel & Tourism Marketing*, **19** (2/3), 9–20.

Petrzelka, P., Krannich, R. S. & Brehm, J. M. (2006) Identification with resource-based occupations and desire for tourism: Are the two necessarily inconsistent?, *Society & Natural Resources*, **19** (8), 693–707.

Pike, S. & Page, S. J. (2014) Destination marketing organizations and destination marketing: A narrative analysis of the literature, *Tourism Management*, **41**, 202–227.

Rubbo, L. (2017) Gloucester residents anxiously await decision on revised Rocky Hill open cut coal mine proposal, May 24, accessed on July 2018 from https://www.abc.net.au/news/2017-05-24/gloucester-residents-feeling-stressed-campaign-against-mine/8554160

Sanders, D. Laing, J., & Houghton, M. (2008) *Impact of Bushfires on Tourism Visitation in Alpine National Parks*, Technical Report prepared for the Sustainable Tourism Cooperative Research Centre, Australia.

Stern, E. & Krakover, S. (1993) The formation of a composite urban image, *Geographical Analysis*, **25** (2), 130–146.

Therkelsen, A. & Halkier, H. (2008) Contemplating place branding umbrellas. The case of coordinated national tourism and business promotion in Denmark, *Scandinavian Journal of Hospitality and Tourism*, **8** (2), 159–175.

Walters, G. & Mair, J. (2012) The effectiveness of post-disaster recovery marketing messages – the case of the 2009 Australian bushfires, *Journal of Tourism and Travel Marketing*, **29** (1) 87–103

Woods, M. (2012) New directions in rural studies?, *Journal of Rural Studies*, **28** (1), 1–4.

Ying, J. (2010). Analysis and suggestions on Chinese industrial tourism development. *International Business Research*, **3** (2), 169–173.

Young, C. & Lever, J. (1997) Place promotion, economic location and the consumption of image, *Tijdschrift voor Economics en Sociale Geographie*, **88**, 332–341

Zenker, S. & Erfgen, C. (2014) Let them do the work: A participatory place branding approach, *Journal of Place Management and Development*, **7** (3), 225–234.

Zenker, S., Braun, E. & Petersen, S. (2017) Branding the destination versus the place: The effects of brand complexity and identification for residents and visitors, *Tourism Management*, **58**, 15–27.

7

8 Rubbish and reputation: How unsustainable waste management impacts tourism

Rohan Miller and Gwyneth Howell

Introduction

Tourism is recognised as having a two-way relationship with the environment (Halleux, 2017). On the positive side, many tourists are attracted to destinations to experience product attributes such as cultural heritage, flora and fauna, sea and sand. Implicitly, sustainability practices and maintaining the destination's environmental integrity are critical to this form of tourism (Ecorys, 2013). On the darker side, however, it is recognised that tourism places significant pressure on a destination's natural environment through pollution, ecosystem degradation and additional strain on natural resources (Weston et al., 2016). Thus, many tourist destinations have reputations that are intrinsically linked to their management of the environment and potentially negative product attributes that can impact on the environment (such as garbage, waste and sewage) (Inversini et al., 2009). In this context, Fombrun et al.'s (1999:72) definition that reputation is considered as "a perceptual representation of a company's [or destination's] past actions and future prospects that describes the firm's overall appeal to all of its key constituents when compared with other leading rivals" is applied in this chapter.

As it is common to identify how organisations and markets change over time (for example see, Knowles & Curtis 1999), this chapter proposes a Reputation Evolution model for application in tourism reputation management. Herein, it is suggested that a tourist destination's reputation is *created* over time, may *recede* over time due to local and international issues related to waste and environmental management, and that once the issue is satisfactorily addressed, then its reputation can be *revised* before the final stage that allows the *rebuilding* of a destination's reputation over time.

In this chapter we highlight Bali's current situation and draw on examples from two global tourism destinations, Boracay and Naples, to demonstrate the impact that waste problems have on the reputation of tourism destinations. Of particular concern is the practice for public waterways to be treated as cheap and convenient dumping grounds for trash and sewage. This has resulted in excess amounts of waste and sewerage being dumped into waterways and these bi-products are increasingly visible and impacting the environment. In 2010 approximately "275 million metric tons (MT) of plastic waste was generated in 192 coastal countries" and between 4.8 to 12.7 million MT entered the ocean (Jambeck et al., 2015:771). Furthermore, an estimated 2 million plus tons of sewage and other effluents drain into the world's salt and non-salt waters each day (United Nations, 2014). There are an estimated "16 shopping bags full of plastic for every metre of coastline (excluding Antarctica)" globally, and by 2025 there will be "enough plastic in the ocean (on our most conservative estimates) to cover 5% of the earth's entire surface in cling film each year" (Hardesty & Wilcox, 2015:2).

Most of the garbage in the oceans originates from land-based legal and illegal dumping, stormwater discharge, extreme natural events, littering and poor waste management practices (Stikel et al., 2012). Over time, much of this garbage seems to form into a toxic sludge of durable materials such as plastics, polystyrene, metal, glass and rubber (Avery-Gomm, et al., 2012; Ebbesmeyer, 2012) that takes many years to decompose. As well as visible waste such as plastic bottles, bags and straws, the sludge includes bacteria, toxic chemicals and microscopic particles from the break-down of solid matter (e.g. microplastics) (Lebreton et al., 2018). The little particles amidst the toxic sludge can be digested by marine life and increase the likelihood that the seafood that families and their future generations eat will contain microscopic pellets of trash and toxins.

Martin and Assenov (2008) posit that if the natural environment is not valued in economic terms, then there is little incentive for government and industry to manage the ocean's water quality and the elimination of rubbish dumping into the oceans. An indicator of the costs of coastal garbage dumping is provided by the U.S. Environmental Protection Agency's estimate that each resident on the US west coast contributes approximately $13 each to combat and clean up ocean-trash (Stikel et al., 2012). That is, an estimated US$520m is spent each year on the US west coast alone to combat rubbish and marine debris before it leaves US shores to pollute international waterways. There are major problems associated with garbage in major tourist destinations such as California and Hawaii, as well as the waters of South-East Asia and the Pacific, and in distant locations such as the Norwegian fiords. Quite simply, garbage is a major threat to the international coastal tourism industry.

The aim of this chapter is to demonstrate the need for established and emerging tourist destinations to proactively manage perceptions and practices associated with waste and sewerage in order to protect their destinations' reputations. Globally, we have reached a saturation point where the out-of-sight, out-of-mind garbage paradigm of dumping waste in our waterways merely pushes a problem elsewhere (although often the waste remains localised) and this is not sustainable given the current levels of waste and sewerage already in our water ways. We argue that the economic costs that poor waste management across the globe has on coastal tourism and coastal tourism's reputation cannot be ignored. Specifically, all tourism stakeholders need to recognise and actively manage for environmental sustainability.

The main context of this chapter is the tropical Island of Bali. The following section provides detailed background into the garbage-related issues that Bali is currently facing and the island's consequent reputational issues. The waste management practices of two global tourism destinations, Naples and Boracay, are scrutinised in this chapter to provide the reader with examples of effective and somewhat ineffective waste management practices and the consequences of these for the tourism industry. Lessons drawn from these examples are used to inform valuable recommendations for Bali and other 3S (Sand, Sea and Sun) destinations that risk the demise of their reputation as a result of garbage and pollution are then presented.

Bali: 'The Island of the Gods'

Bali lies in the southwest aspect of the Coral Triangle; an area some claim as blessed with the most marine biodiversity on the planet (Berdej, 2014). Bali's reputation as a tourism place has primarily focused on elements of its natural environment and the location's image. In tourism marketing, a key purpose of a place's reputation is to attract international tourists that in turn, builds and stimulates the local economy (see for example Law et al., 2016). Bali has been referred to as the Island of Gods since the 1970s and relies heavily on its position as a reknowned 3S tourism destination. Bali's brand reputation promotes many alluring product attributes, such as spiritualism and volcanos, warm and welcoming hospitality from the locals, an exotic local culture, an idyllic beach-side lifestyle, a climate ideal for swimming, diving and surfing, a diverse array of accommodations, and cuisine to suit any traveller.

Apart from some relatively minor cautions pertaining to typical travel risks such as gastroenteritis (e.g. Bali-belly) and over-exposure to the sun, until recently the only obvious issue associated with holidaying in Bali in the tourism media is the chance of heavy monsoonal rain – but then, this should be expected as this destination does rest in the tropics. However, news-broadcasts and Internet sites are now carrying stories that Bali is facing an environmental crisis caused by waste. Some of Bali's biggest fans and most loyal tourists are also taking to e-word of mouth communication to reveal that garbage, sludge and sanitation issues are fundamentally degrading the idyllic island paradise experience. These communications seem to be adversely impacting Bali's traditional reputation and negatively affect two of the three 3S tourism drivers – being sea and sand (Stupart and Shipley, 2012)

A receding reputation

A historical view of the development of tourism in Bali reveals that until the 1970s, Bali was a series of villages, each with many neighbourhoods (*banjars*) representing the territorial, cultural and social identity of each neighbourhood (Hussey, 1989). Bali is one of the many island states under the central governance of Indonesia. However, Bali's growth as a tourist mecca developed organically against the background of frequent Ministry of Tourism reshuffles within the varying political regimes that governed Indonesia from 1945, and since a decentralised system of government was introduced in 2001 (Judisseno, 2015).

Bali attracted more than five million foreign visitors in 2017 and this accounts for 40 percent of Indonesia's total tourism arrivals (Hou, 2018). However, Bali's reputation is receding, precipitated by growing recognition there are shortcomings in the island's infrastructure (e.g. water, waste and sewerage facilities). An examination of publicly available material suggests there was an over-riding lack of concern for the environment by the Indonesian and Balinese governments (see for example, Taylor, 2018; Wright & Waddell, 2017). As commented in Judisseno's (2015: 224) thesis, "government environmental regulations relating to tourism in Bal were inadequate and failed to protect the environment" up to and as late as 2015.

According to the Rivers, Oceans, Lands, Ecology Foundation (R.O.L.E., 2018), Indonesia produces 130,000 tons of solid and liquid garbage, of which only an estimated 50 percent goes into landfill. It is highly plausible that the balance of the garbage is illegally dumped and ultimately ends up in the ocean. Harvey (2018) reports that some of the garbage washed up on Bali's shores comes from the island itself, but that other Indonesian islands, like Java and Sumatra also contribute to the problem. Intuitively then, it is possible for the Indonesian government and local Balinese policy makers to reduce the flow of localised trash into their proximate coast-lines by better waste management policies and practices.

Exacerbating the locally caused pollution problems, Bali is at the mercy of global winds and ocean currents. The Balinese islands are the recipient of global garbage that is moving past the waters of tropical paradises throughout the Pacific Ocean and to the Indonesian Throughflow, before arriving at Bali (Howe, 2005). Thus, the prevention of a substantial proportion of garbage and toxic sludge that is impacting on Bali's reputation will ultimately depend on international negotiation to reduce the flow of garbage, and particular types of garbage such as plastics and toxins, into the ocean.

There seems to be a growing number of adverse posts from dissatisfied consumers and people on social media who are genuinely concerned at the environmental crisis besetting Bali. For example, "Come to the beautiful beaches of Bali, sun bake amongst the rubbish, dive into the trash-filled water and enjoy a skin rash!" (R.O.L.E., 2018:1). Sea-borne toxins now provide an alternative meaning to the historical attribution of Bali-belly (Tripadvisor, 2018). The headline from one of Australia's most popular Internet news-sites reads "Bali beaches swamped by garbage as tourists, hotel workers sweep up each morning" (Harvey, 2018:1). Human-made trash is everywhere (BaliInformationGuide.com, 2018), as Rich Horner revealed on social media (2018) when he posted a video of a huge 'slick' of plastic floating at a popular dive spot, approximately 30 minutes from Bali (Janzen & Kilvert, 2018).

One of the first tourist market segments likely at risk from the sewerage, sludge and pollution is the Balinese surfing industry. Bali has been a major surfing destination for decades, and Bali's 3-S reputation was largely founded by the surfer community. As surfers are exposed for prolonged periods to various pollutants that enter the water, they are among the first to get sick from the sea (Martin & Assenov, 2008). There is a clear need to revise Bali's reputation on the basis of health risks, plus reframe tourist expectations that the island is taking action to deal with the garbage crisis

Bali: The Island of the Gods and Garbage

The waters of South-East Asia are some of the worst affected with plastic waste (see for example, Ocean Conservancy and McKinsey Centre for Business and Environment, 2015). The sludge and garbage issues surrounding Bali are gaining international prominence. The ineffective disposal of unsanitary waste fluid is documented to profoundly and adversely impact tourism in island economies (Dixon et al., 2001). The Balinese sewerage and rubbish crises has affected the water table and traditional water reservoirs to the extent that tap and groundwater are not recommended by most travel sites (Wright, 2016). Somewhat ironically, this is resulting in more trash in the form of plastic water and soda bottles (Lonely Planet, 2018:23). In December 2017 the Balinese government declared a 'trash emergency' closing the Kuta and Legian beaches due to 50 tonnes of garbage washing up in 5 days (Topsfield & Rosa, 2017). This 2017 event finally prompted the Balinese government to officially acknowledge the impact that waste and pollution were having on tourism.

Two competing arguments arise about the extent that Bali's trash problems will impact the industry's reputation in the short and medium terms. The first contends that because people typically prefer to avoid thinking about ethical information (Paharia et al., 2013) tourists will simply choose not to seek out adverse information about the waste problems confronting Bali. Thus, it is possible that many tourism consumers will overlook the available social and news media about Bali's pollution problems, book their holiday destination and adjust their behaviour should the waste problems affect their holiday. In terms of reputation management, this suggests there is little need to adjust Bali's traditional marketing messages other than to reweight the importance of Bali's 3-S tourism attributes to encourage tourism away from the sea and sand.

The second argument rests on a growing body of literature that suggests that consumers are increasingly aware of environmental and ethical/moral issues. Consumers who become conscious of ethical information typically make ethical decisions (Kimeldorf et al., 2006). According to this perspective, unless there is immediate action by the Balinese community and the Indonesian government to address the growing garbage and sewerage crisis surrounding Bali's islands, then dissatisfaction voiced by tourists on social media channels and broadcast in various news bulletins and Internet sites, will become too powerful to ignore and likely undermine Bali's reputation. It follows that the issue of Bali's waste crisis is likely to become judged by consumers as unacceptable or unsafe for a holiday destination, and tourists will shift to purchase other holiday destinations, regardless of any discounting or reputation management strategies.

The importance of the notion of sustainability to Bali's 3S positioning strategy

The vexed issue of environmental sustainability is rapidly growing in tourism and can threaten the essence of a destination's long term reputation. Bali's experience indicates the need to update the 3S positioning strategy that so many island destinations occupy by introducing a fourth 'S' to represent Sustainability. Inove and Lee (2011) found that tourists are evolving, embracing environmental responsibility, seeking destinations that meet their expectations in terms of corporate social responsibility (CSR). This is driving tourism operators to improve their own CSR. Increasingly, corporations identify their actions in relation to both reputation and financial performance. Introducing the concept of sustainability to 3S tourism is consistent with a growing trend in cross-disciplinary research that emphasises the need to explicitly incorporate CSR in strategic planning. Indeed, not only does the literature show there is a link between business strategy, waste management and sustainability (Lamboglia et al., 2018), it is noted that sustainability is likely to influence organisational outcomes

8

(Journeault, 2016). Contemporary consumers are demanding better behaviour from corporations and the 2019 Edelman Trust Barometer (2018) identified the desire of respondents for CEOs to take the lead in terms of environmental management.

A fundamental tenet of commercially-oriented environmental sustainability is that the various stakeholders accept responsibility for their interaction with the environment and specifically avoid action that may degrade it (Wether & Chandler, 2010). In particular, environmental sustainability requires that that each generation should be a custodian of the environment and natural resources for the benefit of future generations. To many of Bali's tourism pioneers, the beachfront land in Bali was unproductive farmland, fishing income in the area was sporadic, and the beachfront was considered spiritually impure (Hussey, 1989) so the conversion of these parts of the island into a low priced authentic island and surfing experience made good economic and social sense. However, the organic style of tourism development that ensued did not allow for the sheer scale of Balinese tourism.

At present, Bali seems to be suffering from its own success and the organic style of development. Tourists produce considerably more waste than non-tourists (Dixon et al., 2001) and the garbage damage caused to the Balinese eco-system is well documented (Bali.com, 2018). The more ecologically spoilt the tourist site, the less appealing the concepts of the sun, sea and sand is likely to become to tourists.

There is considerable competition for tourism dollars between 3S style destinations (including the following Boracay example) and other possible substitutes, such as mountain and tree-change experiences. As the concept of environmental sustainability seems intrinsically linked to Bali's commercial sustainability, there is a need to rectify, and to be seen to rectify, the issues that cause a substantial amount of Bali's ecological issues. The following cases provide comparable insight into two destinations that experienced significant waste management issues, one of which has employed the notion of sustainability and one of which that hasn't.

The historic Italian town of Naples

Located on the coast in southern Italy, Naples enjoyed a reputation as an interesting, well located, climatically favourable and cost-effective tourist area. Although bombed extensively during World War Two, Naples' historic centre is one of the largest UNESCO World Heritage listings in Europe and offers many wonderful historical sites and vibrant street communities. Naples is a traditional 'travellers' town' and home to a busy international sea-port. It is also centrally located as a gateway to popular tourist destinations such as Capri, Ischia and Procida, the Amalfi Coast, Pompei and Rome. Naples draws additional tourism from its reputation as the home of internationally renowned Neapolitan cuisine (e.g. ragu) and the Napoli pizza.

Naples's reputation as a tourist hub started to recede in January 2008 and continued to decline due to a garbage crisis that lasted until 2012. Naples is one of the top three Italian cities regarding population numbers and density, and is home to one of the busiest ports in Europe (Scaramella, 2003). It is almost inconceivable that a garbage crisis could occur in a densely populated city that is subject to the European Commission's strict waste regulations.

It is estimated that at the time of the 2008 garbage crisis, waste production in Naples was 1,600 tonnes per day, of which approximately 40 tonnes of matter were organic waste that came from markets and restaurants. By the beginning of January in 2008, an estimated 60,000 tons of garbage was lying around the streets of Naples. The crisis was caused by landfills and dumps becoming full, and the area's incinerators not in operational condition. The true underbelly of the garbage crisis seems to be opposition to modern incinerators and waste treatment programs from residents near the proposed sites, and organised crime that was making large profits from illegally dumping rubbish (Lambogila et al., 2018).

As a direct result of this crisis, tourism and hospitality were among the industries most affected by Naples' trash trauma, with many stakeholders complaining that the impacts on the tourist industry continued for many years past the crisis's resolution. One reason for this seems to be the enduring impact of illegal dumping, such as environmental degradation, a rise in the number of congenital disabilities and cancers, and the periodic mass media reporting of discoveries of illegal hazardous waste dumps throughout Campania (Triassi et al.,

2015). Not only do residents use social media to raise their concerns about contamination, but the US Navy, whose European command is based in Naples, found substantial evidence of toxicity in the local air, soil and water and advised personnel not to enter certain areas of Campania (Birrell, 2016). As a result, the US Navy banned the use of tap water and avoided ground floor accommodation where the risk of contamination was highest (Birrell, 2016).

It is argued that the Naples' garbage crisis was poorly managed by the local and national governments (Povoledo, 2008) with large financial losses in the tourist industry (D'Auria 2012) and a decline in the numbers of visitors (Siano & Siglioccolo, 2008). Although there are no longer mountains of garbage on the street (this did take several years to resolve) the toxicity (Triassi et al., 2015) and unknowns of the illegal dumps that are being found and dealt with, suggests that the garbage crisis may still be affecting tourism through lower prices and occupancy rates than found in other parts of Italy. Interestingly, the official tourism offerings about Naples seems to omit any discussion of the garbage crisis and the issue of toxic dumps (Kington, 2007).

Naples is not yet able to sucessfully *revise* the area's reputation as toxic garbage is still being found (Triassi et al., 2015). In the era when online search behaviour is intrinsically linked with tourism, any consumer with ethical predispositions (as outlined earlier) researching Naples will quickly become aware of the garbage crisis and the lingering effects of illegal dumping By not properly managing the ongoing legacy of the garbage crisis (Triassi et al., 2015), Naples's reputation has been damaged. Indeed, Naples' reputation is encapsulated in the area's lower-priced tourist offerings relative to the experiences, scenery and climate on offer when compared to similar Italian cities. However, once the crisis is finally resolved, it should be possible for Naples to successfully *revise* their brand and *rebuild* their reputation.

The Phillipine Island of Boracay

Voted as the world's best island in 2012 by *Travel + Leisure* magazine and topping *Conde Nast Traveler's* Best Islands list in 2013, the Philippine island of Boracay was closed for six months from April 2018 to enable significant environmental restoration. After excessive levels of tourism activity, the island had become a 'cesspool' due to years of overcrowding, partying and neglect (Maguigad, 2013). Closing and cleaning the island was an intervention by a government that identifies a link between sustainable environmental practices and long-term commercial outcomes.

Boracay was then *repositioned* with the number of island visitors restricted to about 6000 people daily. One could argue that the Phillipine government is a tourism marketing pioneer by shifting Boracay's 3S tourism model to incorporate an additional 'S' for sustainability. Moreover, the government's intervention seems to have come before the island's reputation receded to the point of being uncompetitive with other offerings. Subsequent to the government's intervention, visitors are asked to sign an oath not to consume liquor, smoke, light bonfires and party wildly on the beach, and to adhere to proper waste disposal practices. The island's Tourism Secretary, Berna Romulo-Puyat informed tourists via the media to "Let us treat the island as our home. Keep it clean and pristine. Don't drink alcohol or smoke on the beach, don't litter" (McGuire, 2018:1).

As part of the Boracay's reputational *revision*, the 157 tourism businesses that could reopen must now comply with a set of regulations that includes connecting to authorised sewer pipes (rather than illegal sewage pipes discharging into wetlands) and maintaining a 30m distance from the ocean (Maguigad, 2013). Swift government intervention drove the clean-up and rebuilding of Boracay's reputation as an idyllic tropical paradise. Little if any long-term damage seems to have occurred to the island's reputation. Rather, it can be argued that the strong and quick government intervention strengthened the island's reputation. This case supports the relevance of the 4S tourism model proposed earlier.

Conclusion

It seems clear that issues related to the environment are adversely impacting on tourism and the reputations of destinations in the 3S marketplace. The garbage and waste crisis is global and transcends the earlier warnings provided by environmentalists – this issue is now impacting on foreign trade, commerce, work and livelihoods, and the health of tourists and locals alike. Bali is an example of a 3S destination whose reputation as a desirable tourist destination is currently under threat due to poor waste management practices and the diffusion of garbage from other origins.

This chapter introduced the importance of effective waste management to a 3S destination's reputation and how effective planning can, over time, over come the consequent image related issues. As observed from the Boracay example, it is possible for an island destination to reposition itself after an environmental crisis. The following recommendations, drawn from our learnings from the Boracay and Naples cases, provide Bali and the other destinations that are struggling with ongoing waste and pollution issues with pathways that will assist destinations to revise and rebuild their reputations over time.

Recommendations for practice

The infrastructure in Bali and Indonesia must be revised to appropriately manage all forms of soft and hard refuse. However, this is expensive to construct and maintain. Someone must meet these costs. Lobbyists for various hotel groups and tourism organisations argue the short-term position that their organisations should not pay heightened levies for better garbage management and their clientele must not be taxed as this is a disincentive that attracts attention to the garbage issue and may affect demand. As shown by the Boracay experience, perhaps government mandating and funding change will be the ultimate solution, with the improvements passed-on over time through a tourist levy and/or increased taxation of foreign tourist operators. Regardless of the funding source, Bali's reputation and image management requires a strong and proactive approach to the garbage crisis. Bali can then be *repositioned* as an environmentally sustainable destination and visitors be encouraged to proactively champion and support 'green – clean' initiatives in Bali and when they return home.

■ A strategic and diplomatic approach is required to influence the international community to stop dumping rubbish, implement better waste management systems and to help clean up the oceans to prevent further ecological degradation. The tourism industry deals with a range of different and often conflicting stakeholder-groups (e.g., developers, politicians seeking to generate economic growth, marine and fisheries departments, tourism stakeholders, ecologists) that can traverse on different scales and levels (Berdej, 2014). Herein it is acknowledged that there are stakeholder-groups throughout many industries and sectors of the economy and community. The forces driving the expansion of international tourism plus polluters such as commercial fishers, and the various other industries that provide non-biodegradable packaging that end up polluting our oceans, are vivid examples of stakeholder-groups using short-term economic business models that are unlikely to succeed in the future. Simply, many of these organisations disregard the external costs to the economy, community and environment of their operations.

■ A number of nations such as Germany and Austria, and land-locked Switzerland, are leading the way with innovations how to manage rubbish and minimise environmental damage (Gray, 2017). Bali should pushing Indonesia to work internationally with other ocean facing nations on innovations to reduce the input of hard and soft wastes into the world's oceans. This can be done through soft power iniatives, public relations and lobbying international bodies, such as the United Nations and financing forums, to argue that dumping can be considerd a waste of potential resource inputs and false economy (as losses are manifest elsewhere, for example the need for drinking water, tourism/service economy employment and sustainable fishing grounds).

■ An alternative intervention strategy to help fund and plan the revision of Bali's garbage related infrastructure is the use of structured Public, Private Partnerships (PPP). The use of PPPs has precedence in Indonesian tourism through the 'Tsunami Ready Toolbox' initiative that was designed to assist hotels in Indonesia prepare for tsunamis (World Tourism Organization, 2015). Demonstrating the potential for PPPs, the 'Tsunami Ready Toolbox' was a partnership between the Bali Hotels Association (BHA) and the Ministry of Tourism. A PPP initiative in Bali to help with the garbage problem would enable a range of stakeholders with different objectives and skills to work together to pool their resources in voluntary relationships to improve the attractiveness and sustainability of Bali as a destination. This would cost-effectively enhance the island's reputation and improve the overall management of tourism on the island and pass on costs to the consumers over time. There is no reason why the industry, government other stakeholders cannot collaborate to establish tourist product offerings to guide and fund cleaning up of the existing environmental pollution and the improvement of infrastructure and regulations to prevent problems in the future. A PPP arrangement seems well suited to Bali as a developing economy with a shallow skill-set regarding sustainability, planning and development.

- In order for mass tourism to be compatible with Bali's environmental sustainability, it seems time for Balinese tourism authorities to determine what the optimum carrying capacity of the island is in order to avoid further adverse impacts on the natural environment. It follows, that ultimately there will likely be a limit to Bali tourism's capacity to host visitors. Under these conditions, it should be expected, just as in Boraquay, there will be adverse consequences for some employees and businesses in the existing marketplace. The alternative for not taking such action may mean, like Naples, sub-optimal tourism outcomes over an extended period of time.

- It also follows that Bali should develop and use an integrated island plan that includes such things as: modelling traffic and transportation needs, water usage, pollutants emitted into the atmosphere, monitoring natural water resources, animal protection, garbage disposal and so on. This level of planning would ideally support and feed into estimates of the optimal number of tourists permitted in and around Bali.

- The Balinese and Indonesian governments could also develop an 'environmental sustainability' accreditation scheme for the tourism industry that focuses primarily on waste management. Recognition and award systems could be used to reward those who comply with waste management regulations while those that fail to comply could be penalised with fines or removal of their operational license.

- An 'environmental sustainability' measurement scale could be developed to assess the needs and challenges of Bali and identify those factors that have the greatest impact on the island's waste management practices. It is vital to make both visitors and locals aware of what is harmful and what is encouraged, supported and rewarded. Such an initative would enable Bali to base future marketing concepts linked to environmental themes. A clean and healthy environment would enhance Bali's reputation as a desirable destination, while appealing to an environmentally responsible tourist segment.

References

Avery-Gomm S., O'Hara P., Kleine L., Bowes V., Wilson L.K. & Barry K.L. (2012) Northern fulmars as biological monitors of trends of plastic pollution in the Eastern North Pacific, *Marine Pollution Bulletin*, September **64**(9),1776-81. DOI: 10.1016/j.marpolbul.2012.04.017

Bali.com (2018) *Efforts for a Sustainable Bali*, https://www.bali.com/sustainable-bali.html (accessed December 10 2018)

BaliInformationGuide.com (2018) Life in Bali: Pros and Cons, https://baliinformationguide.com/ (accessed 28 July, 2018)

Berdej S. (2014) Bridging people, bridging ecosystems in Bali, Indonesia, *Environment Change and Governance Group Blog*, https://uwaterloo.ca/environmental-change-and-governance-group/blog/post/bridging-people-bridging-ecosystems-bali-indonesia (accessed 5th July, 2018)

Birrell I. (2016) Mafia, toxic waste and a deadly cover up in an Italian paradise: They've poisoned our land and stolen our children, *The Telegraph*, 24 June, https://www.telegraph.co.uk/news/0/mafia-toxic-waste-and-a-deadly-cover-up-in-an-italian-paradise-t/ (accessed 22 November, 2018)

D'Auria, R. (2012), *Garbage emergency in Naples: the effects on local economy*, from https://www.researchgate.net/profile/Rosario_DAuria/publication/235791791_Garbage_emergency_in_Naples_the_effects_on_local_economy/links/0fcfd5138aa8f015c9000000.pdf (accessed March 6, 2019)

Dixon J., Hamilton K., Pagiola S. & Segnestam L. (2001), Tourism and the environment in the Caribbean, *World Bank, Environmental Economics Series*, **80** March.

Ebbesmeyer C.C., Ingraham W.J., Jones J.A. & Donohue M.J. (2011) Marine debris from the Oregon Dungeness Crab Fishery recovered in the North-western Hawaiian Islands: Identification and oceanic drift paths, *Marine Pollution Bulletin*, **65**(1-3) 69-75 DOI: 10.1016/j.marpolbul.2011.09.037

Ecorys (2013), Study in support of policy measures for maritime and coastal tourism at EU level, DG Maritime Affairs & Fisheries Rotterdam/Brussels, https://ec.europa.eu/maritimeaffairs/sites/maritimeaffairs/files/docs/body/study-maritime-and-coastal-tourism_en.pdf (accessed 7 December, 2018)

Edelman (2018), *2019 Edelman Trust Barometer*, https://www.edelman.com/sites/g/files/aatuss191/files/2019-02/2019_Edelman_Trust_Barometer_Global_Report_2.pdf (accessed March 10, 2019)

Fombrun, C. J., Gardberg, N. A. & Sever, J. M. (1999) The Reputation Quotient SM: A multi-stakeholder measure of corporate reputation, *Journal of Brand Management*, **7**(4) 241-255.

Gray, A. (2017), Germany recycles more than any other country, *World Economic Forum*, https://www.weforum.org/agenda/2017/12/germany-recycles-more-than-any-other-country/ (accessed on 11 March, 2019)

Halleux, V. (2017), *Sustainable tourism The environmental dimension*, European Parliamentary Research Service Members' Research Service PE 599.327, http://www.europarl.europa.eu/RegData/etudes/BRIE/2017/599327/EPRS_BRI(2017)599327_EN.pdf (accessed December 7, 2018)

Hardesty B. D. and Wilcox C. (2015) Eight million tonnes of plastic are going into the ocean each year, *The Conversation*, February 13, https://

theconversation.com/eight-million-tonnes-of-plastic-are-going-into-the-ocean-each-year-37521 (accessed July 4, 2018)

Harvey, A. (2018). Bali beaches swamped by garbage as tourists, hotel workers sweep up each morning, *ABC News*, mobile.abc.net.au/news/2018-02-21/bali-beaches-swamped-by-garbage/9467974 (accessed March 14, 2018)

Horner, R. (2018) This is honestly hard to watch, *@IFnLoveScience*, March 7, twitter.com/IFnLoveScience/status/971444051219161089/video/1 (accessed 3 July 2018)

Howe, L. (2005) *The Changing World of Bali: Religion, Society and Tourism*, Abingdon Oxon: Routledge.

Hou, A. (2018, May 15) Where do Balis least popular tourist come? *South China Post*, www.scmp.com/lifestyle/travel-leisure/article/2146068/where-do-balis-least-popular-tourists-come-indonesian (accessed November 22, 2018)

Hussey, A. (1989) Tourism in a Balinese village, *American Geographical Society*, **79**(3), 311-325.

Inove, Y. & Lee, S. (2011) Effects of different dimensions of corporate social responsibility on corporate financial performance in tourism-related industries, *Tourism Management*, **32** (4) 790-804

Janzen, A., & Kilvert, N. (2018,). Diver films wave of plastic pollution off Bali on scale 'never seen before'. *ABC News*, March 6, www.abc.net.au/news/2018-03-06/diver-films-wave-of-plastic-pollution-off-bali-coast/9508662 (accessed 15 March 2018)

Jambeck J.R., Geyer R., Wilcox C., Siegler TR., Perryman M., Andrady A., Narayan R. & Law K. (2015) Plastic waste inputs from land into the ocean, *Science* 347(6223) 768-771. DOI: 10.1126/science.1260352

Journeault, M. (2016) The Integrated Scorecard in support of corporate sustainability strategies, *Journal of Environmental Management*, **182**, 214-229. DOI: 10.1016/j.jenvman.2016.07.074.

Judisseno, R.K. (2015) *Destination Strategies in Tourist Development in Indonesia, 1945–2014: Problems of Bali Centredness*, PhD Thesis, College of Arts Victoria University, http://vuir.vu.edu.au/29726/1/Rimsky%20K%20Judisseno.pdf (accessed March 11, 2019)

Kimeldorf, H., Maeyer R., Prasad M. & Robinson I. (2006) Consumers with a conscience: will they pay more?, *Contexts*, 5(1), 24-29.

Kington, T. (2007) Naples burns as residents protest at garbage crisis, *The Guardian*, May 27, www.theguardian.com/environment/2007/may/27/italy.waste (accessed December 8, 2018)

Knowles, T. & Curtis, S. (1999) The market viability of European mass tourist destinations. A post-stagnation life-cycle analysis, *International Journal of Tourism Reseach*, 1: 87-96. doi:10.1002/(SICI)1522-1970(199903/04)1:2<87::AID-JTR135>3.0.CO;2-6

Lamboglia, R., Fiorentino R., Mancini D. & Garzella S. (2018), From a garbage crisis to sustainability strategies: The case study of Naples' waste collection firm, *Journal of Cleaner Production.* **186**, 276-235.

Law, A., De Lacy, T., Lipman, G. & Jiang, M. (2016) Transitioning to a green economy: the case of tourism in Bali, Indonesia, *Journal of Cleaner Production,* **111**(B): 295-305, https://doi.org/10.1016/j.jclepro.2014.12.070.

Lebreton, L., Slat B., Ferrari F., Sainte-Rose, B., Aitken J., Marthouse R., Hajbane S., Cunsolo S., Schwarz A., Levivier A., Noble K., Debeljak P., Maral H., R. Schoeneich-Argent, R. Brambini & Reisser, J. (2018), Evidence that the Great Pacific Garbage Patch is rapidly accumulating plastic, *Scientific Reports* **8**.

Lonely Planet (2018) *Bali Health,* https://www.lonelyplanet.com/indonesia/bali/health (accessed December 10, 2018)

Maguigad, V. (2013), Tourism planning in archipelagic Philippines: A case review, *Tourism Management Perspectives,* July, **7**, 25-35.

Martin, S.A. & Assenov, I. (2008) Interdisciplinary approaches toward sustainable surf tourism in Thailand, *1st PSU Sustainability Conference,* Prince of Songkla University, Phuket.

McGuire, C. (2018) Tourists to sign oath before entering reopened Philippine island, *The Sun,* October 29, https://www.news.com.au/travel/world-travel/asia/tourists-to-sign-oath-before-entering-reopened-philippine-island/news-story/ed0c641539352bf7aae8228e31b7b382 (accessed 30 October, 2018)

Ocean Conservancy and McKinsey Centre for Business and Environment (2015) *Stemming the Tide: Land-based strategies for a plastic-free ocean,* https://oceanconservancy.org/wp-content/uploads/2017/04/full-report-stemming-the.pdf (accessed March 7, 2019)

Paharia, N., Vohs, K. & Deshpande, R. (2013) Sweat shop labour is wrong unless the shoes are cute: cognition can both help and hurt moral motivated reasoning, *Organisational Behaviour and Human Decision Processes,* **121**(1) 81-8.

Povoledo, E. (2008) EU criticizes Italy over trash crisis in Naples, *The New York Times,* January 15, https://www.nytimes.com/2008/01/15/world/europe/15iht-italy.4.9237559.html (accessed 10 December 2018)

R.O.L.E. (2018) *Bali's waste crisis,* accessed on 16 March 2018 from http://rolefoundation.org/wastecrisis/

Scaramella, M. (2003) The case of Naples, Italy, *Global Reports,* University College London (GB), https://www.ucl.ac.uk/dpu-projects/Global_Report/pdfs/Naple.pdf (accessed December 11 2018)

Siano, A. & Siglioccolo, M., (2008) The impact of waste emergency on the number of visitors of the cultural goods of the province of Naples (Italy), EuroCHRIE International Conference, Dubai, United Arab Emirates, October 11th-14th, 2008

8

Stikel, B.H, Jahn, A. & Kier, B. (2012), *The Cost to West Coast Communities of Dealing with Trash, Reducing Marine Debris*, Kier Associates, Blue Lake CA, USA, commissioned by the USA Environmental Protection Agency, Region IX, September.

Stupart, C.A. & Shipley, R. (2012) Jamaica's Tourism: sun, sea and sand to cultural heritage. *Journal of Tourism Insights, 3(1)*

Taylor, M. (2018) Trash heroes and scavenger apps battle Bali 'garbage emergency', Reuters, July 23, https://www.reuters.com/article/us-islands-indonesia-bali-waste/trash-heroes-and-scavenger-apps-battle-bali-garbage-emergency-idUSKBN1KD04K (accessed 6 March, 2019)

Tripadvisor (2018), Bali Belly? What is it? posted 27 Apr., https://www.tripadvisor.com.au/ShowTopic-g294226-i7220-k1926390-Bali_Belly_What_is_it-Bali.html (accessed 18 August 2018)

Triassi,M., Alfano, R., Illario, M., Nardone, A., Caporale, O. & Montuori, P. (2015) Environmental pollution from illegal waste disposal and health effects: a review on the 'Triangle of Death' , *International Journal of Environmental Research and Public Health.* **12**(2), 1216–1236. doi: 10.3390/ijerph120201216

Topsfield, J. & Rosa, A. (2017). Bali beaches buried in rubbish as Indonesia battles oceans of plastic. *The Sydney Morning Herald*, December 30, https://www.smh.com.au/world/bali-beaches-buried-in-rubbish-as-indonesia-battles-oceans-of-plastic-20171229-h0b8e9.html (accessed 14 March, 2018)

United Nations (2014), *Water for Life Decade*, http://www.un.org/waterforlifedecade/quality.shtml (accessed on 24 August, 2018)

Wether, W. & Chandler, D. (2010) *Strategic Corporate Social Responsibility, Stakeholders in a global environment* (2 ed) Thousand Oaks, California Sage Publications.

Weston, R., Peeters, P., Eke Eijgelaar, E., Dubois, G., Strasdas, W., Lootvoet M. & Zeppenfeld, R. (2016), *From Responsible Best Practices To Sustainable Tourism Development*, Policy Department B: Structural and Cohesion Policies, European Parliament, http://www.europarl.europa.eu/RegData/etudes/STUD/2015/573421/IPOL_STU(2015)573421_EN.pdf (accessed 7 December 2018)

Wright, T. (2016) Beneath the surface of tourism in Bali, *The Conversation*, https://theconversation.com/beneath-the-surface-of-tourism-in-bali-64673 (accessed December 10, 2018)

Wright, T. & Waddell S. (2017) How can Indonesia win against plastic pollution, *The Conversation*, https://theconversation.com/how-can-indonesia-win-against-plastic-pollution-80966 (accessed March 3, 2019)

World Tourism Organization (2015), *Affiliate Members Global Reports, Volume eleven – Public-Private Partnerships: Tourism Development*, UNWTO, Madrid.

9 Reputation and perceived resilience in developing countries bidding for major sports events

Richard Shipway and Lee Miles

Introduction

Increasingly, international sports events (ISEs) are viewed as attractive opportunities for developing nations seeking to enhance their global profile in terms of both global prestige, economic development, and tourism (Chappelet & Parent, 2015; Shipway & Fyall, 2012). From a resilience perspective, the dimension of changing host locations, often due to the increasingly competitive bidding agenda of many host cities and nations, represents a significant proposition that has major implications with regards to the resilience of such events, in terms of crisis and disaster management. As such, changing host locations, from a resilience perspective, requires not only attention to the capacity of sports venues and infrastructure to absorb shocks and still maintain function, but to also include the propensity to facilitate adaptation, renewal and even re-organisation (Shipway, 2018). Whether these are natural disasters or man-made terrorist attacks, any disturbance creates an opportunity for both undertaking new actions (innovation), and for more effectively reacting to their onset (ongoing development) (Berkes et al., 2003; Holling, 1973; Gunderson 2000). Similarly, crisis management is influential in being an assessment of the ability of the country, including its emergency services, political elite, medical services, military and disaster management system to handle emergencies and/or disasters (Shipway & Miles, 2018).

Using two case studies from new emerging host nations, one from the Middle East (Qatar) and one from Africa (Cameroon), this chapter critically explores the resilience landscape, and identifies some of the challenges associated with how destinations faced with either political instability or image issues, due to negative perceptions held by both tourists and global media, have chosen to manage their destination image through bidding to host major sports events. Both nations, Qatar and Cameroon, have been proactive in the bidding processes to host tournaments linked to 'The People's Game', Association Football, and to manage the various challenges that exist with their effective organisation and delivery (Sugden & Tomlinson, 1998). This planning has been particularly controversial and tumultuous for both nations. The chapter will also critique some of the broader strategies being adopted by other African countries and Gulf States, in close proximity to Cameroon and Qatar, to both reassure potential tourists with regards to safety and security, and to also ensure suitable measures are in place to minimise any reputational damage that might result from potential future crises or disasters.

From a global perspective, it is apparent that new emerging host nations and destinations will have differing levels of resilience based on their relative (in)experience of previously hosting high profile ISEs. These broadly correlate with two interlinked dimensions. First, there could be challenges linked to the actual ability of the respective sports federations, clubs, organisations, stakeholders to ensure that the sporting tournament will be completed smoothly. As such, on this basis it is vital to establish whether they have sufficient measures in place to ensure this, whilst also being able to handle any emergencies and/or disturbance. Second, there is the symbiotic relationship with the resilience of the wider country and its effect on national reputation and branding.

Defining resilience and reputational risk

As discussed in the Introduction to this volume, the concept of resilience overlaps to a large degree with the concepts of vulnerability and adaptive capacity (Gallopin, 2006). Specifically, vulnerability is the susceptibility of a system to disturbances and is determined by exposure and sensitivity to perturbations and the capacity to adapt (Nelson et al., 2007). It is therefore logical to assume that the more vulnerable a sports event or venue is, the more extreme the impact of a given shock will be. Hence, the link to resilience: if a sports event or venue is vulnerable and has little adaptive capacity, then a shock is more likely to shift it from one state to another, such as from stable to chaotic (Biggs et al., 2012). In the sports event context, this shift might not be classed as 'chaotic' per se, however the shock and subsequent impact on both event and destination could be highly significant. As such, this concept will now be explored in relation to the hosting of ISEs in developing countries, which view these tournaments and championships as an effective means to assist with their own tourism development and to enhance destination image.

Yet, if this is the case, it is also important to recognise the evolving and sometimes symbiotic relationship between perceptions of existing and future resilience. This is particularly pertinent with regards to handling and delivering ISEs and some of the specific implications for the overall reputation of the ISEs, venues, and even the host nation(s). In simple terms, understanding the perceived level of resilience of an ISE and the host destination for event organisers, sports fans, and also for potential future tourists, will have implications for the reputation and reputational risk associated with specific country more generally, and vice-versa.

Indeed, this is even more challenging in developing countries that may have experienced political instability and thus may have existing negative reputational issues. Hence, a *resilience-reputational paradox* often exists. On the one hand, developing countries may secure a successful bid for hosting a major international sporting tournament precisely because global sports federations and wider political entities believe that hosting that tournament will be a stabilising force and ethical 'force for good' in building the reputation of sport in developing countries (Dowse & Fletcher, 2018). It represents part of the 'soft power' influence and strategies of the international community (Grix & Lee, 2013). Equally, it is often the case that one of the main reasons why host nations in the developing world are chosen is because of the desire of international sporting communities and global governing sports federations to be seen to contributing actively to building better reputations for host countries and encouraging stability. In contrast, developing countries will wish to secure ISEs precisely because, as

Cornelissen (2010) illustrates, that (while economic imperatives are important), many governments attempt to use sports mega events to fulfil larger political aims, including enhancing national branding and international reputation (Knott et al., 2017). Thus, during bidding phases, the link between resilience and reputation is often seen in an 'upward-spiralling' positive mode as a 'dual enhancement' both of sports governance and the wider stability and political reputations of nations. As such, it is apparent that a 'win-win' argument exists during the bidding processes for many sporting tournaments. However, it would appear that a contrast may exist between the strategic objectives of global sports federations awarding tournaments to developing nations for their own 'soft power' reasons, and the objectives of host nations in developing countries that are bidding more for political and/or image building reasons. Ultimately, in the long-term, this paradox might not necessarily contribute towards enhancing either venue or destination resilience.

Bidding for and securing global sports events: Resilience implications

Initiatives encouraging the globalisation of the sports events industry, as well as the contemporary policies and strategies of world sports governing bodies and international federations, have often sought to extend the reach of their respective events to audiences not reached before. This often involves host cities and nations with little or no prior experience gaining the right and contracts to host such events. (Shipway & Fyall, 2012). Yet, in practice, and certainly once a bid is secured and there is a movement to the planning and implementation phases of ISEs, this can lead to changes and tensions within the resilience-reputation paradox mentioned earlier. As such, this chapter argues that this highlights how a resilience perspective needs to be more firmly linked to the way we consider both ISEs and the host destinations where they take place. Certainly, varying degrees of (in)experience can lead to differing degrees of resilience for every individual sporting event, where no two mega events will ever be the same, not just in space but over time. These variations in the host cities and nations of ISEs will also lead to greater complexity in gauging risk to crisis and disasters that will be differentiated across the globe (Shipway, 2018). This increased public awareness of vulnerability and the need for greater resilience, merged with the growing global profile of ISEs, now makes mitigation and prevention not just socially and economically acceptable, but also imperative. This is particularly pertinent at the implementation and completion phases of ISEs.

However, this ironically feeds the aforementioned resilience-reputation paradox where the very 'dual enhancement' rationales that are often apparent in securing bids can then lead to 'down-spiralling' tensions and a 'dual criticism' of both weak sports federations and the wider respective host nations level of preparedness for hosting ISEs (Shipway, 2018). Put more simply, the frequent inexperience of hosting events in developing countries combined with their often weaker sporting governance suggests that in practice they are less resilient to handle major emergencies and crisis. In essence, sports governance and the supporting apparatus to deliver ISEs are less resilient and suffer from weaker reputations. In addition, the host nation and destinations may also suffer a poor reputation in terms of 'incapacity', with a weaker resource-stretched disaster management system. They may also be subject to varying degrees of political instability and turmoil (Grix & Lee, 2013), as will be highlighted in the case study of Cameroon that follows. Hence, in the implementation phase the resilience-reputation paradox may be illustrated via these ongoing 'dual criticisms'. This is due to existing poor reputations and perceptions that neither the sport federations and sports stakeholders, clubs and venues, or the country, have the necessary expertise or the adaptive resilience to deliver the ISE when subject to any likely disturbance. This may ironically lead to some external stakeholders, invariably global media sources and outlets, calling for the ISE to be taken away from the developing countries during the implementation phase running up to the main tournament or sporting event (Dowse & Fletcher, 2018; Shipway & Miles, 2018). Again, this was the case in both the case studies that follow. This is usually based on a criticism of the reputation and resilience incapacities of both the sports bodies and the wider apparatus of the host nation and its host destinations.

Contrasting size and scale: Cameroon and Qatar

Despite the globalised nature of sports events and debates about the size components of more recent mega sports events (Shipway & Miles, 2018), none of these classifications pay attention to criteria relating to resilience, nor to the arguments relating to the 'resilience-reputation paradox' discussed here. Given that the characteristics of sports events will vary across their size, scope and structure, it is suggested that this will present different challenges in terms of managing crises and disasters. As Shipway and Fyall (2012) suggest, this is even more problematic when defining the different types and characteristics of ISEs especially with the emergence of new events and ongoing bidding activity for high profile mega sports events in regions such as the African continent or across the Gulf States, given this potentially significant variance in scope, scale and structure.

More specifically, and as specified by Shipway and Miles (2018), in terms of resilience, first, there will be multi-faceted implications due to the complexity of the sports events and these will affect resilience in spatial (space/scale) terms. In the case of the two case studies chosen, both linked to the globally popular sport of Association Football, there will be a complex menu of differing venues and sport-specific requirements that will include coverage over multiple cities/destinations across Qatar and Cameroon respectively. Second, both of the identified Association Football tournaments have international significance in terms of global reach, where both global and continental media coverage are watching not just the football tournaments but also their levels of resilience. In the initial planning and preparation stages it is logical to assume that in both Qatar and Cameroon, crisis managers were extremely keen to avoid incidents happening whilst the international media and public were watching. As such, this requires subtle and extensive communication with national as well as international audiences and publics. Third, for both of these tournaments there are clear implications for resilience in temporal terms (time), in that the matches would be held over an extended period of weeks rather than days. Therefore, both sporting tournaments require more complicated and longer lasting crisis and disaster management arrangements within the host destinations to ensure greater resilience whilst the sporting event is being both planned and hosted. Finally, and to illustrate some of these complex challenges in the planning stages for a major tournament, in late November 2018 Cameroon were stripped of the right to host the 2019 African Cup of Nations, six months before the event was due to begin. As will become apparent, this highlights more fundamental obstacles and challenges within Cameroon, and also has significant negative implications for both reputation and image.

From a resilience perspective, the additional dimension of changing host location, due to the increasingly competitive bidding agendas of host nations like Qatar and Cameroon, has implications for the way we think about the resilience of such events in terms of crisis and disaster management. To clarify this point, such variations in the sites of tournaments like the FIFA Football World Cup, and to a lesser extent the AFCON (African Cup of Nations) leads to much greater complexity in assessing the potential risk of future crises and disasters. Likewise, in terms of vulnerability to natural disasters, differing regions and host countries will also be subject to variances in types, forms and frequency of natural hazards, such as earthquakes, volcanic eruptions, cyclones and/or tsunamis (see Miles et al., 2017). Additionally, in the developing world, man-made threats and risks such as crime rates, kidnapping, insurgencies, terrorism or conflict may be more significant. The resilience challenges of providing integrated planning and procedures to handle such natural hazards and man-made threats whilst the Association Football tournaments are operational will place new pressures on the capacities of destinations in both Cameroon and Qatar as the proposed host nations. These outcomes are also a result of the contemporary policies and strategies of world sports governing bodies and international federations like FIFA and the Confederation of African Football (CAF) seeking to extend the reach of their respective football tournaments to audiences not reached before. As such, another direct result is host cities / destinations and nations, with little or no prior experience, and differing degrees of resilience, gaining the rights and contracts to host major international sports events.

Given some of the challenges associated with the delivery of both major and mega international sports events that are identified above, the focus now moves towards a critique of the issues, challenges and broader strategies adopted by two emerging tourism nations, Cameroon and Qatar, in their planning and preparations for hosting major sports events. In doing so, it also addresses the positive and negative implications for both reputation and image recovery within the tourism industry. Fundamentally, when scoping resilience landscapes, the foundational literature within crisis and disaster management studies highlight that 'context is everything' (Haldrup & Rosen, 2013:137), and as such the two case studies that follow are embedded within the context of hosting ISEs in developing countries.

2019 Africa Cup of Nations: Cameroon

The 2019 Africa Cup of Nations (also known as AFCON 2019 or CAN 2019) was due to be hosted in Cameroon in June and July 2019. However, in late November 2018, with stadiums only half-built and a violent separatist rebellion taking place close to planned venues, Cameroon was stripped of the right to host the tournament, less than six months before the event was due to commence. Concerns were raised following the delayed preparations and the escalating security situation in the south-west and north-west of the country involving English-speaking separatists and government sources (The Guardian, 2018). The decision was taken by the tournament organisers, the Confederation of African Football (CAF) following a special meeting of its executive committee in November 2018 in Ghana, where they also announced the opening of a new bidding process with interested countries given until the end of December 2018 to submit bids for the tournament.

Cameroon had been due to enter the tournament as the reigning champions, previously winning the previous event in 2017. This bi-annual international men's football championship of Africa is organised by the Confederation of African Football (CAF), and 2019 was the first Africa Cup of Nations to be expanded from 16 to 24 teams. This growth added further size, scale and complexity to the tournament. In the initial planning for the event, the expansion resulted in the proposed use of six venues, varying in capacity from 20,000 to 50,000 (CAF, 2018). The tournament was due to be staged in five cities across Cameroon: Bafoussam, Douala, Garoua, Limbe and Yaounde. In the lead-up to the tournament, and as part of the implementation phase, each venue developed independently and consequently with differing states of readiness. This was a result of the varying proximity of some of the cities to disaster-prone regions in the Cameroon, and their susceptibility to future violent incidents as a results of the worsening political crisis between the Anglophone and Francophone communities in the country (Miles et al., 2017).

In terms of image reputation, the governing body of football in Cameroon, the Cameroonian Football Federation (*Fédération Camerounaise de Football*), known more widely as FECAFOOT, had a history of alleged unsavoury links with the world governing body of football, FIFA (*Fédération Internationale de Football Association*). Prior to being stripped of the hosting rights, the 2019 Africa Cup of

Nations was widely perceived as an opportunity to challenge many of these long-held, primarily western world perceptions of the (lack of effective) organisation and governance of football in both Cameroon and across the African continent. To further elaborate, and turning to sports dimensions specifically, external perceptions of football in Cameroon had been previously tainted due to the global high profile political and financial scandals associated with FIFA, and allegations of uncontrolled spending, fraud and the misappropriation and embezzlement of funds within Cameroon that were intended for grassroots football and facility developments (Madiya, 2018). Hence, the case of Cameroon did suggest that in line with thinking on the resilience-reputational paradox, there were clear arguments for using the ISE to reinforce national sports governance in the Cameroon. However, it soon became apparent there were rising and legitimate concerns about whether the incapacity of Cameroon's existing sports governance and the political instability and turmoil would put an impossible strain upon the host nation and subsequently upon the host destinations, as their failed preparations unfolded.

The build-up to the tournament had already been shrouded in both controversy and confusion, with CAF voicing regular concerns over the ability of Cameroon to host the event (BBC, 2017), especially since this particular tournament coincided with an increase in participating teams from sixteen to twenty four nations, and the inevitable added pressure this places on any host country. This turmoil and organisational crisis clearly had a negative impact on both the reputation and image perceptions of Cameroon as a host nation. These delays and challenges with preliminary planning and organisation for AFCON2019 suggest that broader resilience issues were most certainly *not* the most pressing challenge on the agendas of the organising committee and other key stakeholders in the lead up to the tournament. The media spotlight was focused on Cameroon, for all the wrong reasons. There were clearly more underlying fundamental concerns, that were voiced by Mr Ahmad Ahmad, the president of the Confederation of African Football (CAF), about the hosting of the tournament. In fact, prior to the tournament, Madiya (2018) highlighted the extensive ongoing discussions that occurred during 2017 and 2018 about whether the newly expanded twenty four team format for the tournament would still proceed in Cameroon. Ultimately, it did not.

In August 2017, auditors PriceWaterhouseCoopers were due to undertake an inspection throughout Cameroon, which was subsequently cancelled at short notice, with no reasons given. In January 2018, representatives from a firm of independent assessors, Roland Berger, visited Cameroon to assess the nation's preparations. At that stage it was also suggested that Morocco and South Africa might have been willing to commit to hosting the 2019 event should the event hosting rights be removed from Cameroon by CAF, which later transpired into reality in November 2018. However at the time, in August 2018, CAF reaffirmed its seal of approval on Cameroon's 2019 AFCON hosting rights, stipulating that the tournament would not be taken away from the country (Madiya, 2018).

It is perhaps inevitable that differing levels of resilience and issues relating to crowd control and crowd management would exist at Association Football tournaments in some developing African countries, and this is perhaps in contrast to some of the more 'established' European, Asian, Australasian, or North American host nations. However, such perceived delays and negative global media surrounding AFCON2019 raised serious concerns about their ability, and that of Cameroon more widely, to cope with any potential onset of either man-made or natural disasters that might occur during the hosting of the tournament. These episodes can also be perceived as evidence of how during the implementation phase, concerns about weak resilience relating to handling disturbance of the tournament can contribute to the downward spiral effect on the reputation and ability of the country, host destinations, the sports governance systems and stakeholders to effectively deliver an ISE.

Additionally, at the time, media criticism also included discussions of whether the ISE should take place in a country that was also on verge of civil war, and also susceptible to natural disasters (Madiya, 2018). The implications of these criticisms of the (in)capacity of Cameroon to handle natural crises and disasters were not inconsequential, not least because Cameroon has experienced notable challenges in handling relatively frequent natural hazards and disasters. First, Cameroon includes Africa's most frequently active volcano and volcanic area which borders cities that were due to host events in the 2019 Africa Cup. The proposed AFCON participating cities also included the capital, Yaounde, which is increasingly susceptible and has experienced major and more regular flash flooding in recent years. In addition, major issues exist with drought in the northern areas, which have placed considerable strain and illustrated significant vulnerabilities of the country's critical infrastructure (Miles et al., 2017). Second, and what inevitably proved to be a major contributory factor in Cameroon being stripped of hosting rights, there were the significant on-going issues with political stability, such as growing conflict and tensions between the Franco-phone central areas and Anglo-phone minorities. This had resulted in widespread violence in the south west of the country that cast a shroud around the integrity and governance of the country. Third, there were numerous man-made disasters, including notable rail crashes that raised searching questions relating to the effectiveness of Cameroon's disaster management system to handle even rudimentary man-made emergencies effectively.

Ultimately, the negative perceptions on the capability of the country to host major sports events spilled over, and has had significant detrimental impacts upon the broader perceptions and reputational risks relating to the tourism industry within Cameroon (Miles et al., 2017). Cameroon now faces a period of adjustment as it tries to minimise the reputational damage that resulted from this sport event related crisis.

FIFA 2022 World Cup: Qatar

The 2022 Federation Internationale de Football Association (FIFA) World Cup to be hosted in the Gulf State of Qatar will be the first World Cup tournament hosted in the Middle East. It will be the 22nd hosting of the international men's football championship, held every four years. The securing of this bid was partly based on an argument that sport was being brought not just to new audiences but also to developing lands. The reputation of the sport in Qatar and that of the national sports federations and bodies would be enhanced alongside that of a developing nation being vindicated as being resilient enough to hold such events, in spite of notable inexperience. Thus, the reputation and resilience enhancing features were evident during the bidding process.

Henderson (2016) highlighted that some of the primary motivations behind Qatar's bid to host the FIFA 2022 World Cup were related to supporting national branding and enhancing foreign relations. Additional objectives also included stimulating tourism development and economic diversification strategies (Morakabati et al., 2014). The ongoing government expenditure on the construction of facilities and infrastructure underlines the significance attached to sports events and sports tourism (Hukoomi, 2018). This has been supported by high profile global promotion and publicity campaigns engineered by the

Qatari organising committee for FIFA 2022, known as the Supreme Committee for Delivery and Legacy.

Nevertheless, once the bid was secured, the tournament has been subject to significant negative publicity in the prelude to the event, linked to alleged corruption in the bidding process for both the 2022 event, and the 2018 tournament in Russia (Pielke, 2013). There has also been significant negative publicity linked to alleged human rights abuses associated with the treatment of foreign workers during the construction of venues and tournament infrastructure that has damaged the reputation of the host nation. Most interestingly, in their preliminary bid evaluation report, FIFA (2010) raised concerns about safety and security issues associated with hosting the tournament in the Gulf State. As such, it is possible to observe that, as part of the implementation phase, concerns about the disaster management preparedness of the sports bodies as well as that of the nation more widely are prevalent. There is potential this could lead to a further future downward spiral on both the resilience and reputation of sports governance and the disaster management system in Qatar.

Yet, we can also see a notable difference here with the Qatar case compared to that of the ill-fated Cameroon preparations. As Chappelet and Parent (2015) identify, Qatar has developed a recent history and track record for hosting one-off sports events. Perhaps the first significant major sports event was the 2006 Asian Games. Qatar was the first Middle East country to hold the Asian Games (Amara, 2005). This initial major sports event is supported by a longer-term ambition to host the Olympic and Paralympic Games, after the 2022 FIFA World Cup. They will also host the 2021 Confederation Cup (Football) in the build-up to the FIFA tournament. To support this developing major sports events strategy, Qatar has already hosted World Championships in Squash (2012); Handball (2015); Fencing (2017); Gymnastics (2018); and Athletics (2019). Qatar has developing expertise in hosting several recurring annual sports events, including the Doha Tennis Open, Qatar Masters Golf, Tour of Qatar Cycling, and the Qatar Moto Grand Prix, to name a few (Hukoomi, 2018). Qatar's robust reputation for holding successful events helped therefore to placate concerns about whether preparedness in terms of crisis management was sufficient. In practice this was despite misgiving being expressed about the actual effectiveness of existing measures in place (Henderson, 2016). Hence in the case of Qatar as a host nation, reputational factors are helping to alleviate practical concerns over levels of resilience in the run-up to 2022.

Nonetheless, in the build-up to the FIFA 2022 tournament Qatar received extensive (both positive and negative) publicity with regards to the development of the state of the art facilities that are often associated with sports mega events (Chappelet & Parent, 2015; Shipway & Miles, 2018). There were concerns raised about the escalating construction costs, in times of broader global austerity. In addition, there have been rising concerns that wider political issues relating to deteriorating relations between Qatar and other Middle East states, like Saudi Arabia, have affected travel routes. As such, it is perhaps logical to speculate that these issues may have an indirect impact on the attractiveness of these events to local and regional audiences and tourists. As such, this high profile mega sports event hosted in Qatar is not immune to wider political factors. This clearly illustrates that any assessment of reputational risks are not restricted to simply the running and completion of the respective event.

Nevertheless, in the context of crisis and disaster management, it is suggested that the Qatari facilities, whilst embedded in cutting edge state of the art 21st century technology, may not necessarily be accompanied with the levels of resilience or experience of managing crises and disasters that are associated with other globally recurring mega and major sports events that have proven and tested expertise and track records in risk management and mitigating against the potential onset of natural and/ or man-made disasters.

Conclusion

The aim of this chapter was to make a contribution to current thinking on International Sports Events (ISEs) and resilience in developing nations who have chosen to bid and host major sports tournaments, despite previously facing either political instability or image issues due to negative perceptions held by both tourists and global media. In doing so, through the use of two contrasting Association Football based case studies from Africa and the Gulf States, it has been possible to identify some of the challenges faced by host nations to develop and enhance greater resilience during the planning and preparation for hosting major global tournaments. In addition, through the *resilience-reputation paradox* concept, there are some important reflections and considerations on the symbiotic relationship between reputation and resilience, notably when both bidding and hosting ISEs.

More specifically in the case of the chaotic and failed preparations for the AFCON2019 tournament, there were clearly broader underlying concerns with regards to the timely construction and delivery of the most basic infrastructure requirements in terms of hotels, stadiums, hospitals and road access within host destinations. It is apparent that issues relating to developing, managing and supporting higher levels of resilience and preparedness for the tournament were clearly not the main priority for either Cameroonian Football Federation or other key stakeholders. As such, this particular African case study highlights that significant further work is still required if major ISEs that are hosted in developing nations are truly to embed crisis and disaster management planning as an integral part of both their bidding, organisation, delivery and longer-term legacy plans. Once again, the reality of these findings, in the African context, indicate that suitable measures were most certainly not in place to minimise any reputational damage that might have resulted from any potential crises or disaster. The turbulent periods of organisational crisis that led to the tournament being removed from Cameroon have clearly had a significantly adverse impact upon the image and reputation of the country.

Moving forwards, there remains a need for further knowledge on ISEs in developing countries which explores more sophisticated appreciations of resilience at both venue and destination level when deciding which sports events or tournaments on their respective continents are perceived as 'successful' or 'effective' by a wide range of stakeholders including international federations (including both CAF or FIFA), governments (such as Cameroon and Qatar respectively), and global media commentators. Additionally, there is further need for future knowledge that develops a better understanding of the concept of resilience, and more specifically the relationship between resilience and reputation, under the auspices of the proposed resilience-reputation paradox. This closer scrutiny would then provide host nations and destinations with further tools to support both future bidding and hosting not just within Africa and the Gulf States, but amongst emerging developing nations on the global stage that perceive these sporting events as a mechanism to promote destination image and support longer term tourism development.

Recommendations for practice

As a consequence of the resilience issues raised in this chapter, a series of recommendations for bidding host nations in developing countries seeking to both recover and maintain their destination image are now proposed. These recommendations also extend to global sports federations that award these high profile global tournaments and major sports events.

■ In an increasingly uncertain world, destinations faced with either political instability or image issues due to negative perceptions held by both tourists and global media should reflect, review and possibly re-appraise the compatibility, suitability and attractiveness of using ISEs as a strategic objective for managing their long term destination image.

■ Developing nations contemplating bidding for sports events and tournaments should consider the resilience-reputation paradox surrounding major events as an integral part of their decision making process. A contrast clearly exists between the strategic objectives of global sports federations awarding tournaments to developing nations for their own 'soft power' reasons and the objectives of host nations in developing countries that are bidding more for political and/or image building reasons. Ultimately, in the long-term, this paradox might not necessarily contribute towards building and developing resilience at either venue, destination or nation levels.

■ Global sports federations, including FIFA, should reflect, review and re-appraise their long term strategic objectives when deciding on host nations for major sports events, given some of the existing resilience challenges that exist in developing nations. This chapter illustrates the dilemma when host nations and destinations experiencing political instability and turmoil, with little or no prior experience, and with differing degrees of resilience gain the contracts to host major ISEs. These varying degrees of (in)experience will lead to differing degrees of resilience for every individual sporting event and destination, where no two major sports events will ever be the same, not just in space but over time.

References

Amara, M. (2005). 2006 Qatar Asian games: A 'modernisation' project from above? *Sport in Society,* **8**: 493–514.

BBC (2017). CAF president Ahmad reiterates Cameroon 2019 warning. http://www.bbc.co.uk/sport/football/42430227. Accessed 10 April 2018.

Berkes, F., Colding, J. & Folke, C. (Eds.) (2003). *Navigating Social–Ecological Systems: Building Resilience for Complexity and Change.* Cambridge: Cambridge University Press.

Biggs, D., Hall, C. M. & Stoeckl, N. (2012). The resilience of formal and informal tourism enterprises to disasters: reef tourism in Phuket, Thailand. *Journal of Sustainable Tourism,* **20**(5), 645-665.

CAFonline.com (2018). http://www.cafonline.com/en-us/competitions/32ndedit ionoftotalafricacupofnations/home. Accessed 30 March 2018

Chappelet, J.-L. & Parent, M. (2015) *The (Wide) World of Sports Events.* In Parent, M. & Chappelet, J.-L. (eds), *Routledge Handbook of Sports Event Management,* Abingdon: Routledge, pp. 1-17.

Cornellissen, S. (2010). Sport mega-events in Africa: processes, impacts and prospects, *Tourism and Hospitality Planning and Development,* **1**(1), 39-55.

Dowse, S. & Fletcher, T. (2018). Sport mega-events, the 'non-West' and the ethics of event hosting, *Sport in Society,* **21**(5), 745-761.

FIFA. (2010). *2022 FIFA World Cup bid evaluation report: Qatar.* Zurich: FIFA.

Gallopín, G.C. (2006). Linkages between vulnerability, resilience, and adaptive capacity. *Global Environmental Change,* **16** (3) 293–303.

Grix, J. & Lee, D. (2013). Soft power, sports mega-events and emerging states: the lure of the politics of attraction, *Global Society,* **27**(4): 521-536

Gunderson, L.H. (2000). Resilience in theory and practice. *Annual Review of Ecology and Systematics,* **31**, 425–439.

Haldrup, S.V. & Rosen, F. (2013). Developing resilience: a retreat from grand planning. *Resilience,* **1** (2), 130-145.

Henderson, J.C. (2016). Hosting the 2022 FIFA World Cup: opportunities and challenges for Qatar, *Journal of Sport & Tourism,* **19** (3-4), 281-298.

Holling, C.S. (1973). Resilience and stability of ecological systems, *Annual Review of Ecology and Systematics* 4, 1–23.

Hukoomi (2018). Qatar E-government. http://portal.www.gov.qa/wps/portal/topics/Tourism+Sports+and+Recreation. Accessed 9 April 2018

Knott, B., Fyall, A. & Jones, I., (2017). Sport mega-events and nation branding: Unique characteristics of the 2010 FIFA World Cup, South Africa. *International Journal of Contemporary Hospitality Management,* **29** (3), 900-923.

Madiya, M. (2018). CAF stamps final approval on Cameroon as 2019 Afcon hosts. http://www.goal.com/en-gb/news/caf-stamps-final-approval-on-cameroon-as-2019-afcon-hosts/m8etxn15y12bzwbcrhgsccnd. Accessed 19 August 2018.

Miles, L., Gordon, R. an&d Bang, H. (2017). Blaming active volcanoes or active volcanic blame? volcanic crisis communication and blame management in the Cameroon. In C. Fearnley, D. Bird, G. Jolly & B. McGuire (Eds.) *Observing the Volcanic World: Volcanic Crisis Communication* (pp. 1-15). New York: Springer.

Morakabati, Y., Beavis, J. & Fletcher, J. (2014). Planning for a Qatar without oil: Tourism and economic diversification, a battle of perceptions. *Tourism Planning and Development,* **11**(4): 415–434.

Nelson, D.R., Adger, W.N. & Brown, K. (2007). Adaptation to Environmental change: contributions of a resilience framework. *Annual Review of Environment and Resources,* **32** (1), 395-419.

Pielke, R. (2013). How can FIFA be held accountable? *Sport Management Review,* **16**, 255 – 267.

Shipway, R. (2018). Building resilience and managing crises and disasters in sport tourism. *Journal of Sport and Tourism,* **22** (3), 265-270.

Shipway, R. & Fyall, A. (eds) (2012). *International Sports Events: Impacts, Experiences and Identities.* London: Routledge.

Shipway, R. & Miles, L. (2018). Bouncing back and jumping forward: scoping the resilience landscape of international sports events and implications for events and festivals. *Event Management.*

Sugden, J. & Tomlinson, A. (1998). *FIFA and the contest for world football: who rules the people's game?* Cambridge: Polity Press.

The Guardian (2018). Cameroon stripped of right to host 2019 Africa Cup of Nations. https://www.theguardian.com/football/2018/nov/30/cameroon-stripped-right-host-africa-cup-of-nations-2019. Accessed 2 December 2018.

9

10 E-communication in crisis communication: Best practice for tourism destination management organizations

Antonella Capriello and Simone Splendiani

Introduction

The role of crisis communication is becoming increasingly important in disaster management, especially considering the impact that disasters can have on the image and reputation of tourist destinations. Although the literature has begun to focus on this topic in recent years, the greater number of natural disasters and the impact of new media communication tools, make this theme particularly interesting for further scholarly investigation. Developing an effective crisis communication strategy requires consideration of the role that local authorities, including destination management organizations (DMOs) play, the channels they use, and the content that should be included. Numerous authors have analyzed this issue from a chronological perspective in terms of the difference phases of a crisis starting from preparation and ending with recovery. However, a series of strategic requirements emerge alongside these phases for successful crisis management, including:

- Cooperation with the media in providing information to the public; in particular, imparting a consistent message to all stakeholders to build credibility and preserve the image of organizations and destinations.

- Preparedness and the capacity to plan an effective communication response to a crisis in advance, paying attention to the specific characteristics of each case.

- The development of a public relations plan that creates a support network for the dissemination of communication across multiple channels facilitated by the web and Information Communications Technologies (ICTs).

This chapter presents a number of strategic approaches to crisis management communication for DMOs and tourism organizations. It discusses these approaches in alignment with the prevention and preparedness, response and recovery phases of a crisis. Within each stage, various communication approaches, including the use of e-public relations (E-PR) are presented. Examples of crisis-related communication practices from a variety of destinations around the world are incorporated to illustrate the application and effectiveness of these approaches.

Crisis communication: A review of current literature

As Ritchie et al. state, "Crisis communication is mainly concerned with providing correct and consistent information to the public and enhancing the image of the organization or industry sector faced with a crisis" (2004: 205). The key factors of an effective crisis communication strategy can be summarized as follows: existence of a crisis communication plan and recovery marketing plan; speed of development and implementation of the marketing plan; access to funding for marketing activities; consultation with stakeholders; consistency of messages; use of messages to correct unfounded destination image perceptions; and honesty and openness (adapted from Armstrong & Ritchie, 2008: 176).

Crisis communication has its origins in public relations (Palttala et al., 2012), and is typically associated with managing public perceptions to contain or limit the damage to the organization and its stakeholders (Reynolds & Seeger, 2005). The emphasis in communication and public relations should be to limit the potential negative effects on current and future tourists' perceptions that position the destination as dangerous (Rittichainuwat, 2013; Kozak et al., 2007; Fall & Massey,

2005). In disaster management, public relations can improve the business capabilities of tourism destinations, but the level of stakeholder engagement – especially between DMOs and destination stakeholders will often depend on the stakeholder relationships that existed prior to the disaster (Granville et al., 2016).

Prevention/preparedness

Most scholars agree that preventive communication planning is required for successful post-crisis recovery strategies (AlBattat & Mat Som, 2013; Ritchie, 2008; Huang et al., 2008; Hickman & Crandall, 1997). According to Ritchie et al. (2004: 215), "the cost of developing a crisis management strategy would be far less than the cost of not having one, and a key aspect to any crisis strategy is crisis communication." These authors also propose a communication planning model that articulates the following essential criteria for crisis communication to be effective:

1) Respond quickly and develop two-way dialog with the media;

2) Provide all necessary and detailed information on what occurred;

3) Ensure communication is coherent and discourage the dissemination of unofficial information;

4) Be open and accessible at all times to offer clear and honest information about the crisis;

5) Acknowledge and express sympathy to victims and their families.

Communication before the crisis can help in disaster preparedness, particularly through targeted and well-planned information dissemination activities regarding future possible emergencies (Volo, 2008). Such activities may prove difficult, because tourist destinations are often multifaceted contexts in which many actors work, often without common guidelines (Splendiani, 2017). Therefore, communication activities must be based on cooperation, coordination, and collaboration among the various stakeholders (Martin et al., 2016). Likewise, as Curtis (2015) states, "Disaster preparedness and mitigation depend on how well governments and service organizations communicate and coordinate with one another." Analyzing the gaps in crisis communication, Palttala et al. (2012) highlight that coordination among local entities in terms of the development of effective crisis communication strategies is a challenge, because everyone tends to work in their own way. Therefore, the different roles related to crisis communication in the preparation phase should be clarified to avoid the risk of poor and inadequate cooperation. From the organizational point of view, several authors underline the importance of creating a taskforce to manage communications in the event of a crisis (Faulkner, 2001; Ritchie et al., 2004; Hickman & Crandall, 1997),

Response

Any crisis situation is more complex in the emergency phase. First to consider is the role of reporters and the risk that their sensationalist reporting style could lead to significant damage to the destination's image. To avoid this, destination managers should attempt to convince media operators to mention the exact location of the disaster, as well as those locations that remain unaffected (Walters et al., 2016), An example of best practice in this regard was New Orleans' response to hurricane Katrina, when a DVD titled *Make Way for the Rebirth* was freely distributed to show the undamaged tourist areas and hence able to host tourists (Chacko & Marcell, 2008). This approach could have been effective in response to the 2016 Central Italy earthquake where, as a result of no specific details being released as to the regions that were and were not affected, the entire country experienced a significant decrease in tourist numbers.

In addition to the hype and sensationalist reporting that is common among mainstream media channels, destinations are now faced with the challenge of managing social media content. The numbers of messages relating to a disaster can reach extremely high levels, for example, again considering the case of the 2016 Italian earthquake, more than 200,000 tweets were posted in the first six hours following the event. User-generated content (UGC) that commentates on disasters and crises is not always reliable and is potentially harmful to the destination's or organisation's image (Quarantelli, 1997). However, the internet also provides destinations with an essential communication platform for the dissemination of information relating to the disaster or crisis itself. As Volo states, "the internet, because of its reach, speed and flexibility is an ideal communication channel in times of actual or potential disasters" (2008:84). The internet is now the most commonly used tool for sharing information during an emergency event and beyond. Fischer's (1998) study predicted the potential benefits of websites for disaster management, albeit 20 years ago: "The next 'generation' of website development involving disaster education and training will quite likely include a much larger website role in the dissemination of basic knowledge about disaster agents, the need for mitigation and disaster planning, response needs and recovery procedures."(p.32). The management of web content, whether this be for essential crisis-related safety information or the monitoring of public commentary surrounding the event, is nonetheless an essential element of crisis communications during the response phase. In fact, PR practitioners need to reflect on compelling strategies to deal with different stakeholders on the web (Van der Merwe et al., 2005) across all three phases.

Recovery

In the recovery phase, the key objective of communication is to counter the negative destination images that may have emerged as a result of the crisis and subsequent media coverage. In some cases, reinventing the destination image may even be necessary (Walters & Mair, 2012; Scott et al., 2008).

Marketing communication in the recovery stage should focus on two points (Walters & Mair, 2012):

1) Changing (mis)perceptions of the destination caused by intense media coverage; and

2) Restoring visitors' confidence in the destination.

In terms of the most effective content to transmit in the recovery phase, worth mentioning is the study of Walters and Mair (2012) which shows that the most credible advertising campaigns are those that use celebrity endorsements. An example of such communication policy is the Risorgi Marche festival (www.risorgimarche.it), which literally means, "Rise again, Marche!". This Italian region was particularly affected by the 2016 earthquake, and the festival hosted a series of music events organized by a group of famous Italian artists who – performing for free – used the disaster areas as stages, with the aim of economically re-launching the region.

Finally, when considering the timing of response communications, this greatly depends on the readiness of the destination and the host community (Mair et al, 2016). When it comes to 'how' such communications are designed and delivered, Public relations (PR) activities are often employed to enhance the credibility of the message and regain public confidence. The importance of PR, and in particular E-PR (Public Relations on the Internet) as a crisis communication strategy is discussed in the following section.

Public relations and crisis communication

Solis and Breakenridge (2009) underline that with the advent of social media we need to consider e-public relations (E-PR) to communicate in the stakeholder ecosystem, because E-PR has important effects on empowering consumers. The idea of E-PR is to establish the principle of information dissemination to create awareness among tourists of the potential risks of a destination, as well as problem solving and decision making, information gathering, and co-sharing experiences. The plethora of social media tools has considerably changed the crisis management landscape in recent years, with the possibility of social actions now becoming a reality. E-PR makes use of websites and other internet technologies (Hallahan, 2004). In this vein, tourism authorities and DMOs are adopting E-PR with a focus on social media platforms. For example, the Hawaii Tourism Authority used its social media channels to provide continuous updates on the status of the Kilauea volcano eruption, as did Sonoma County Tourism in the wake of the wildfires in 2017 (Moskowitz, 2018).

As mentioned, this recent form of media creates a number of additional challenges for managing a crisis. Dynamic approaches to digital communication, interactive actions, and open online dialogue are essential E-PR drivers for managers when attempting to respond to a crisis. These are discussed in detail below.

1) **Dynamic approaches** in digital communication have an impact on social media applications such as Twitter and various blog sites, providing a platform for immediate global news coverage. Time-pressured traditional media are more competitive (also using Web 2.0 methods) in their attempts to maintain and attract audiences. In the past, tourist organizations had time after the crisis unfolded to prepare the crisis communication plan, create a crisis response team, prepare a press release, and hold a press conference. Today, social media channels have the potential of creating awareness or reporting certain crises or disasters *prior* to their occurrence – for example, in the case of forecasted extreme weather events PR practitioners must now be prepared to act immediately to confront the crisis conditions. Unlike traditional media, Web 2.0 technologies are not subject to time constraints, because bloggers and Twitter posts are constantly active. If a tourism organization is unable to deal with specific issues immediately, these issues can manifest online with negative implications on destination reputation.

2) **Interactive actions** are needed because of the new rules of social media, which increase the need for companies to proactively communicate with their internal and external stakeholders to mitigate or neutralize negative comments. These efforts must be proactive, because it is even more important to establish and maintain good relationships with the media industry (industry bloggers and other key online influencers). Web 2.0 technologies have also created opportunities to directly engage and interact with tourists.

3) **Open online dialogues** are instrumental to establishing trust and credibility, and the best approaches to build conversations before a crisis occurs. Well-respected tourist destination organizations are investing financial and human resources to establish these networks. These aspects all have implications on building a social media team to monitor the WebSphere. In addition, there is an emerging need to educate senior leaders in tourist organizations on the importance of social media, not just in crises, but also in the overall corporate communication strategy.

Social media are a source of uncontrolled information, and may seriously impede the dissemination of trustworthy information. While social media and social media tools enable individuals to express themselves freely and without restraint, gaps in the law may transform online communication into a channel for disinformation. The potential manipulation of information is particularly harmful at every stage of a natural disaster, and destination managers cannot ignore its ability to aggravate an unfolding crisis. They therefore need to prevent disinformation by adopting effective tools. With readily available software tools such as online discussion platforms and news aggregators, tourism organizations can now acquire and analyse information more efficiently and comprehensively.

In E-PR, social media plays a key role in all three phases of the crises (prevention/preparedness, response, recovery). The following section describes the function of social media tools at each of these specific stages.

Social media and prevention and preparedness

Tourist destinations are extremely vulnerable to negative perceptions regarding public health and safety. Tourism is information intensive, and the dissemination of information regarding emerging or potential crises is instrumental to the tourist's decision-making processes and

10

more importantly to their evaluation of risk when considering their destination choice. The use of social media platforms during the disaster preparedness phase allows tourism managers to provide updated information for tourists and locals, particularly for those events that can be forecast in advance. Table 10.1 illustrates a series of examples of the adoption of social media in accordance with the variables that are likely to influence the tourists' decision-making process.

Table 10.1: Example of social media use in the preparation and planning phase

Weather

The National Oceanic and Atmospheric Administration's National Weather Service Twitter account (@NWS) provides regular storm updates, including crucial information during the hurricane season.

Regional and related accounts are identified such as the National Weather Service San Juan (@ NWSSanJuan) and the National Hurricane Center Atlantic Ops (@NHC_Atlantic), although @NWS often reTweets the most important updates from these accounts.

Some meteorologists used their own accounts to offer perspectives on storms during Irma, including Taylor Trogdon (@TTrogdon), a senior scientist with the Storm Surge Unit at the National Hurricane Center (@NHC_Surge).

Safety

The Center for Disease Control & Prevention (@CDCgov) posts health & safety updates. After Irma, it tweeted a link to its food & water safety guidelines, as well as home cleanup recommendations.

FEMA (@fema) provides information on activities during a crisis. The State Department's Bureau of Consular Affairs posts travel-related security messages, weather-related evacuations, etc. at @ TravelGov.

The local emergency management office in New York City, the Emergency Management feed (@ nycoem), local fire and police department feeds are also helpful. The Metropolitan Police Service (@metpoliceuk) Tweeted updates on the investigation and threat-level changes on the Parsons Green attack in London. In the Florida Keys, the Monroe County Sheriff's Office (@mcsonews) posted links about hurricane recovery, as well as curfew and checkpoint information.

The Italian National Institute of Geophysics and Volcanology has used social channels since 2012 to disseminate information on seismic activity, especially during strong earthquakes, seismic sequences, and tidal waves, and on the results of INGV studies and research. It has a Twitter account (@INGVterremoti), but also a Facebook page and a YouTube channel.

The Italian National Civil Protection Department uses social channels to inform the population on every possible form of natural risks (@DPCgov).

Transport and accommodation

On a national and international level, there are a variety of accounts to follow, including rail (@ Amtrak and @RailEurope), bus (@GreyhoundBus, @MegaBus), and cruise lines, such as Royal Caribbean (@RoyalCaribbean) and Norwegian Cruise Line (@CruiseNorwegian), car services such as @Uber and @Lyft, and airports and airlines (@United).

Airbnb (@Airbnb and @AirbnbHelp) has a disaster response program that helps find temporary accommodation. Booking sites such as @Expedia and @Priceline post relevant information in emergencies.

Local government and tourism boards

Local government accounts. Throughout Hurricane Irma, Monroe County, which includes the Florida Keys, posted updates, including to its Facebook page (@MonroeCountyFLBOCC). The Caribbean Tourism Organization provided up-to-date information on Irma's effects on the islands on its Facebook (@CaribbeanTourismOrganization) and Twitter (@ctotourism) accounts.

News organizations such as the Miami Herald and Orlando Sentinel were especially helpful during Irma.

Other local institutions are identified, such as London Ambulance (@Ldn_Ambulance), the London Fire Brigade (@LondonFire), and Terrorism Police UK (@TerrorismPolice).

The role of social media in the response phase

In the response stage, social media and networking processes are effective tools for broadcasting real-time information for both affected areas and people interested in receiving real-time data from the areas, mobilizing and coordinating immediate relief efforts. Table 2 reports a range of potential uses for collaborative problem solving and decision-making during the response phase.

Table 10.2: Social media for collaborative problem solving and decision making in the response phase

Contacting emergency responders

With phone lines often congested after a natural disaster, contacting emergency responders via social media, websites, or email and online friends can be a compelling alternative. Emergency responders need to be trained and accessible via social media.

Locating family members

Social media such as Facebook are a valuable way of reuniting family members with "safe and well" listings on the Red Cross website.

Instant communication with social networks

Twitter and following conversations via hashtags not only help involve people around the world in relief efforts, but also guarantee a way for victims to reach out to family members and find resources.

Lost and found

Facebook pages (such as Moore Oklahoma Lost and Found, and groups such as Oklahoma Tornado Photo Recovery) were used to help reunite victims with items they thought they would never see again. The OKC Metro Area Lost & Found Pets website acts as a virtual bulletin board to help people find and reunite them with their animals.

Mobilizing help

Through social media, many organizations are able to tap into this human need and mobilize potential volunteers. Non-profit organizations (such as Operation BBQ Relief, founded after the 2011 tornado in Joplin) help feed victims and emergency personnel after a disaster. Operation BBQ Relief uses social media to mobilize those looking to volunteer, while also telling their story through images and videos.

Fundraising

Social media and mobile phones have streamlined the fundraising process. Many non-profit associations now have a "text to donate feature" (such as mGive). This tool makes donating to a cause as easy as sending a text message.

Finding resources

Crowdsourcing tools such as Google Docs enable people to work together to share tips and resources, the Resource Directory for Oklahoma Tornadoes and Google's online Oklahoma crisis map helped detail the area hit.

The role of social media in the recovery phase

In rebuilding the reputation of a tourism destination that has been hit by disaster, social media can optimize recovery activities, because they can collect public opinions and identify emerging trends. This data collection enables the promotion of tourist destinations with a new and positive vision. Through the Facebook platform, tourists can post and share their own photographs on social media to counter damaging stories. The Pensacola Bay Area Convention & Visitors Bureau developed a blog, '*Curious about Our Coast*' to provide daily updates from the beach (including unedited photos, videos, and reports from the health department). This tourism organization also introduced an 'Invite a Friend' campaign that gave away a free trip (including airfare, lodging, meals, and attraction tickets) to encourage visitors to the region(Anderson & Thorstensen, 2013).

Destination marketers need to provide factual information regarding safety and the status of attractions, accommodation, restaurants, and other facilities. Providing access to factual and reliable information helps to combat media sensationalism and ensures visitors can make an informed choice. After the Gulf of Mexico Oil spill, the Florida Tourist Board released an emergency response campaign that directed consumers to their tourism website visitflorida.com to watch live webcams, read Twitter feeds, and view up-to-the-minute photos posted by people in real time of different beach destinations throughout Florida (Modiano, 2011). Visit Florida also launched a blog to respond to the travel industry's request for information on the Deep Water Horizon Oil Spill (http://sunshinematters.org). Tourists need to be aware of areas that are not affected so that they can be encouraged to seek alternative destinations within the same region if they need to re-evaluate their travel plans. Travel websites such as TripAdvisor and Virtual Tourist, as well as travel forums such as Fodors and Lonely Planet, are effective tools for establishing a constructive dialogue with tourists about a community's capacity to receive guests. Many tourists constantly check these travel websites while planning their trip and ask questions on forums. For example, since 2008, TripAdvisor has included a page focused on the hurricane season in New Orleans.

As the community recovers, marketing messages on social media should be tailored to reflect the progress made. However, it is important to be strategic and honest about the availability of resources and attractions for visitors (Walters et al., 2015). If most attractions have not yet returned to operation, the messages should be tailored to specific audiences that are likely to enjoy the activities that are available. Events can also foster the rebuilding progress by diverting attention away from the crisis and attracting visitors to the region (Walters & Mair, 2012).

Conclusion

The advent of the digital era has created the need to redesign crisis communication models and reflect on the importance of e-public relations. The new challenge for tourism organizations and DMOs is to manage online communications in an emerging crisis to preserve the destination's brand image and reputation. In comparing case studies, creativity emerges as fundamental to success in engaging with and persuading tourists, but the actions identified highlight that in this time-restricted operating environment, standardized digital content should be prepared well in advance and then adapted to the specific situation.

Recommendations for practice

With a focus on protecting and/or recovering a destination's image, this chapter identifies effective online E-PR communication strategies and how these strategies apply to the preparation, response and recovery phases of a disaster or crisis. For DMOs and tourist organizations, we propose the following practical guidelines:

■ Ensure the crisis plan has clearly specified actions concerning e-public relations in addition to post-disaster marketing campaigns and mainstream media management strategies

- Have a standardised E-PR strategy in place that can be modified quickly to suit different disasters or crises.

- Communicate with key stakeholders and ensure there is clear communication in terms of the emerging issues and the day to day improvements, and that any public sharing of this information is consistent.

- Nurture relationships with loyal visitors and encourage this group to endorse the destination and the destination experience via the destination's social media networks in the recovery stage.

References

AlBattat, A.R. & Mat Som, A.P. (2013) Emergency preparedness for disasters and crises in the hotel industry, *Sage OPEN*, July-September, 1-10.

Anderson, L. & Thorstensen, E. (2013) *Recreating destinations: Rebuilding the tourism industry after disaster*, IEDC Research Report, International Economic Development Council, Washington, D.C., United States, August.

Armstrong, E.K. & Ritchie, B.W. (2008) The heart recovery marketing campaign: destination recovery after a major bushfire in Australia's National Capital, *Journal of Travel & Tourism Marketing*, **23**(2/4), 175–189.

Chacko, H.E. & Marcell, M.H. (2008) Repositioning a tourism destination: The case of New Orleans after hurricane Katrina, *Journal of Travel & Tourism Marketing*, **23**(2/4), 223–235.

Curtis, C.A. (2015) Understanding communication and coordination among government and service organisations after a disaster, *Disasters*, **39**(4), 611–625.

Fall, L, T & Massey, J, E. (2005).The significance of crisis communication in the aftermath of 9/11: a national investigation of how tourism managers have re-tooled their promotional campaigns. *Journal of Travel and Tourism Marketing*, **19**(2/3)77-90.

Faulkner, B. (2001) Towards a framework for tourism disaster management, *Tourism Management*, **22**, 135–147.

Fischer, H.W. (1998) The role of the new information technologies in emergency mitigation, planning, response and recovery, *Disaster Prevention and Management*, **7**(1), 28–37.

Granville, F., Mehta, A. & Pike, S. (2016) Destinations, disasters and public relations: Stakeholder engagement in multi-phase disaster management, *Journal of Hospitality and Tourism Management*, **28**, 73–79.

Hallahan, K. (2004) Online public relations in Hossein Bidgoli (ed.) *The Internet Encyclopedia*, Hoboken, NJ: John Wiley, 769–783.

Hickman, J.R. & bCrandall, W. (1997) Before disaster hits: A multifaceted approach to crisis management, *Business Horizons*, **40**(2), 75–80.

Huang, Y., Tseng, Y. & Petrick, J.F. (2008) Crisis management planning to restore tourism after disasters: A case study from Taiwan, *Journal of Hospitality and Tourism Management*, **23**(2/4), 203–221.

Kozak, M., Crotts, J.C. & Law, R. (2007) The impact of the perception of risk on international travellers, *International Journal of Tourism Research*, **9**, 233–242.

Mair, J., Ritchie, B.W. & Walters, G. (2016) Towards a research agenda for post-disaster and post-crisis recovery strategies for tourist destinations: a narrative review, *Current Issues in Tourism*, **19**(1), 1–26.

Martin, E., Nolte, I. & Vitolo, E. (2016) The four Cs of disaster partnering: Communication, cooperation, coordination and collaboration, *Disasters*, **40**(4), 621–643.

Modiano, D. (2011) DMO best practices. Innovative uses of social media, Retrieved from https://aboutourism.wordpress.com/tag/visitflorida/. Accessed 20th August 2018.

Moskowitz, S. (2018) Weathering the effects of a natural disaster, *O'Dweyer's Communications & New Media*, **32**(6), 9.

Palttala, P., Boano, C., Lund, R. & Vos, M. (2012) Communication gaps in disaster management: Perceptions by experts from governmental and non-governmental organizations, *Journal of Contingencies and Crisis Management*, **20**(1), 2–12.

Quarantelli, E.L. (1997) Problematical aspects of the information/communication revolution for disaster planning and research: Ten non-technical issues and questions, *Disaster Prevention and Management*, **6**(2), 94–106.

Reynolds, B. & Seeger, M.W. (2005) Crisis and emergency risk communication as an integrative model, *Journal of Health Communication*, **10**, 43–55.

Ritchie, B. (2008) Tourism Disaster Planning and Management: from response and recovery to reduction and readiness, *Current Issues in Tourism*, **11**(4), 315–348.

Ritchie, B.W., Dorrel, H., Miller, D. & Miller, G.A. (2004) Crisis communication and recovery for the tourism industry: Lessons from the 2001 foot and mouth disease outbreak in the UK, *Journal of Travel & Tourism Marketing*, **15**(2/3), 199–216.

Rittichainuwat, B.N. (2013) Tourists' and tourism suppliers' perceptions toward crisis management on tsunami, *Tourism Management*, **34**, 112–121.

Scott, N., Laws, E. & Prideaux, B., (2008) Tourism crisis and marketing recovery strategies, *Journal of Travel & Tourism Marketing*, **23**(2/4), 1–13.

Solis, B. & Breakenridge, D. (2009) *Putting the Public Back in Public Relations: How social media is reinventing the aging business of PR.* Upper Saddle River, NJ: FT Press/Pearson Education.

Splendiani, S. (2017) *Destination Management e Pianificazione Turistica Territoriale. Casi e esperienze in Italia,* Milano: Franco Angeli.

Van der Merwe, R., Pitt, L.F. & Abratt, R. (2005) Stakeholder strength: PR survival strategies in the internet age, *Public Relations Quarterly,* **50**(1): 39–48.

Volo, S. (2008) Communication tourism crises through destination websites, *Journal of Travel & Tourism Marketing,* **23**(2/4), 83–93.

Walters, G. & Mair, J. (2012) The effectiveness of post-disaster recovery marketing messages – the case of the 2009 Australian bushfires, *Journal of Travel & Tourism Marketing,* **29**, 87–103.

Walters, G., Mair, J. & Lim, J. (2016) Sensationalist media reporting of disastrous events: Implications for tourism, *Journal of Hospitality and Tourism Management,* **28**, 3–10.

11 Managing the reputation of cruise lines in times of crisis: A review of current practices

Bingjie Liu-Lastres and Amy M Johnson

Introduction

Serving as both a luxury hotel and a traveling city, the cruise line industry acts as one of the fastest growing sectors within the tourism and hospitality industry. With a 62% growth in demand from 2005 to 2015, the cruise line industry expects to welcome 28 million global passengers on board (Cruise Line International Association [CLIA], 2018). According to CLIA (2018), the top five source markets of the global cruise industry are the United States (11.5 million passengers in 2016), China (2.1 million passengers in 2016), Germany (2 million passengers in 2016), United Kingdom (1.9 million passengers in 2016), and Australia (1.3 million passengers in 2016). Although the United States ranks as one of the most important markets for the cruise industry, the number of domestic cruise line companies remains relatively small, which is due to the necessity of obtaining substantial capital investment, and the intense competition (Ryschka et al., 2016).

Within such a competitive market, reputation has become one of the key assets that cruise line companies cannot simply overlook (Weaver, 2005). Reputation refers to "the prestige or status of a product of service, as perceived by the purchaser, based on the image of the supplier" (Petrick, 2002:125). Reputation helps distinguish a particular brand from others as well as affecting peoples' attitude, perceptions, and purchasing intentions (Petrick 2002, 2011; Weaver, 2005). The strong relationship between reputation and consumer decisions and behaviors has been well reported by numerous empirical studies, including both the general marketing literature (e.g. Olshavsky & Granbois, 1979) and the cruise tourism literature (e.g. Perick, 2002, 2011).

Notably, the onset of a crisis can pose a direct threat to an organization's reputation (Coombs, 2007). This is especially true for the cruise industry. Cruise travel is considered one of the safest travel modes and is regulated by multiple international authorities (e.g., U.S. Coast Guard, the Centers for Disease Control and Prevention, and the Environmental Protection Agency, and European Maritime Safety Agency). However, there have been several high-profile crisis events on cruise ships in the past few years. Examples include the 2012 sinking of the Costa Concordia, where the cruise ship ran aground and overturned after striking an underwater rock, resulting in 32 deaths; and the norovirus outbreaks with Princess Cruises and Celebrity Cruises between 2010 to 2015, where a total of 30 gastroenteritis outbreaks took places on board and affected over 5300 passengers. These events not only threaten the safety of passengers and crew members, but also can be costly to affected cruise lines in terms of economic loss and reputational damage (Marti, 1995). Although reputational damage is normally intangible, it is the main cause of people's distrust in major cruise lines as well as of hesitations about taking cruises in the future (Harris Poll, 2013, 2014).

The development of an organization's reputation relies on time and the information stakeholders receive about the organization (Fombrun & van Riel, 2004). In particular, media reports serve as one of the most prominent information sources for stakeholders as well as for the general public, and thus, media coverage has become an important element in reputation management (Carroll & McCombs, 2003). History has demonstrated that crises have the ability to significantly harm an organization's reputation built over years or even decades. This is largely due to the fact that reputations are evaluative in essence and the public has a tendency to build their own reality based on the information they receive via media and personal networks (Champoux et al., 2012). Thus, without proper responses to negative incidents on cruise ships, the audience may misjudge the situation and lose confidence in the cruise line company, which can lead to long-term reputational damages (Liu-Lastres et al., 2018). Ineffective crisis responses can also cause ripple effects, whereby the incident not only affects one ship, but also generates company-wide and even industry-wide ramifications (Ryschka et al., 2016).

Although the importance of crisis responses has been stressed by cruise line professionals and scholars (Liu-Lastres et al., 2018), it is necessary to stay informed regarding the current measures adopted by cruise lines in response to major incidents. Very few articles, however, can provide a comprehensive understanding of this topic. Thus, the purpose of this chapter is to review and analyze cruise lines' responses to major incidents between 2013 and 2017. In doing so, it is expected that the findings of this chapter can provide important implications for both researchers and practitioners. Guided by the Situational Crisis Communication Theory (SCCT), this chapter addresses the following research questions:

■ How did cruise lines respond to major incidents onboard?

■ How effective are these responses?

■ What lessons can be learnt to better handle future crises experienced by the cruising industry?

Situational Crisis Communication Theory

This study is guided by the Situational Crisis Communication Theory (SCCT). The SCCT is one of the most widely used theories within crisis communication research (Avery et al., 2010). Based on an attribution approach and a situational approach, the SCCT aims to provide instructions for organizations to establish effective crisis responses (Coombs, 1995, 2007). More specifically, the attribution approach deals with how the information is perceived and gathered by individuals to form a casual judgement (Fiske & Taylor, 1991); while the situational approach suggests that contextual factors should be taken into account and a crisis response should always align with the actual crisis situation (Coombs, 1995). It is expected that these messages can help organizations protect their reputational assets as well as achieve other desirable outcomes from the communication process following the outbreak of a crisis (Coombs, 1995, 2007).

Furthermore, based on the attribution level (i.e., to what extent an organization is responsible for the crisis), the SCCT groups various crises into three types, also known as crisis clusters. They are: the victim cluster; the accidental cluster; and the preventable cluster. The *victim* cluster refers to a situation where the organization holds minimal responsibility for a crisis and there have been no similar crises in the past. The *accidental* cluster refers to a situation where the organization holds low responsibly for a crisis and a small number of similar crises have happened in the past. The *preventable* cluster refers to a situation where the organization is mostly responsible for the crisis. Different response strategies should be used to address the crisis situation accordingly.

In the same vein, the SCCT proposes several guidelines related to crisis responses.

■ First, a complete message should contain three types of information: *instructing* information, which deals with public safety information; *adjusting* information, which involves corrective actions and sympathy; and *reputational management* options, which aim at protecting an organization's reputational assets. Definitions and explanations of each type of information are provided in Table 11.1.

■ Second, the reputational management options cover four types of strategies: *denial,* which tries to remove the relationship between the organization and the crisis event; *diminishing,* which tries to improve the image of the organization during the crisis communication process; *rebuilding,* which tries to re-establish a positive image of the organization; and *bolstering,* which aims to remind the public of the organization's previous positive performance and reduce the negative impacts of a crisis. Detailed information on each type of strategy can also be found in Table 11.1.

■ Third, the SCCT recommends the specific choice of a reputational management strategy and the combinations of different information depending on the crisis situation. According to Coombs (2007, 2014), such strategic responses and combinations can reshape the attribution of the crisis, change the public's perception of the organization, protect the reputation of the organization, and reduce the negative effects associated with the crisis. When it comes to tourism research, the SCCT has been used in several studies to evaluate the effectiveness of tourism organizations' crisis responses. For example, Liu et al. (2015) used SCCT to examine the effectiveness of hotels' responses to a bed bug issue on social media. Likewise, based on a case study approach, Liu and Pennington-Gray (2015) utilized the SCCT to analyze cruise lines' responses to norovirus outbreaks. A recent study has also used the SCCT to evaluate destinations' responses to terrorism attacks on Twitter (Barbe et al., 2018). Collectively, the findings of these studies have demonstrated the pragmatic utility of SCCT as a guiding framework to evaluate the effectiveness of organizations' crisis responses.

Table 11.1: An overview of SCCT guidelines

Strategy	Definition	Content
Instructing information	Basic information about the crisis and how to protect individuals during the crisis	Basic information about the crisis What to do to protect oneself during the crisis
Adjusting information	Information that aims to help the audience to cope with the crisis psychologically	Factual information about what happened
		Corrective actions: information that explains what measures have been undertaken to correct the situation and to prevent its occurrence in the future
		Controllability: information that addresses the fact that the situation is under control.
		Expressions of concern and sympathy.
Reputation management	Strategies for crisis responses	Denial Posture: aims to remove the connection between the crisis and the organization
		Diminishment: aims to reduce the responsibility of the organization toward the crisis
		Rebuilding: aims to improve the organization's reputation and provide apology and compensation.
		Bolstering: aims to rebuild positive relations between the organization and the audiences.

Adopted from Coombs, 2007, 2014

11

Method / procedure

The major objective of this chapter is to examine the current crisis response practices of cruise lines and evaluate these practices using the SCCT guidelines featured above. Following the suggestions provided by Hsieh and Shannon (2005), a directed approach was used to analyze the content of 14 cruise line incidents that occurred between 2013 and 2017. A directed approach means that the authors first developed a coding scheme following the SCCT guideline and then used this coding scheme to guide the process of content analysis. When it comes to the timeframe, 2013 marks a year when a series of incidents occurred on cruise ships that impacted the cruise industry (Harris Poll, 2013, 2014) and 2017 is the year when this study was conducted.

The sample was collected using a keyword search (e.g., "cruise", "cruise line" "incident") over the database EBSCOhost (Newswires section). Newswire services are commonly used by companies and PR agencies to disseminate news stories to journalists, bloggers, and other online audiences. It is one of the major channels for researchers to capture timely news and organizations' statements related to incidents. Thus, examining the content of the newswire is meaningful and appropriate in the context of this study. The news articles were selected based on their relevance. All initial responses were examined in terms of relevance and a total of 14 specific statements/stories were included in the sample. Each statement/story served as a unit of analysis.

The data analysis procedure consisted of three steps. First, based on the SCCT and related literature, a coding scheme was developed which outlined all the key concepts as initial coding categories (See Table 11.2). Second, according to the findings of previous studies (e.g., Liu & Pennington-Gray, 2015) and the literature, operational definitions are provided for each category (See Table 11.2). Third, based on the coding scheme, the researchers examined and coded the appearance of each theme/category within the unit of analysis.

Table 11.2: Coding scheme of cruise line's crisis responses

	Definition	Example
Instructing Information		
	Public safety information related to the incident.	The illness was confirmed as norovirus, which is highly contagious and typically transmitted from person to person.
		Those affected by the short-lived illness were treated by our ship's doctors with over-the-counter medication.
Adjusting Information		
Sympathy	The cruise line expressed sympathy toward the situation.	We extend our deepest sympathies to the family during this extremely difficult time and are providing full assistance and support
Corrective Actions	Information related to how cruise lines manage the situation and prevent the occurrence of a similar event in the future.	Sanitation experts were flown in to perform enhanced sanitary procedures to supplement routine cleaning protocols and minimize the risk of a recurrence.

Reputation Management		
Denial	The cruise line tries to remove the connection between the incident and the cruise line.	The company believes a passenger who brought it abroad exposed the 19 passengers to the virus.
Diminish	The cruise line tries to lessen its responsibility of the incident through strategies such as excuses and justification.	These types of outbreaks and requests for medical assistance for passengers are "not uncommon" in big ships.
Rebuilding	The cruise line tries to improve its image via strategies such as compensation and apology.	Passengers will receive refunds of their cruise fares, future cruise certificate, arranging chartered air travel home.
Bolstering	The cruise line tries to re-build a positive connection between the company and the passengers.	At XXX Cruise Line, the safety of our guests is our highest priority

Results and discussion

To examine cruise lines' crisis response behaviors, this study analyzed the content of their press releases addressing various incidents. As shown in Figure 11.1, there are a total of 14 crisis responses/statements disseminated via newswires over the past five years (2013-2017), among which over one third (35.7%) of them were published in 2014 and around one fifth (21.4%) of them were published in 2013 and 2016. The average number of responses seems relatively stable over the years.

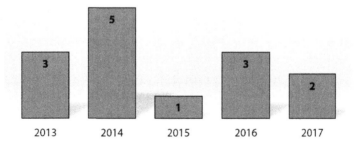

Figure 11.1: Number of crisis responses by year

As shown in Figure 11.2, the most commonly reported incidents were: passenger-related incidents (28.5%), such as passengers falling overboard as well as crimes; and norovirus outbreaks (28.5%). Other incidents include operational incidents (21.4%), such as engine failures and natural/weather issues (21.4%) (e.g., extreme weather/storm-related incidents).

11

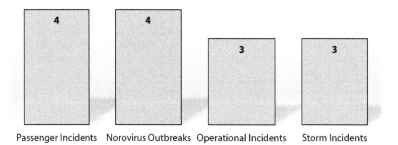

Passenger Incidents   Norovirus Outbreaks   Operational Incidents   Storm Incidents

Figure 11.2: Number of responses by the type of incident

Overall, the results of the descriptive analyses suggest that the scope of cruise lines' crisis response behavior is wider than expected, which is reflected through the type of incident. In terms of the type of the incident, the CLIA identified two major types of risky issues related to cruise travel, namely, operational incidents and health-related outbreaks (e.g., norovirus infections) (CLIA, 2014). The results of the descriptive analysis, interestingly, indicate that the typology of cruise travel incidents should be expanded to include passenger-related incidents and storm/weather-related incidents. The inconsistencies here suggest that more up-to-date research is in need to help practitioners and researchers to stay informed regarding the current status of crisis management in the cruise line industry.

To further explore cruise lines' response behaviors, the content of their statements was also analyzed (Table 11.3). Regarding instructing information, half (50%) of cruise lines provided information on how they managed the situation and specified their general safety policies. For example, following a norovirus incident, a cruise line provided specific information on how they managed the situation by stating that "sanitation experts were flown in to perform enhanced sanitary procedures to supplement routine cleaning protocols and minimize the risk of a recurrence." With respect to the adjusting information, more than one quarter (28.5%) of the responses in the sample displayed a sympathetic attitude toward the victims. For instance, after an incident involving two children on cruise ships, the spokesperson displayed a sympathetic attitude by addressing the fact that "we extend our deepest sympathies to the family during this extremely difficult time and are providing full assistance and support."

When it comes to the reputational management strategies, it is noted that multiple reputational management strategies have been employed. Rebuilding (71.4%) was the most popular strategy where information related to compensations and apologies were frequently mentioned. For instance, after a technical incident, one cruise line offered passengers a full refund of cruise fares, future cruise certificates, as well as assistance with airfares. Diminishing (64.3%) was another popular strategy where cruise lines tended to justify the situation and minimise its responsibility of the crisis. For example, one cruise line addressed the fact that "(norovirus) is not a cruise ship disease, it happens elsewhere." Furthermore, bolstering was used among 50% of the cruise line or anizations in this study to remind the public of their previous good performance. For example, cruise lines would constantly stress the importance of shipboard safety by announcing that "the safety of our guests is our highest priority" in the responses. Lastly, the utilization of denial was found in a small number (14%) of responses, here the cruise line attempted to disassociate itself from the e crisis. For example, they would blame other passengers as the major cause of a norovirus outbreak on board or refuse to reveal details related to the incident.

Table 11.3: Results of content analysis

Theme	Frequency	Percentage
Instructing Information	7	50.0%
Adjusting Information	4	28.5%
Reputation Management Strategies		
Denial	2	14.3%
Diminishing	9	64.3%
Rebuilding	10	71.4%
Bolstering	7	50.0%

Conclusions

Guided by the Situational Crisis Communication Theory, this chapter reports the findings of a critical evaluation of how cruise lines respond to crises or major incidents in a bid to protect their reputation. Interestingly, this study noted that not all cruise lines act in the best interests of the image and reputation of their organisations when responding to crises. However, the majority of those in our sample did adopt appropriate reputational management strategies such as rebuilding (i.e., offering compensation and apology) and diminishing (i.e., using justifications to minimize organizations responsibility to a crisis). Such response strategies imply that the organization is taking responsibility for the incident (Coombs, 2007). Previous research (Liu & Pennington-Gray, 2015) suggested that denial was the most frequent crisis response strategy among cruise line, which according to the SCCT approach is an inappropriate response for the kinds of crises experienced by cruise lines. When compared with the results of this previous study by Liu and Pennington-Gray (2015), our findings demonstrate a significant improvement.

Additionally, it was found that not all responses in the sample featured instructing and adjusting information. Although reputational management strategies can assist in protecting an organization's reputation during the crisis communication process, instructing and adjusting information are essential elements that should not be ignored. Coombs (2007) argues that both instructing and adjusting information can help contextualize the crisis, reduce public uncertainties, and comfort the stakeholder during the difficult time. The lack of a sympathetic attitude, particularly, can be problematic as most audiences are searching for emotional solidarity during crisis times, thus, emotional responses tend to be more effective than informative-factual type statements on some occasions (Kim and Cameron, 2011). It is apparent in our evaluation that generally, cruise lines are not aware of the necessity of having all these elements in their messages.

Important insights generated from our findings speak to the necessity for cruise companies to be proactive and prepared for crises likely to impact their industry. Figure 11.2 indicates that norovirus for example is likely to be the most common type of crises experienced by cruise passengers – it is not unreasonable to expect cruise lines to have a tested and tried pre-prepared communications strategy to minimize reputational damage and ensure the company is shown in a favourable light. It seems that most cruise lines are not prepared and are unlikely to release announcements until after the news media have picked up the story. This is reflected by the fact that not all incidents were addressed in a timely manner and that sometimes the affected cruise lines tended to be non-responsive to media inquiries and/or reveal detailed information in the statements. Such a reactive approach may not be able to satisfy the public's needs of information, which in turn, could place cruise lines' reputations at risk.

Recommendations for practice

Reputation plays a vital role in determining consumers' choices and decisions. Consumers who rely on reputation are more likely to align themselves with companies with positive publicity and possess stronger desires to purchase these products rather than the competitors (Fombrun & Van Riel, 2004). This also applies to the cruise travel context where passengers have the tendency to stay with cruise lines with good reputations (Petrick, 2011). Crisis events are unexpected by nature and can threaten organizations' reputational assets (Coombs, 2014). More specifically, the outbreak of a crisis event can lead to public doubts in an organization's ability as well as bad impressions and evaluation of the organization, both of which can result in damages in the organization's reputation (Coombs, 2007). Post-crisis communication utilizes effective strategies to amend the reputation and even prevent reputational damages (Coombs & Holladay, 2008). Accordingly, this study analyzed major cruise lines' crises responses via newswires over the past five years and aimed at providing insights for tourism professionals and researchers.

The following section provides recommendations regarding how to create effective crisis communication messages and how to manage cruise lines' reputations in crisis times:

- Assume a proactive attitude in tourism crisis communication and management. One of the most notable shortcomings in current cruise lines' practices revealed in this study involves the lack of comprehensiveness and responsiveness. This is reflected through the fact that not all incidents have been well managed and that very few sample statements have incorporated all three recommended information elements. In fact, most cruise lines tend to be reactive in nature and wouldn't respond to an incident openly and clearly until a news report is released. Being unable to provide timely and appropriate updates may be one of the biggest challenges for practitioners in the cruise line industry. The lack of information not only can cause public panic, but also will lead to public distrust, which would eventually, does harm to the reputation of an organization.

To become proactive in tourism crisis management, practitioners need to pay attention to two aspects. The first one is *risk reduction*. There is a constant need of monitoring emerging risk issues (Paraskevas, 2006). Identifying potential risk elements and employing risk-reduction plans beforehand is one of the best strategies in tourism crisis management. Also, having an appropriate interpretation of the environment and accurate assessment of risks can help cruise lines better position themselves during a crisis and adjust their strategies to cope with the evolving environment. Once an incident occurs, the best strategy is to *stay engaged*. Actively participating in conversations with stakeholders and the general public not only can deliver the most accurate information, but also can maintain a positive image in public by displaying a concerning and sympathetic attitude. This emotional connection can be one of the most powerful weapons in protecting the cruise line's reputation during crisis times.

- Create the most effective crisis communication message. According to the findings of previous studies (e.g., Liu et al., 2015; Liu-Lastres et al., 2018), most incidents that occurred on cruise ships are perceived as preventable. Coombs (2014) suggested that the most appropriate strategies to use to address this situation should involve the postures of rebuilding and diminishing. The goal of utilizing these strategies is to lessen the connection between the organization and the crisis and switch public focus off the crisis by taking positive actions.

To create an effective crisis response, practitioners need to incorporate three types of information elements in the message: *instructing* information, *adjusting* information, and the postures of *rebuilding and diminishing*. In terms of instructing information, the cruise line should clarify the situation by stating what happened and what they have done to manage the situation (e.g., emergency measures). Safety information on how to protect oneself should also be included. Regarding the adjusting information, cruise lines need to: display a sympathetic attitude (e.g., showing concerns over the victims); and specify the corrective actions by stating what changes will be made in the future to avoid the re-occurrence of a similar event. Lastly, with respect to the reputation management strategies, the cruise line should make sure that they apologize for the situation and that they offer compensations (e.g., refund, credit for future cruises, and other special arrangements). Cruise lines can also remind the public of their previous positive performance and address the fact that shipboard safety is one of their most important priorities.

There is also a need to devote efforts to *testing the effects of different crisis communication messages*. Considering that most studies in tourism crisis communication are descriptive in nature and that the findings of the current study have revealed differences between theoretical guidelines and industry practices, empirical studies testing the effects of messages have become especially important.

- Have a strategic, coordinated and rehearsed crisis communication plan. As important as it is to have a proactive attitude and an effective message template, cruise line companies should always have a strategic, coordinated, and rehearsed crisis communication plan in place. One of the advantages of having such a plan is that it helps the major decision-makers to interpret the underlying dynamics beforehand and therefore, have enough time to come up with strategies to address any arising crisis situation. The abovementioned aspects (i.e., a proactive attitude and an effective crisis communication message) are essential parts of this plan. The ultimate goal of the plan is to minimize the negative consequences brought by an unexpected crisis event as well as to call attention to the positive steps taken to ensure shipboard safety.

The function of organizational learning should also be acknowledged in tourism crisis management and communication. This is an element that has long been neglected by mainstream research (Blackmam & Ritchie, 2008). When it comes to the current case, it is apparent that most cruise lines have learned from their previous lessons, as they have started to use multiple reputational management strategies in their crisis response instead of simply denying everything. However, the findings of this study noted that most crisis responses are missing the elements of instructing information and adjusting information. The discrepancies between the theoretical guidelines and practice not only provide directions for future research, but also signify the importance of organizational learning during the crisis management process.

- Pay attention to loyal customers. Walters et al. (2015) suggest that tourism organizations can rely on their loyal customers in crisis time. Similarly, cruise travel research (e.g., Petrik, 2011; Liu-Lastres et al., 2018) found that an important element that should be featured during the crisis communication process involves customer loyalty. Repeated and loyal customers are among the most valuable assets for cruise lines. Major cruise lines have established VIP programs and loyalty programs to attract and retain this market segment. Similarly, some studies (e.g., Liu-Lastres et al., 2018) found that this group of customers are more likely to stay aligned with the cruise line during crisis times. Thus, this segment should be seen as one of the most valuable resources for cruise lines to restore/protect their reputation assets during crisis times. Future studies should take this into account and establish crisis communication messages corresponding to different segments.

References

Avery, E.J., Lariscy, R.W., Kim, S. and Hocke, T. (2010) 'A quantitative review of crisis communication research in public relations from 1991 to 2009', *Public Relations Review*, 36(2), 190-192.

Barbe, D., Pennington-Gray, L., and Schroeder, A. (2018) 'Destinations' response to terrorism on Twitter', *International Journal of Tourism Cities*. Available at https://www.emeraldinsight.com/loi/ijtc/(Accessed 5 April. 2018).

Carroll, C.E. and McCombs, M. (2003) 'Agenda-setting effects of business news on the public's images and opinions about major corporations', *Corporate Reputation Review*, 6(1), 36-46.

Champoux, V., Durgee, J. and McGlynn, L. (2012) 'Corporate Facebook pages: when "fans" Attack', *Journal of Business Strategy*, 33(2), 22-30.

Coombs, W.T. (1995) 'Choosing the right words: The development of guidelines for the selection of the "appropriate" crisis-response strategies', *Management Communication Quarterly*, 8(4), 447-476.

Coombs, W.T. (2007) 'Protecting organization reputations during a crisis: The development and application of situational crisis communication theory', *Corporate Reputation Review*, 10(3), 163-176.

Coombs, W.T. (2014) *Ongoing Crisis Communication: Planning, Managing, And Responding*. New York City: Sage Publications.

Coombs, W.T. and Holladay, S.J. (2008) 'Comparing apology to equivalent crisis response strategies: Clarifying apology's role and value in crisis communication', *Public Relations Review*, 34(3), 252-257.

Cruise Line International Association [CLIA]. (2014) *'Report on Operational Incidents 2009 to 2013'*, [Online]. Available at http://cruising.org/ (Accessed 5 April. 2018).

Cruise Line International Association [CLIA]. (2018) *'2018 Cruise Industry Outlook'*, [Online]. Available at http://cruising.org/ (Accessed 5 April. 2018).

Fiske, S.T. and Taylor, S.E. (1991) *Social Cognition*, New York: McGraw-Hill

Fombrun, C. and Van Riel, C. (2004) 'Managing your company's most valuable asset: Its Reputation', *Criticaleye Review*, (5), 71-74.

Harris Poll. (2013) *'Cruise Line Perceptions Continue to Sink'*, [Online]. Available at https://theharrispoll.com/ (Accessed 5 April. 2018).

Harris Poll. (2014) *'Cruise Line Industry Continues to Battle Unfavorable Tides'*, [Online]. Available at https://theharrispoll.com/ (Accessed 5 April. 2018).

Hsieh, H.F. and Shannon, S.E. (2005) 'Three approaches to qualitative content analysis', *Qualitative Health Research*, 15(9), 1277-1288.

Kim, H.J. and Cameron, G.T. (2011) 'Emotions matter in crisis: The role of anger and sadness in the publics' response to crisis news framing and corporate crisis response', *Communication Research*, 38(6), 826-855.

Liu, B. and Pennington-Gray, L. (2015) 'Understanding the Cruise Industry's Responses to Health-Related Crises: A Case Study Approach', paper presented at the 2015 ttra International Conference, 15-17 June, Oregon.

Liu, B., Kim, H., and Pennington-Gray, L. (2015) 'Responding to the bed bug crisis in social Media', *International Journal of Hospitality Management*, 47,76-84.

Liu-Lastres, B., Schroeder, A., and Pennington-Gray, L. (2018) 'Cruise Line Customers' Responses to Risk and Crisis Communication Messages: An Application of the Risk Perception Attitude Framework' *Journal of Travel Research*, Available at https://journals.sagepub.com/home/jtr/(Accessed 5 April. 2018).

Marti, B. E. (1995) 'The cruise ship vessel sanitation program', *Journal of Travel Research*, 33(4), 29-38.

Olshavsky, R. W., and Granbois, D. H. (1979) 'Consumer decision making—fact or fiction?',*Journal of Consumer Research*, 6(2), 93-100.

Paraskevas, A. (2006) 'Crisis management or crisis response system? A complexity science approach to organizational crises', *Management Decision*, 44(7), 892-907.

Petrick, J.F. (2002) 'Development of a multi-dimensional scale for measuring the perceived value of a service', *Journal of Leisure Research*, 34(2), 119-134.

Petrick, J.F. (2011) 'Segmenting cruise passengers with perceived reputation', *Journal of Hospitality and Tourism Management*, 18(1), 48-53.

Ryschka, A.M., Domke-Damonte, D.J., Keels, J.K. and Nagel, R. (2016) 'The effect of social media on reputation during a crisis event in the cruise line industry', *International Journal of Hospitality & Tourism Administration*, 17(2), 198-221.

11

Walters, G., Mair, J., & Ritchie, B. (2015) 'Understanding the tourist's response to natural disasters: The case of the 2011 Queensland floods,' *Journal of Vacation Marketing,* 21(1), 101-113.

Weaver, A. (2005) 'The McDonaldization thesis and cruise tourism', *Annals of Tourism Research,* 32 (2), 346-366.

12 Managing media sensationalism in the event of an airline disaster

Kate Delmo and Sean Chaidaroon

Airlines are a critical sector in the tourism industry. Progress in travel and mobility presents both opportunities and challenges to airline companies (Henderson, 2003). Airlines put a premium on the safety of travellers in their journey to and from destinations. They are meant to be prepared for potential disruptions to their operations. Airlines are, however, susceptible to certain tragic events that come without warning and bring fatal consequences (Fishman, 1999; Henderson, 2003). An airline crash is one of them. Causes of plane crashes vary from technical failure, manufacturing defects, extreme weather conditions, human error, or a combination of these. Post the September 11 World Trade Centre attacks, acts of terrorism are added to the list. Regardless of what causes a plane to crash, the unpredictability and high concentration of death and injury in a single event commonly lead to extreme grief and anger among members of the public (Gerken et al., 2016; Henderson, 2003). When a plane crashes, the host airline company encounters intense government, media and public scrutiny (Faulkner, 2001; Fishman, 1999; Henderson, 2003).

Airline crashes provide an emotionally compelling as well as highly visual and textual media story (Vincent et al., 1997 cited in Fishman, 1999). Events surrounding an airline crash provide journalists and media practitioners with various narratives and perspectives that they can choose to use in writing stories about the incident. Media stories influence organisational reputation, which is defined as "collective representation of images of an organisation established over time" (Cornelissen, 2011:8). In media coverage of airline crashes, framing is a way for media practitioners to promote salient angles or storylines about the crash (Entman, 1993). It is critical for airline management to examine storylines about the airline crash because media reports influence stakeholder perceptions. Media reports of a plane crash provide audiences with "visible public expressions of approval or disapproval of [airlines] and their actions" (Valentini & Romenti, 2011:361). Therefore, effectively managing media in news reports of an airline crisis is crucial to an airline company to restore its reputation. An airline's reputation influences travel decisions and thus impacts tourism and hospitality industry as a whole.

This chapter presents a case study of a local airline in Australia that demonstrates media framing in airline disasters. The case study describes the role of post-crisis investigations as sources of media stories. Findings of this case study emphasise that post-crisis investigations conducted by third-party authorities present frames (Goffman, 1974) that media use in making sense of an airline crash. Third-party investigations, although intending to shed light on what transpired in a crash, add complexities to crisis communication because their findings are used as key narratives or storylines for media reports. Media practitioners have direct access to investigative reports about a plane crash. They are no longer reliant on information subsidies (Park et al., 2016) such as press releases or media statements otherwise provided by airline companies.

This chapter aims to examine how media reported on the Whyalla Airlines Flight 904 crash in 2000 in South Australia. It describes how the attribution of blame in media reports based on post-crisis investigations severely tarnished the airline's reputation, which eventually led to its demise. It aims to extend knowledge and understanding of complexities in upholding organisational reputation through managing media representations in the event of an airline disaster. Past studies on airline disaster response emphasise the importance of information subsidies in framing the crash from the host airline's perspective. Post-crisis inquiries at times override the preferred narratives of airline companies. This is critical to note because stakeholders (especially the media) are more inclined to uphold views of investigating authorities even though results of investigations are sometimes questionable.

Even though Flight 904 incident is a local case, it is an important airline disaster to examine because: it took years for government authorities to determine the cause of the crash; a lack of proper crisis attribution led to sensationalised media reporting; and Whyalla Airlines was unable to recover from the disaster. The longer it took for post-crisis inquiries to determine the reason behind the crash, the longer the media speculated on crisis attribution. In the following sections, details of the case are presented followed by a brief discussion on relevant theoretical concepts that underpinned analysis for this case. This chapter discusses insights generated from a careful investigation of news frames from May 2000 to early 2003, the period inclusive of the airline crash until conclusion of post-crisis investigations. Practical implications for the airline industry on effective stakeholder communication at the post-crisis stage are provided.

Whyalla Airlines Flight 904 Case Study

> *"Adelaide, Adelaide. This is Mayday! Mayday! Mayday! Mike Zulu Kilo has experienced two engine failures. We'll be, um, landing. We're going to have to ditch. We're trying to make Whyalla at the moment... We've got no engines so we'll be ditching. We have eight POB (people on board). I repeat again eight POB, and ah, most likely we're currently, ah, about one five miles off the coast of Whyalla on the Gibon Whyalla Track. Request someone come out and help us please."*

These were the last words of Ben Mackiewicz, pilot of Whyalla Airlines Flight 904, minutes before the aircraft plunged into Spencer Gulf, 10 km southeast of Whyalla, South Australia at 6:23 pm on 31 May 2000. The twin-engine commuter plane departing from Adelaide International Airport crashed into the Gulf a few minutes short of reaching its destination. All eight people on board, including the pilot, lost their lives.

Whyalla Airlines Flight 904 is considered as one of South Australia's worst air disasters. An intricate disaster rescue operation ensued that entailed collaboration among state emergency responders and volunteers who worked together for the entire duration of the rescue initiative (Nicholson, 2001). It took six days before the bodies of the victims were recovered. The wreckage was located at the Yarraville Shoals, 20 meters below sea level, 30km short of its destination. Ten days after the crash, Whyalla Airlines' Air Operator's Certificate (AOC), a document that allows an airline to transport paying passengers, was suspended by the Civil Aviation Safety Authority (CASA). The airline eventually ceased operations for good.

12

Post-crisis investigations about the cause of the Flight 904 airline crash resulted in debates among authorities. Inquiry reports submitted by the Australian Transport Safety Bureau (ATSB), the Civil Aviation Safety Authority (CASA) and the South Australian Coronial inquiry highlighted varied speculations on the cause of the incident such as Whyalla Airline's safety culture (e.g. lack of mandate on the use of life jackets despite official safety policy), pilot competency, employee fatigue, and engine failure. It took three years before authorities provided a clear narrative about the cause of the airline disaster. Post-crisis media reporting similarly focused on conflicting attributions of the cause of the crash, based on investigations conducted by relevant government authorities.

Attribution of causes and managing airlines' reputation amidst media sensationalism

When a crisis occurs, especially in the case of an airline crash that leads to fatal consequences, stakeholders closely watch actions and decisions made by airlines in dealing with the aftermath of a plane crash (Henderson, 2003). An airline company's immediate concern is to locate and help air crash victims. In the first few hours after the crash, airline management deals with multi-layered, urgent demands in a highly time-pressured environment where stakeholders, especially the media, pay close attention (Goodrich, 2002). Airline management assesses the scale of damage caused by the crash, coordinates safety and rescue operations with crisis responders, comforts victims' next of kin, liaises with authorities' post-crisis investigations, and communicates information about the crash to various stakeholders, among other tasks. Initial crisis response measures also aim for organisational operations to return to normal as soon as possible. If messages released by organisations in the post-crisis stage are unclear or ambiguous, stakeholders speculate on possible causes of the incident. Speculations lead to various interpretations that influence organisational reputation.

Three theoretical concepts have been extensively researched by communication and business scholars to understand and predict effective crisis communication. First, as derived from Attribution Theory in psychology (Weiner, 1985, 1986), organisational crises are characterised as either smouldering (e.g. ongoing issues) or sudden events that threaten organisational objectives and reputation (Coombs, 2007). Crises bring high uncertainty to organisations and demand urgent response. In crises, stakeholders identify and explore possible causes in order to determine organisational responsibility (Coombs & Holladay, 2005; McDonald & Hartel, 2000). The cause of a crisis influences stakeholders' perceptions formed of an organisation (Coombs, 2016). For example, if a crisis is allegedly caused by mistakes made by an organisation, stakeholders tends to view the latter negatively (Schwarz, 2012). Crisis response includes management of stakeholders' attribution processes because of the critical role that stakeholder perceptions, including those of victims, customers, media, community members, investors, government or the general public, play in determining post crisis recovery and survival.

Second, organisational responsibility in a crisis is a fundamental concept of the Situational Crisis Communication Theory (SCCT) (Coombs, 2016; Coombs & Holladay, 1996; Schwarz, 2008) that has been widely adopted by industry as a guide for effective crisis communication. SCCT proposes that there are two factors in selecting effective crisis responses strategies. First, organisations analyse the type of the crisis that has occurred and determine their level of responsibility in causing it. Second, an organisation's existing reputation prior to the crisis could either help or exacerbate the situation. Organisations that have a positive reputation among their stakeholders prior to a crisis are generally better placed to call on this goodwill when a crisis occurs (Ulmer, 2001). For organisations with existing good reputations, stakeholders tend to be slow to perceive organisations negatively when crises occur (Ulmer, 2001). According to SCCT, this is an important factor in selecting crisis response strategies.

The media play a vital role in providing information to stakeholders in all phases of managing a crisis. Media practitioners select certain angles for stories in reporting about crises. This process of selecting narratives and perspectives to report in the news is called media framing (Goffman, 1974). Frames are "schemata of interpretation" (Goffman, 1974: 21) used by a person in constructing meaning (Gerken et al., 2016). They are tools in selecting, emphasising and presenting information that guide interpretation and direct action of others (Gitlin, 1980). An airline crash is susceptible to media's use of specific frames in making sense of events that led to the crash, as well as reporting abo ut initiatives that take place after. A study on media coverage of the disappearance of Malaysian Airlines Flight 370, a commercial flight travelling from Kuala Lumpur, Malaysia to Beijing, China in March 2014, reported that there are generally five media frames used

12

in reporting airline crashes: attribution of responsibility, conflict, economic consequences, human interest, and morality (Neuman et al., 1992 cited in Park et al., 2016). Any of these frames can damage an airline's reputation by questioning its commitment to travellers' safety and by sensationalising the incident (Gerken et al., 2016).

This process of framing leads to media sensationalism, which is one of the critical factors that travel, tourism and hospitality organisations need to consider in managing crises (Mair et al., 2016; Walters et al., 2016). Sensationalism entails biased representations in media reporting (Walters et al., 2016) that creates hype among the readers (Paracha et al., 2013). Reports of this nature use sensationalist language through figures of speech (e.g. metaphors, hyperboles) and are emotion-laden to attract readers (Davis & McLeod, 2003; Tierney et al., 2006). It is significant to investigate multifaceted portrayals of crisis attributions reported in the media because media reporting informs the formulation of perceptions. The perceived reputation of airline companies is immensely impacted by media reports, especially during crises. Perceptions of airlines influence decisions to travel which makes airline safety a crucial factor that drives tourism (Fleischer et al., 2012; Koo et al., 2019; Yang et al., 2018).

The link between media portrayal of the Whyalla Airlines Flight 904 airline crash and post-crisis inquiries that followed suggest that media representations of Whyalla Airlines varied based on conflicting findings gathered by the inquests. This case study sheds light on how post-crisis inquiries framed media reports (Nisbet & Mooney, 2000) that eventually affected the organisation's reputation (Coombs & Holladay, 2010). The following media analysis of Flight 904 crash illustrates how media framing and attribution (Coombs, 2016; Coombs & Holladay, 1996; Schwarz, 2008) contributed to the demise of the airline's reputation, and ultimately its operations.

Findings presented in this chapter used a qualitative media analysis (Altheide & Schneider, 2013) of 116 news articles published by Australian newspapers, both national and regional, about Flight 904 from 2000 to 2003. The authors of this chapter open coded all articles to identify initial themes (Charmaz, 2014). Axial coding was performed to explore relationships among emerging themes (Charmaz, 2014).

Insights from news media analysis: Conflicting post-crisis reports as sources of media sensationalism

Media analysis conducted for this chapter found that Australian media reports framed the causes of the airline crash differently based on varying findings from the post-crisis investigations of the incident. It is important to note that while the media waited for results of post-crisis investigations, news media speculated on the cause of the crash such as engine failure, pilot competency, and the airline's safety culture. Our analysis of the published media reports revealed that there was a direct relationship between media reporting and post-crisis investigations. The latter issued conflicting findings about crisis attribution about the incident. Similarly, media shifted its framing about the airline crash numerous times over the three years. This consequently created changing narratives about the airline's responsibility during this period as well.

Table 12.1 highlights key turning points in the post-crisis investigations for Flight 904. It describes the shift in media framing of the airline crash based on conflicting findings released by relevant authorities. Published media articles were based on reports submitted by three government agencies during the crisis recovery stage, namely the Australian Transport Safety Bureau (ATSB), Civil Aviation Safety Authority (CASA), South Australian Police (SAPOL) and South Australian Coroner (SA Coroner). ATSB's report was submitted to CASA, whereas SAPOL's findings were turned over to the SA Coroner. All four agencies aimed to identify what caused Flight 904 to crash minutes away from its port of destination.

As illustrated in Table 12.1, post-crisis investigations influenced the way the media framed their stories about the airline crash. Media frames not only shifted or changed as investigations progressed, but the media also sensationalised their chosen storylines about attributions of the crash. If a recent finding of an investigating body alluded to pilot error as the probable cause, for example, this angle became the focus of published media stories around that time. Was the pilot exhausted during the flight? Did the pilot lack training, given Mackiewicz's relatively young age? These angles were unconfirmed and yet were topics of stories published in relation to findings of government authorities. The focus of media reports changed when the next round of post-crisis investigations released alternative findings. Conflicting findings of investigations over a period of three years added to the dismay of families and relatives of victims of Flight 904.

12

Table 12.1: Timeline of authorities' reports on Whyalla Flight 904 crash & corresponding media framing

---

June 2000

Authority investigation & report: Australian Transport Safety Bureau (ATSB) opened post-crisis investigations by examining weather condition, state of aircraft, and pilot's competency and health condition before the flight.

News media reports: News media mentioned that investigation was in progress. Early reports focused on emotions of victims' next of kin.

June 2000

Authority investigation & report: Civil Aviation Safety Authority (CASA) audited Whyalla's safety compliance immediately after the crash

News media reports: Media did not report the cause(s) directly but left the audience to question Whyalla Airlines' safety culture as they focused reporting on the safety audit conducted by CASA.

May 2001

Authority investigation & report: Australian Transport Safety Bureau (ATSB)'s subsequent findings identified engine failure as cause of the plane crash. As later investigations revealed, this implicates the airline's pressure on pilots to save fuel costs that ultimately overworked plane engines making the latter susceptible to air crash.

News media reports: Media framed the cause of the disaster as direct responsibility of the airline. Pilot competency was also questioned in published media reports. There were media stories that reported on the pilot's health condition due to stress and fatigue before the flight. Besides engine concerns, other issues such as the lack of life jackets was now reported thereby intensifying negative narratives around the airline's safety culture.

July 2003

Authority investigation & report: South Australia Coroner concluded the investigations by conducting a final, five-month intensive inquiry into the airline crash. SA Coroner debunked previous findings of ATSB that questioned pilot's competency. Its findings concluded that the plane crashed due to mechanical failure. The report indicated that Whyalla Airlines was mainly responsible for appropriate routine checks of the aircraft to ensure safety.

News media reports: After release of the Coroner's report, media shifted its frame of reporting about the airline crash. Whereas initial media reports highlighted alleged pilot error as the cause of the disaster (based on ATSB report), media started to shift emphasis to mechanical failure after findings of the Coroner's investigation were released. Media stories shifted emphasis to Whyalla Airlines' failure to check planes prior to departure. They published stories that cleared the name of the pilot and instead framed the latter as a victim of the airlines' negligence.

On the one hand, post-crisis investigations of Flight 904 provided emotional closure to families of victims. One of the articles published by *The Age*, an Australian newspaper, on 22 July 2002 quoted Marie Schuppan, widow of one of the victims:

> *"I waited in the airport lounge for one-and-a-half hours not knowing what had happened. My husband Chris is (was) still missing. (I'd like to see) procedures put in place so that what happened to me does not happen to anyone else. I'm waiting for the inquest to hear from the experts about reasons for the crash."*

On the other hand, conflicting findings of post-crisis investigations over a period of time caused further unrest to victims' next of kin.

The Australian Transport Safety Bureau (ATSB) was the first agency tasked to investigate the crash in the early post-crisis stage. Once bodies of the victims were recovered, and after plane wreckage was found, ATSB commenced its investigation. ATSB examined the aircraft's airworthiness vis-à-vis weather conditions on the day of the crash.

Apart from investigating the state of the aircraft to operate that day, ATSB also probed into Mackiewicz's competency and health condition leading to and during the flight. ATSB's report was crucial to the overall post-crisis investigation because its report was critical to the Civil Aviation Safety Authority's (CASA) wider investigation on the airline crash. CASA, as the regulating agency for aviation safety in Australia that reports directly to the office of the Federal Transport Minister of Australia, determined if Whyalla Airlines could resume its operations. Its report primarily assessed Whyalla Airlines' safety culture as an air transport provider. After ATSB's preliminary investigation, CASA conducted a snap audit on Whyalla Airlines' safety compliance one week after the crash. Investigations conducted by various agencies complicated the process of identifying the reason why Flight 904 crashed.

During this initial stage after the crisis occurred, the news media did not seem to make any direct attribution about the causes of the incident. Media reports used the traditional "investigation in progress" approach in reporting about the crash. However, the sensationalised tone was placed on stories about how families and friends of victims learned about the crash, and their initial reactions about safety and rescue operations.

ATSB's preliminary report identified engine failure due to manufacturing design as the primary cause of Flight 904 disaster. Media reports

12

published after ATSB released its findings framed Whyalla Airlines responsible for the disaster. Media mainly described the airline's failure to conduct routine maintenance and pre-flight checks as the key factor that led to the airline's demise. ATSB reports indicated that Whyalla Airlines' lean fuel policy caused the aircraft's engine to malfunction. A lean fuel policy required Whyalla Airlines pilots to save fuel costs during flights. There appears to be a link between saving fuel costs in this way and engine malfunction (REF). This finding was important because it implied that the pilot made an incorrect decision to boost power to the right engine when the aircraft's left engine lost power. This decision may have overworked the right engine that eventually caused the plane to crash. From this perspective, pilot incompetency caused the plane to crash.

As published by *The Australian* on 25 July 2003 (Plane, 2003):

"The ATSB has not yet reported on its latest investigation of the crash, undertaken since last November, when it reopened its inquiry. But it continues to maintain that the right engine failed when pilot Ben Mackiewicz boosted power to compensate for loss of the left engine."

The strategic use of ambiguous language in the above quote can be interpreted either as pilot incompetency or a case of one circumstance leading to another that eventually resulted in the crash. Other readers may perceive that the pilot made an incorrect decision of boosting power to the right engine when the left engine failed in the first place.

Apart from pilot incompetency, Whyalla Airlines' safety procedures were also questioned.

On 20 May 2001, *Sunday Mail* reported:

"...June 7: Relatives of victims call for laws making it mandatory for aircraft operating over water to carry life jackets. June 10: CASA grounds Whyalla Airlines indefinitely after audit found series of deficiencies."

ATSB's initial report submitted to CASA resulted in the suspension of Whyalla Airlines' license to operate. It took ATSB 18 months to complete the investigation. Media stories published after ATSB's initial report was made public included emotive words and phrases such as 'ill-fated flight', 'ill-fated airline', 'stunning tragedy', 'tragic mystery', 'untrained pilot', 'inexperienced employee', 'depths of despair', 'mangled wreckage', 'shattered lives', 'grim reality', 'cruelly surreal', and 'the end of Whyalla Airlines', among others. These emotive words framed Whyalla Airlines in a negative light.

The media also reported on CASA's former chairman Dick Smith's allegations that CASA had been lenient on Whyalla Airlines. Media reported that Smith believed the airline's licence should not have been re-issued after its fleet was similarly grounded in 1997. The airline was grounded back then due to regulatory breaches and safety concerns. Several media articles such as the one published on 14 July 2000 by the *Adelaide Advertiser* highlighted four incidents between January and April of 2000 criticising Whyalla Airlines' safety procedures. The article enumerated the incidents:

- An aircraft (similar to Flight 904) left Whyalla travelling to Wudinna to Adelaide in April with one fuel cap missing;

- The pilot of a flight from Adelaide to Wudinna in February realised 15 minutes into the flight that the plane had insufficient fuel;

- A pilot landed a plane at Cleve in April in foggy conditions below the permissible level; and

- A pilot had to make an emergency landing in another destination due to failure detected in one of two aircraft engines on 7 January during a flight from Whyalla to Adelaide. (Andrew, 2000)

These media reports followed ATSB's finding on pilot incompetency and Whyalla Airlines' poor safety measures. Former CASA Chairman Dick Smith's hard stance on this news angle occupied media reports for several months after the crash.

On 22 July 2002, a few months after the ATSB has completed its full investigation on Flight 904, the SA Coroner opened an inquest into Whyalla Flight 904 airline crash to challenge ATSB's finding that pilot error caused the crash. The SA Coroner's five-month investigation concluded that Flight 904 crashed into Spencer Gulf due to mechanical failure thereby clearing the name of the pilot. This concluded all investigations pertaining to Flight 904. (Dornin, 2002)

Media reports that followed the SA Coroner's investigation took a different turn by reporting on positive attributes of the pilot this time. The Australian Associated Press General News quoted Peter Eriksen, counsel assisting the Coroner, on 23 July 2002,

> *"From the time the pilot called mayday to the time the plane ditched, all evidence suggests this young pilot maintained his cool, maintained appropriate communications and performed as a well-trained pilot in a very serious emergency."*

12

One key finding in analysing media reports of Flight 904 was the lack of Whyalla Airlines' voice as host airline in stories published from 2000 onwards. Most frames focused on speculations and results from investigations that blamed the airline. It was not until 2003 when further investigations released Flight 904's pilot from being seen as a 'culprit' that a few quotes from the airline's CEO appeared on the news. Although it was understandable why the airline did not intervene in post-crisis investigations, the airline's decision to be silent on the news did not help. Absence of the airline's voices indirectly implied insecurity of its position as host airline and reinforced the negative image created by the sensationalised media reporting for three years. This case shows the importance of providing useful and honest information to the media to complement post-crisis investigations in the post-crisis stage. This is key if airlines want to provide clear narratives about what the investigations meant from their perspective. Providing information subsidies to the media alongside investigations gives airlines an opportunity to manage organisational reputation.

Conclusion

Findings of this media analysis shows that perceptions of Flight 904 were based largely on what post-crisis investigations released to the media. This case emphasises that Whyalla Airlines was not proactive in helping its stakeholders, especially the wider public, make sense of what the findings of the post-crisis investigations meant. The airline did not provide information subsidies (Park et al., 2016) to the media that explained its position as an organisation amidst investigations of what transpired in this disaster. The media, therefore, freely framed (Entman, 1993) the incident, and eventually Whyalla Airlines, in their own terms. Media also sensationalised (Walters, et. al., 2006) crisis attributions based on crisis investigations, which Whyalla Airlines did not challenge. Although airlines are required to uphold post-crisis investigations, Whyalla Airlines in this case could have released statements to the media that findings were still inconclusive in 2000, for example, regardless of whether their license to operate had been cancelled or not. It was crucial for the airlines to proactively issue this statement to the media in order for the latter to avoid choosing their own angles in framing the incident due to a lack of clear and direct narrative coming from the company. The wider public should have seen more of Whyalla Airlines' presence in post-crisis discussions in the media sphere, instead of giving the media a free rein in reporting about the crash in particular, and the company in general, in whatever frames suited them.

This chapter also highlighted that in an airline crisis, the media tend to initially find an airline company responsible for the crash. In other types of crisis such as natural disasters or terrorism, the locus of responsibility is usually beyond an organisation's control as explained by the Situational Crisis Communication Theory (Coombs, 2016). In these types of incidents, media and external stakeholders are inclined to be more sympathetic to organisations mainly because the crises were caused by factors external to the organisation. For airline crashes, in contrast, the media and external stakeholders are poised to question an airline's crisis responsibility (Coombs, 2016). When third party authorities step in to investigate the crash, either media storylines are confirmed, or new ones emerge. Nonetheless, an airline is still entitled to release statements to the media and the wider public about their views on or reactions to the air crash investigations. This gives their voice as the host airline saliency (Gerken et al., 2016) and allows them to still be a part of ongoing discussions about the crash. Presence in media discussions gives airlines a chance to manage their reputation proactively.

This case study on airline disaster crisis response emphasises that media coverage of post-crisis investigations plays a significant role in managing organisational reputation. On the one hand, an airline's reputation is tarnished if investigations conclude that it is responsible for a crash. Some airlines recover, others do not like Whyalla Airlines. On the other hand, if an investigation confirms airline safety, positive organisational reputation is reinforced. This results in increased confidence amongst travellers. Therefore, managing media representations of airline disasters plays a critical role in the tourism ecosystem.

The following are key practical implications for the airline industry in crisis communication as shown by the case discussed:

Recommendations for practice

- First, airline companies should promote a culture of safety. Airlines put the lives of their passengers on the line, hence enforcement of safety measures are of utmost importance to the business. The

Whyalla Flight 904 case, for example, demonstrated that the airline's failure to properly document its safety practices made it difficult for them to provide evidence that they had them during investigations, if at all. In the crisis planning stage, it is imperative that airlines are up to date with all safety regulations required by the aviation industry. As mentioned by Fink (1986), organisations are always in a pre-crisis mode. Keeping transparent and comprehensive records of safety practices is essential. During crises, routine safety practices are heavily scrutinised. Airlines that abide by industry safety regulations are able to salvage their reputation and recover. This is similar to what Singapore Airlines (SIA) did in managing the Flight SQ006 crash in 2000 (Henderson, 2003). The crash had 100 casualties out of 179 passengers. It was considered as the first and only air crash tragedy for the airline, and one that challenged its place in the aviation industry. Despite the number of casualties, SIA's post-crisis initiatives gathered positive stakeholder feedback. Post-crisis investigations revealed that the airlines complied with all safety requirements. SIA was ever-present in walking the public through the investigations as demonstrated by timely and accurate provision of information to the media. Whereas, Whyalla Airlines was not prepared to demonstrate its safety protocols to investigating authorities. Although the issue of life jackets, for instance, was not relevant to the reason for the Flight 904 crash, the lack of provision of jackets was brought up as an evidence that further questioned the airline's safety practices.

- Second, airlines should strategically develop key messages to create a proper closure to the crisis narrative. In the case of the Whyalla Airline plane crash, relevant government authorities served as key drivers of determining crisis attribution (Weiner, 1985, 1986). When conflicting findings were released, it was more difficult for Whyalla Airlines to communicate a clear narrative on why the aircraft crashed. While airlines cannot intervene in investigations by authorities in general, they should assert their voices in media spaces during the post-crisis stage by interpreting what the investigations meant in relation to their position as the host airline. This will help balance news coverage and avoid one-sided and/or sensationalised media reporting (Paracha et al., 2013; Walters et al., 2016).

- Third, airlines, regardless of their size, should have a strong crisis communication and media relations plan. This includes conducting training for an official spokesperson, and media release writing that will help the airline provide effective information subsidies proactively to the media during and after crises (Park et al., 2016; Henderson, 2003). Establishing protocols on how to liaise with relevant authorities during crises is also key (Schwarz, 2008; Ulmer, 2001). An airline's crisis communication plan should also identify various platforms for stakeholder communication, both face to face or online (Greer & Moreland, 2003), to gather feedback that could inform decisions and actions in crisis response.

References

Andrew, G. (2000). Pilots lose jobs after airline stays grounded. *Adelaide Advertiser*.

Altheide, D. L., & Schneider, C. J. (2013). *Qualitative Media Analysis* (2nd ed.). Los Angeles, CA: Sage Publications.

Charmaz, K. (2014). *Constructing Grounded Theory* (2nd ed.). Los Angeles, CA: Sage Publications.

Coombs, W. T. (2007). Attribution Theory as a guide for post-crisis communication research. *Public Relations Review*, **33**, 135-139.

Coombs, W. T. (2016). Reflections on a meta-analysis: Crystallizing thinking about SCCT. *Journal of Public Relations Research*, **28**, 120-122.

Coombs, W. T. & Holladay, S. J. (1996). Communication and attributions in a crisis: An experimental study in crisis communication. *Journal of Public Relations Research*, **8**, 279-295.

Coombs, W. T. & Holladay, S. J. (2005). Exploratory study of stakeholder emotions: Affect and crisis. In N. M. Ashkanasy, W. J. Zerbe, & C. E. J. Härtel (Eds.), *Research on Emotion in Organizations: Volume 1: The effect of affect in organizational settings* (pp. 109-119). New York, NY: Elsevier.

Coombs, W. T. & Holladay, S. J. (2010). *The Handbook of Crisis Communication*. Malden, MA: Wiley-Blackwell.

Cornelissen, J. P. (2011). *Corporate Communication: A guide to theory and practice*. London: Sage Publications, Ltd.

Davis, H. & McLeod, S. L. (2003). Why humans value sensational news: An evolutionary perspective. *Evolution and Human Behavior*, **24**, 208-216.

Dornin, T. (2002, 23 July). SA- Experts to disagree with official reports on Whyalla. Australian Associated Press General News.

Entman, R. M. (1993). Framing: Toward clarification of a fractured paradigm. *Journal of Communication*, **43**(4), 51-58.

Faulkner, B. (2001). Towards a framework for tourism disaster management. *Tourism Management*, **22**, 134-147.

12

Fink, S. (1986). *Crisis Management*. New York: American Association of Management.

Fishman, D. A. (1999). ValuJet Flight 592: Crisis communication theory blended and extended. *Communication Quarterly*, **47** (4), 345-375.

Fleischer, A., Tchetckik, A. & Toledo, T. (2012). The impact of fear of flying on treveler's flight choice: Choice model with latent variables. *Journal of Travel Research*, **51**, 653-663.

Gerken, F., Van der Land, S.F. & Van der Meer, T.G.L.A. (2016). Crisis on the air: An investigation of AirAsia's crisis-response effectiveness based on frame alignment. *Public Relations Review*, **42**, 879-892.

Gitlin, T. (1980). *The whole world is watching: Mass media in the making & unmaking of the new left*. New York: Harper and Row.

Goffman, E. (1974). *Frame analysis: An essay of the organization of experience*. New York: Harper and Row.

Goodrich, J.N. (2002). September 11, 2001 attack on America: A record of the immediate impacts and reactions in the USA travel and tourism industry. *Tourism Management*, **23**, 573-580.

Greer, C.F. & Moreland, K.D. (2003). United Airlines' and American Airlines' online crisis communication following September 11 terrorist attacks. *Public Relations Review*, **29**, 427-441.

Henderson, J.C. (2003). Communicating in a crisis: flight SQ 006. *Tourism Management*, **24**, 279-287.

Koo, T. T. R., Collins, A. T., Williamson, A. & Caponecchia, C. (2019). How safety risk information and alternative forms of presenting it affect traveler decision rules in international flight choice. *Journal of Travel Research*, **58**, 480-495.

Mair, J., Ritchie, B. W. & Walters, G. (2016). Towards a research agenda for post-disaster and post-crisis recovery strategies for tourist destinations: A narrative review. *Current Issues in Tourism*, **19**, 1-26.

McDonald, L. & Härtel, C. E. J. (2000). Applying the involvement construct to organizational crises. In *Proceedings of the Australian and New Zealand Marketing Academy Conference 2000 Visionary Marketing for the 21th Century: Facing the Challenge* (pp.799—803). Gold Coast, Qld: Griffith University.

Neuman, W.R., Just, M.R. & Crigler, A.N. (1992). *Common Knowledge*. Chicago, IL: University of Chicago Press.

Nisbet, M. C. & Mooney, C. (2007). Framing science. *Science,* **316** (5821), 56-69.

Paracha. S. A., Shahzad, M., Ali, S. & Nazir, J. (2013). To analyze the news contents of electronic and print media in Pakistan, whether media is terrorizing or informing the community. *International Journal of Academic Research in Business and Social Sciences*, **3**, 59-67.

Park, S., Bier, L. & Palenchar, M. (2016). Framing the flight MH370 mystery: A content analysis of Malaysian, Chinese, and U.S. media. *International Communication Gazette,* **80**(2), 158-184

Schwarz, A. (2008). Covariation-based causal attributions during organizational crises: Suggestions for extending situational crisis communication theory (SCCT). *International Journal of Strategic Communication,* **2**, 31-53.

Schwarz, A. (2012). Stakeholder attributions in crisis: The effects of covariation information and attribution inferences on organizational reputation. *International Journal of Strategic Communication,* **6** (2), 174-195.

Nicholson, B. (2001). A young pilot's skill could not save Flight 904. *Sunday Age,* 23 December, p. 7.

Sunday Mail, (2001). Official report Flight 904 - Why eight people died. *Sunday Mail,* 20 May, p. 4.

Plane, T. (2003). Coroner castigates air-safety watchdog. *The Australian,* 25 July, p. 5.

Tierney, K., Bevc, C. & Kuligowski, E. (2006). Metaphors matter: Disaster myths, media frames, and their consequences in Hurricane Katrina. *Annals of the American Academy of Political and Social Science,* **604**, 57-81.

Ulmer, R.R. (2001). Effective crisis management through established stakeholder relationships. *Management Communication Quarterly,* **14**, 590-615.

Valentini, C. & Romenti, S. (2011). The press and Alitalia's 2008 crisis: issues, tones, and frames. *Public Relations Review,* **37**, 360-365.

Vincent, R.C., Crow, B.K. & Davis, D.K. (1997). When technology fails: The drama of airline crashes in network television news. In D. Berkowitz (ed.). *Social mMeanings of the News.* Thousand Oaks, CA: Sage, 351-361.

Walters, G., Mair, J. & Lim, J. (2016). Sensationalist media reporting of disastrous events: Implications for tourism. *Journal of Hospitality and Tourism Management,* **28**, 3-10.

Weiner, B. (1985). "Spontaneous" causal thinking. *Psychological Bulletin,* 97, 74-84.

Weiner, B. (1986). *An Attribution Theory of Motivation and Emotion.* New York: Springer.

Yang, L., Tjiptono, F. & Poon, W. C. (2018). Will you fly with this airline in the future? An empirical study of airline avoidance after accidents. *Journal of Travel & Tourism Marketing,* **35**, 1145-1159.

12

13 Service failures as triggers of superior brand evaluations?

Clemens Hutzinger and Wolfgang Weitzl

Introduction

In pursuit of better purchasing decisions (e.g., choosing the right restaurant or hotel), prospective customers increasingly turn to social media, such as Facebook, to source information about new products, services and brands. On Facebook, a brand's former, current and potential customers are not only exposed to marketer-created brand postings, but also to other customers' subjective evaluations, personal thoughts and feelings regarding their consumption experiences (Hennig-Thurau et al., 2010). Research has shown that consumers strive for multifaceted goals when sharing consumption-related postings online. For instance, some satisfied customers want to help the company by posting favorable statements about a positive brand experiences, known as positive electronic word of mouth or PeWOM (Hennig-Thurau et al., 2004), while others want to help their fellow shoppers by giving a neutral description of a regular brand experience (ReWOM). However, many dissatisfied customers also use Facebook brand-pages as a public platform to express their unfavorable thoughts and negative emotions (e.g., anger) after a service failure by means of an online complaint or negative electronic word of mouth (NeWOM; Ward & Ostrom, 2006; Weitzl et al., 2018).

Consumers that are directly affected by the service failure and involved in the recovery process are referred to as complainants.

The reasons why customers spread NeWOM are diverse. They range from venting (i.e., lessening his/her frustration and reduce anger), via revenge (i.e., intentionally sabotaging and harming the company; Grégoire et al., 2009), warning others (Willemsen et al., 2011), to advice seeking (to acquire new skills/information to better use and/or repair the product; Willemsen et al, 2013). Earlier research demonstrates that online complaints can have strong and diverse detrimental effects, particularly on a brand's potential customers (so-called online complaint bystanders), including unfavorable attitudes and an increased willingness to criticize the involved brand to others (e.g., Chevalier & Mayzlin, 2006; Sen & Lerman, 2007). However, evidence also exists that 'webcare', which is company's online complaint handling response to a public complaint can repair negative reactions of these bystanders to some extent (e.g., Weitzl & Hutzinger, 2017). It remains, nevertheless, unclear how far such positive reactions can be stimulated with webcare among NeWOM bystanders.

Hart et al. (1990: 148) claim that "a good recovery can turn angry, frustrated customers into loyal ones. It can, in fact, create more goodwill than if things had gone smoothly in the first place". There is strong evidence (e.g., McCollough et al., 2000; Michel & Meuter, 2008) that a service failure followed by a superb recovery response by the company can cultivate even more positive reactions (e.g., favorable attitudes, satisfaction) among complainants than regular/neutral brand experiences. This is often referred to as the 'service recovery paradox' (SRP; McCollough & Bharadwaj, 1992). This chapter assesses whether this phenomenon is also applicable to complaint bystanders (i.e., consumers passively observing a public complaint (NeWOM) and the recovery process online). Considering the potentials of the SRP, the guiding, somewhat provocative, research question reads as follows:

"Is it ever wise for a company in the tourism or hospitality industry to deliberately mess up a service experience which is then 'repaired' successfully afterwards by means of (credible) online complaint-handling? Does this achieve more positive bystanders' brand attitude than after customer postings of regular experiences (ReWOM)?"

This research provides answers to these important questions by investigating bystanders' reactions after a service failure in a coffee house and hence adding knowledge about the SRP on relatively uninvolved individuals in the under-researched tourism/hospitality context.

Complainants' reactions to successful service recoveries

Service failures are mistakes or problems that customers experience while consuming or communicating with a brand (Maxham, 2001). These often-occurring negative events (e.g. an unfriendly waiter, a malfunctioning product, a late delivery) lead to customer dissatisfaction and customer complaint behaviors shown both in offline channels (complaining directly in the involved store) as well as online. Online complaints can be direct (posting a negative comment on the brand's Facebook page) or indirect via a third-party discussion forum. These failures – or more precisely, the attempt to recover dissatisfied customers – furnish companies with a great opportunity. Companies can alter the minds of complainants and restore the collapsing customer-brand relationship with a successful service recovery, which is a strategy that tries to rectify the failure (Kaltcheva et al., 2013) and remove the associated bad memories.

Extant literature in the offline complaining context shows that service recovery can elicit various positive outcomes among complainants who have personally experienced the failure and filed a complaint afterwards, such as satisfaction (Maxham & Netemeyer, 2002b), justice restoration (McQuilken et al., 2013), and establishing repurchase intention (Huang & Lin, 2011). Some research, however, sheds light on the outstanding outcomes or vast potential of successful recoveries. According to the service marketing literature, the Service Recovery Paradox (McCollough & Bharadwaj, 1992) occurs when a high recovery performance leads to a customer's greater post-recovery satisfaction, as compared to his/her pre-failure satisfaction. The SRP among complainants has been supported by literature for several different scenarios and outcome variables. For instance, Hansen and Danaher (1999), studied the SRP in the airline industry. In their experiment, they compared a positive performance trend (i.e., service experience with poor initial performance and with high final performance) with a neutral performance trend (i.e., service experience with average initial and final performance). They found that participants faced with a positive performance trend experienced a higher service satisfaction than those faced with the neutral performance trend. Likewise, Michel and Meuter (2008), found that consumers had a higher recommendation intention after experiencing successful service recovery as compared to a situation of no service failure. Furthermore, Bijmolt et al. (2014) showed that complainants who experienced a positive service recovery had a higher repurchase intention on the internet as compared to complainants who did not experience a service failure at all. In a hospitality context, Magnini et al. (2007) demonstrated that the SRP is more likely to occur if, for example, the failure is not considered to be severe or the customer had no prior failure with the hotel. While literature on *online* complaining – a different and *more* demanding complaining context (Grégoire et al., 2009) – suggests that recoveries can lead to various positive outcomes (see van Noort et al. (2015) for a recent review), research on the SRP among complainants and particularly NeWOM bystanders is sparse.

Bystanders' reactions to successful (online) service recoveries

Given the potential negative consequences of online complaints among its bystanders, many companies started to counteract NeWOM by online complaint handling or *webcare* (Hong & Lee, 2005; Lee & Song, 2010). Webcare can be defined as "the act of engaging in online interactions with (complaining) consumers, by actively searching the web to address consumer feedback (e.g. questions, concerns and complaints)" (van Noort & Willemsen, 2012: 133). With these actions, companies hope to improve complainants' and bystanders' perceptions of the failure as well as of their products and services. Companies can employ webcare either proactively (i.e., the company tries to anticipate problems) or reactively (i.e., the company reacts to a specific service failure experienced by a customer). While both forms can provide benefits to the company, interestingly, reactive strategies are especially powerful in bringing a smile back on the face of the customer (Köhler et al., 2011).

Companies can choose between two reactive webcare strategies: *Accommodative webcare* (AW) and *defensive webcare* (DW) (Marcus & Goodman, 1991). These two strategies differ in the level of how much responsibility the involved company takes for the failure (Coombs, 2007): while AW comprises a high degree of responsibility, DW comprises the opposite. In the former, the company admits that it has caused the service failure and typically reacts with an apology, acknowledgement of the problem and/or a redress offer (e.g., free product, refund, or discount) (Lee & Cranage, 2014). On the other hand, by using DW the company typically stresses that someone else (e.g., a supplier) has caused the service failure. Consequently, DW comprises denial of fault, attacking the complainant and blaming the complainant or a third party (Lee & Song, 2010). We have learnt that this strategy can be successful when the failure circumstances are unclear (Weitzl & Hutzinger, 2017).

Mainly, webcare aims at pacifying (involved) complainants, which can be current or recently lost dissatisfied customers. However, there is a huge group of other consumers: relatively uninvolved online bystanders (i.e., potential customers considering the brand for purchase; Weitzl & Hutzinger, 2017). By observing negative postings of consumers (NeWOM) and follow-up reactions of companies, bystanders obtain valuable information which they use for making consumption decisions. There is clear evidence (e.g. Chevalier & Mayzlin, 2006; Sen & Lerman, 2007; Vermeulen & Seegers, 2009) that NeWOM has a striking (negative) impact on bystanders' choice and loyalty towards brands.

Webcare's direct effect

We acknowledge that AW and DW differ in their effectiveness in triggering favorable outcomes among NeWOM bystanders: specifically, AW is assumed to be especially successful in eliciting positive reactions (e.g. Chang et al., 2015; Lee & Song, 2010). We base our assumption about the positive, direct effect that AW has on bystanders on social learning theory (Bandura, 1977) and reinforcement theory (Skinner, 1969). According to the former, individuals observe others' behaviors and/or consecutive reactions for personal learning. According to reinforcement theory, a reward for a specific behavior makes people learn that behavior (even) faster. Consistent with Schamari and Schaefers (2015), we propose that webcare (e.g., a redress offer) can be regarded as such a 'reward'. Earlier research (e.g., del Río-Lanza et al., 2009) has shown that the reward transmitted through webcare has an impact on recipients' reactions. Further, we argue that when bystanders notice that complainants get a reward by the company through webcare, they imagine that they would also receive that reward as a company's future customer. We argue that – for bystanders – DW provides *low* rewards (unsatisfactory recovery) and that AW provides *high* rewards (satisfactory recovery). This can be explained by perceived justice (Adams, 1963) which is associated with the tw o webcare strategies. Specifically, we suggest that AW – as compared to DW – triggers higher levels of distributive justice (the perceived adequacy of compensations; Mattila,

13

2001), procedural justice (the perceived appropriateness of service problem solving; Smith et al., 1999) and interactional justice at the same time (the perceived fairness of interpersonal treatment; Tax et al., 1998). Consequently, we argue that AW (with its many positive justice cues) contrasts more to neutral Facebook customer comments about regular brand experiences (i.e., ReWOM) than DW (with its few positive justice cues). Therefore, we want to investigate whether the service recovery paradox does exist for accommodative webcare. We assume that an act of accommodative webcare after a service failure leads to more favorable brand attitude of bystanders as compared to customer comments about a regular service experience. Similarly, we attempt to empirically show that the service recovery paradox does *not* exist for defensive webcare. Because we assume that an act of defensive webcare after a service failure leads to less favorable brand attitude of bystanders as compared to customer comments about a regular service experience.

Moderating effect of webcare credibility

The Elaboration Likelihood Model (ELM) and the Heuristic-Systematic Model (HSM) both provide an explanation of how individuals (e.g., bystanders) process information. Specifically, the 'central route' (ELM) or 'systematic processing' (HSM) routine are activated when involved individuals are interested in and are capable of using higher cognitive effort to elaborate information. On the contrary, the 'peripheral route' or 'heuristic processing' is used by individuals who apply heuristics and/or simple decision rules to quickly form judgments. In many situations, people follow the 'least effort principle' and opt for heuristic information processing to minimize personal effort and to save time (Bohner et al., 1995). This is especially true for NeWOM bystanders, when they are exposed to a great amount of information (e.g., customer complaints, responses) on social media. To avoid confusion and save mental energy, these relatively uninvolved potential customers automatically rely on heuristic cues to judge webcare responses and the focal brand (Fogg et al., 2003). For information recipients, the credibility of a message or its source has been shown to be one of the most important heuristic cues for evaluating a message online (Metzger et al., 2010). Accordingly, we suggest that webcare credibility, which we define as the extent to which the corporate online complaint handling response is perceived as trustworthy by the recipient (Weitzl & Hutzinger, 2017), acts as an important moderator of heuristically or peripherally processed webcare responses (Petty & Capcioppo, 1986). Extant literature suggests that a highly credible – compared to a less credible – message is more influential and more likely to trigger attitude changes (e.g., Hovland et al., 1953). Therefore, we suggest that credible AW – proving high webcare benefits in a sincere manner (i.e., highly satisfactory webcare) – is the only response strategy that is likely to outperform the positive influence of customer postings discussing a regular brand experience (i.e., ReWOM). Hence, we want to show empirically that the service recovery paradox does exist for credible, accommodative webcare because we assume that an act of credible, accommodative webcare after a service failure leads to more favorable brand attitudes of bystanders as compared to customer comments about a regular service experience.

Method

An online experiment with a 2 × 2 (webcare: defensive webcare [DW] vs. accommodative webcare [AW]) and (credibility of webcare: non-credible vs. credible) factorial design was applied. Participants were told to imagine a scenario in which that they intend to visit a new coffeehouse with their friends. To seek information, they visit the coffeehouse's own Facebook page on which they either (i) observed a customer comment about a regular service experience (ReWOM) (i.e., the control group) or (ii) a customer's complaint about an unsatisfactory coffee purchase (NeWOM) (i.e., experimental groups). We have selected this hospitality context because earlier literature remained silent about uninvolved bystanders' reactions to service problems related to a leisure activity. Respondents were randomly assigned to these conditions. The experimental groups were subsequently exposed to one of the recovery conditions, receiving either DW or AW. All conditions were carefully developed and pretested.

Data was collected for the main experiment by means of an online questionnaire, which contained only multi-item scales from established academic literature to measure this research's key constructs, such as perceived webcare credibility (Weitzl & Hutzinger, 2017). The application of a median-split to this variable enabled us to form five quasi-experimental groups to perform our analyses. This was done after ensuring all measures' psychometric qualities. For testing the research assumptions, responses from 529 adult consumers

13

(91.30% used Facebook at least once a day) were used for this study. A non-probability snowball sampling technique was applied to invite appropriate participants. The mean age of participants was 26.46 years (SD=8.80) and 95% of them where between 18 und 51 years old. 71.10% (n=376) were female, 49.30% graduated from high school, and 30.60% were employees.

Results

Manipulation check

We first checked whether our experimental manipulation of the valence of the customer comment (i.e., regular service experience [ReWOM] vs. complaint [NeWOM]) was successful. For this, participants rated the valence of the customer comment on a 7-point scale ranging from 1 ('The comment was very negative.') to 7 ('The comment was very positive.'). As evidenced by an one-way ANOVA ($F_{(2,523)}=165.47$, $p<0.001$), the regular service experience (M=4.43, SD=1.28) was perceived as significantly more positive than the complaint later followed by the DW condition (M=1.98, SD=0.90, $p<0.001$) and the AW condition (M=1.94, SD=0.89, $p<0.001$). Thus, the experimental manipulation of the valence of the customer comment (Facebook posting) was successful. Further analyses on the respondents' characteristics (e.g., social media usage) revealed that the experimental groups and the control group were homogeneous. For instance, we showed that the groups (ReWOM vs. complaint followed by DW vs. complaint followed by AW) did not differ in participants' Facebook review usage ($F_{(2,523)}=0.08$; $p=0.92$; rated with 4 items on a 7-point scale ranging from 1 ('I totally disagree') to 7 ('I totally agree')).

Assumption testing

Webcare's direct effect

To test our assumptions about the direct effects of webcare, we ran an ANCOVA with 'brand attitude' (bystander's overall favorable evaluation of a brand) as dependent variable, service condition (i.e., type of communication) as fixed factor, and age, gender, involvement and problem severity as covariates. The results are shown in Table 13.1.

Table 13.1: Effects of service condition and covariates on brand attitude

Sources	df	Dependent Variable: Brand Attitude
Main effect		
Service condition (R vs. DW vs. AW)[a]	2	60.133***
Covariates		
Age	1	.039ns.
Gender	1	.000ns.
Involvement	1	.705ns.
Problem severity	1	4.321*

Note: Table shows F-values with significance levels: ns. = not significant, * p<.05, ** p<.01, *** p<.001;
[a] Service condition: R = Regular service experience; DW = Defensive webcare; AW = Accommodative webcare

Planned comparison (F=58.38, p<.001) showed that, compared to a regular service experience (M=3.66; SD=1.23) participants' brand attitude was significantly higher in the AW condition (M=4.24; SD=1.08; p<.001). Thus, our assumption about the existence of the service recovery paradox for online bystanders was supported. However, participants' brand attitude was significantly lower when they observed DW after the complaint about a service failure (M=3.13; SD=1.13; p<.01) as compared to ReWOM. This is consistent with our second assumption about the paradox's absence. For results see Figure 13.1.

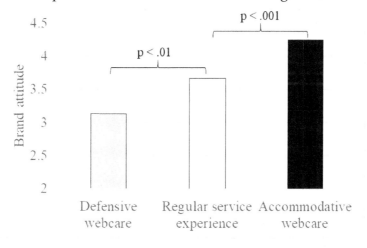

Figure 13.1: Effect of regular service experience and webcare on brand attitude

13

Moderating effect of webcare credibility

To explore the role of webcare credibility, we ran an ANOVA with brand attitude as dependent variable and the five recovery conditions as factor. Results showed that – as compared to a customer posting about a regular service experience (ReWOM) – after an online complaint, only credible AW leads to a significant increase in bystanders' brand attitude (p<.001), while noncredible AW does not. In comparison to ReWOM, noncredible DW leads to a significantly lower brand attitude (p<.001) following a customer complaint. However, credible DW leads to comparable levels of brand attitude as ReWOM. The results are summarized in Figure 13.2.

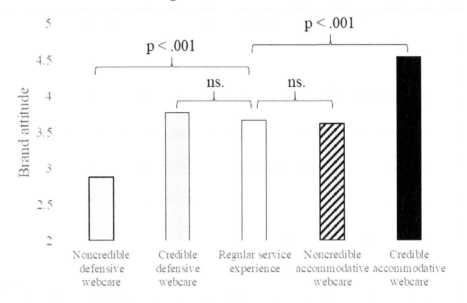

Figure 13.2: Effect of regular service experience and (non)credible webcare on brand attitude.

Discussion

In this work, we examine the role of webcare (i.e., online complaint handling) observed by online complaint bystanders which has the potential to trigger the so-called 'service recovery paradox' (SRP; McCollough & Bharadwaj, 1992). The SRP traditionally denotes a situation when high recovery performance leads to a complainant's greater post-recovery satisfaction, as compared to his/her pre-failure satisfaction. It has been supported by literature (Hansen & Danaher,

1999; Michel & Meuter, 2008; Bijmolt et al., 2014), however generally only in the offline setting (see Bijmolt et al. (2014) for a notable exception) and for directly involved complainants. Research on the effect on online bystanders remained scare (see Marx & Nimmermann (2015) for pioneering insights). Our work empirically shows that, compared to a postings about a regular service experience (i.e., neutral/slightly positive customer comments; ReWOM), bystanders' favorable brand attitude (i.e., overall brand evaluation) was significantly higher when they observed a credible accommodative webcare (AW) as a response to an online complaint. On the contrary, online bystanders' favorable brand attitude was significantly lower when they observed a noncredible defensive webcare (DW). Credible DW and noncredible AW lead to similar results as ReWOM. Thus, our results supported the existence of the SRP for bystanders only when they received credible AW (e.g., a sincere apology, a serious explanation, appropriate redress offer) but not when marketers applied another recovery strategy (i.e., less satisfying responses).

What is the bad news?

Given the nature of services and the heterogeneity of customer demands, service failures (i.e., situations in which a service does not meet customers' expectations) occur regularly. A few years ago, harsh critique by dissatisfied customers were often not heard by more than half a dozen of ears (e.g., close friends, family). Today, this situation has changed as a multitude of complainants are willing and able to post their unfavorable thoughts and feelings about negative experiences on social media (e.g., on a Facebook brand page). These direct, public complaints (i.e., negative electronic word-of-mouth; NeWOM) have been shown to have negative effects on their observers (i.e., 'complaint bystanders' or a brand's potential customers), such as a rise in their bad brand evaluations and consequently their willingness to disseminate brand-skeptical information (e.g., Chevalier & Mayzlin, 2006; Sen & Lerman, 2007).

What is the good news?

The good news is that companies can combat NeWOM with webcare by responding to online complaints with respective communicative actions (van Noort & Willemsen, 2012). Companies can choose among accommodative webcare (taking responsibility for causing the service failure and pacifying the complainant by providing social and financial benefits like an apology and a free gift; Lee & Cranage, 2014) and

13

defensive webcare (neglecting responsibility and blaming someone else or external conditions; Lee & Song, 2010). Predominantly, webcare strategies aim at restoring a brand's relationship with its current customers (i.e., complainants). However, recent work (Weitzl & Hutzinger, 2017) has shown that webcare also strongly impacts online bystanders.

What are the strengths, limitations and future research?

In our analysis, we followed McCollough et al. (2000)'s call to control for several confounds that could affect the SRP. Specifically, we included bystanders' age, gender, involvement and problem severity as control variables. Furthermore, our study is first evidence that the webcare strategy determines whether the SRP exists among bystanders or not. We broadly distinguished between the classic forms of DW as well as AW. Future work should investigate the effects of more fine-grained facets of these strategies. An example of the former is the comparison of a simple apology with a financial compensation. An example of the latter is the comparison of blaming the complainant and blaming a third party for having caused the service failure. Finally, consistent with Maxham and Netemeyer (2002a), we found that the SRP occurs after a single service failure. However, future work should explore whether and under which conditions the SRP does also exist for a series of different types of service failures (e.g., financial vs. non-financial failures). In addition, customer characteristics (e.g., relationship status) should be considered.

What are the practical implications and recommendations?

It has been stressed that having better insights into service recovery is crucial for managers (McCollough et al., 2000). Companies should be aware that webcare does not only impact the complainant but also an indefinite number of online bystanders. These potential customers have a huge impact on the well-being of the company. Choosing the right webcare strategy is a key to success. Although many companies use DW (e.g., denial of fault, attacking the complainant) this strategy can lead to detrimental brand reactions. In contrast, AW (e.g., an honest apology, acknowledgement of the problem and redress offer by means of a financial compensation) can have far-reaching positive effects that can even outperform slightly positive customer postings (ReWOM). This implies that companies can benefit from a publicly reported service failure when they are willing to provide a sincere online service recovery in which they stay friendly and earnest as well as demonstrate that they are doing their best to solve the complainant's problem (i.e., highly satisfying webcare). This means, in theory at least, that companies could think about ways to mess up their services first, before providing outstanding service recovery online afterwards. This strategy, however, should naturally be handled with care as it comes at the cost of the current customers. In addition, multiple reports of negative experiences on the internet are likely to trigger negative bystander reactions due to mental accounting. Hence, the SRP is likely to diminish at some point.

Recommendations for practice

This chapter has highlighted four key learnings:

- Many dissatisfied customers complain publicly on companies' social media sites.

- Since these online complaints negatively impact bystanders, it is crucial for managers in hospitality and tourism to gain better insights into service recovery effects on complaint bystanders.

- The right communication after a service failure (i.e., a posting about a negative service experience) can even lead to more favorable brand attitudes of online complaint bystanders as compared to a situation without a service failure (i.e., a posting about a regular service experience).

- The most effective communication is one that is highly credible, that takes responsibility for causing the service failure and that provides social and financial benefits like an apology and a free gift.

References

Adams, J. S. (1963) Toward an understanding of inequity, *Journal of Abnormal and Social Psychology*, **67** (5), 422–436.

Bandura, A. (1977) *Social Learning Theory*. Englewood Cliffs, NJ: Prentice Hall.

Bijmolt, T. H., Huizingh, E. K. & Krawczyk, A. (2014) Effects of complaint behaviour and service recovery satisfaction on consumer intentions to repurchase on the internet, *Internet Research*, **24** (5), 608–628.

Bohner, G., Moskowitz, G. B. & Chaiken, S. (1995) The interplay of heuristic and systematic processing of social information, *European Review of Social Psychology*, **6** (1), 33–68.

13

Chang, H. H., Tsai, Y.-C., Wong, K. H. & Cho, F. J. (2015)'The effects of response strategies and severity of failure on consumer attribution with regard to negative word-of-mouth, *Decision Support Systems*, **71**, 48–61.

Chevalier, J. A. & Mayzlin, D. (2006) The effect of word of mouth on sales: Online book reviews, *Journal of Marketing Research*, **43** (3), 345–354.

Coombs, W. T. (2007) Protecting organization reputations during a crisis: The development and application of situational crisis communication theory, *Corporate Reputation Review*, **10** (3), 163–176.

del Río-Lanza, A. B., Vázquez-Casielles, R. & Díaz-Martín, A. M. (2009) Satisfaction with service recovery: Perceived justice and emotional responses, *Journal of Business Research*, **62** (8), 775–781.

Fogg, B. J., Soohoo, C., Danielson, D. R., Marable, L., Standord, J. & Tauber, E. R. (2003) How do users evaluate the credibility of web Sites? A study with over 2,500 participants, DOX'03: Proceedings of the 2003 conference on designing for user experiences. San Francisco, CA: ACM Press.

Grégoire, Y., Tripp, T. M. & Legoux, R. (2009) When customer love turns into lasting hate: The effects of relationship strength and time on customer revenge and avoidance, *Journal of Marketing*, **73** (6), 18–32.

Hansen, D. E. & Danaher, P. J. (1999) Inconsistent performance during the service encounter: What's a good start worth?, *Journal of Service Research*, **1** (3), 227–235.

Hart, C. W., Heskett, J. L & Sasser, W. E. (1990), The profitable art of service recovery, *Harvard Business Review*, **68** (4), 148–156.

Hennig-Thurau, T., Malthouse, E. C., Friege, C., Gensler, S., Lobschat, L., Rangaswamy, A. a&nd Skiera, B. (2010) The impact of new media on customer relationship', *Journal of Service Research*, **13** (3), 311–330.

Hennig-Thurau, T., Gwinner, K. P., Walsh, G. & Gremler, D. D. (2004) Electronic word-of-mouth via consumer-opinion platforms: What motivates consumers to articulate themselves on the internet?, *Journal of Interactive Marketing*, **18**, 38–52.

Hong, J.-Y. and Lee, W.-N. (2005) Consumer complaint behavior in the online environment; in Y. Gao (Ed.), *Web Systems Design and Online Consumer Behavior* (pp. 90–106). Hershey, PA: IGI Global.

Hovland, C. I., Jannis, I. & Kelley, H. H. (1953) *Communication and Persuasion*, New Haven, CT: Yale University Press.

Huang,W.-H. & Lin, T.-D. (2011) Developing effective service compensation strategies, *Journal of Service Management*, **22** (2), 202–216.

Kaltcheva,V. D., Winsor, R. D. & Parasuraman, A. (2013) Do customer relationships mitigate or amplify failure responses?, *Journal of Business Research*, **66** (4), 525–532.

Köhler, C. F., Rohm, A. J., de Ruyter, K. & Wetzels, M. (2011) Return on interactivity: The impact of online agents on newcomer adjustment, *Journal of Marketing*, **75** (2), 93–108.

Lee, C. H. & Cranage, D. A. (2014) Toward understanding consumer processing of negative online word-of-mouth communication: The roles of opinion consensus and organizational response strategies, *Journal of Hospitality and Tourism Research*, **38** (3), 330–360.

Lee, Y. L. & Song, S. (2010) An empirical Investigation of electronic word-of-mouth: Informational motive and corporate response strategy', *Computers in Human Behavior*, **26** (5), 1073–1080.

Magnini, V. P., Ford, J. B., Markowski, E. P. & Honeycutt, E. D. (2007) The service recovery paradox: Justifiable theory or smoldering myth?, *Journal of Services Marketing*, **21** (3), 213–225.

Marcus, A. A. & Goodman, R. S. (1991) Victims and shareholders: The dilemmas of presenting corporate policy during crisis, *Academy of Management Journal*, **34** (2), 281–305.

Marx, P. & Nimmermann, F. (2015) Online complaints in the eye of the beholder: Optimal handling of public consumer complaints on the internet, *Proceedings of the 44th EMAC Annual Conference*, Leuven, Belgium: European Marketing Academy.

Mattila, A. S. (2001) Emotional bonding and restaurant loyalty, *The Cornell Hotel and Restaurant Administration Quarterly*, **42** (6), 73–79.

Maxham, J. G. (2001). Service recovery's influence on consumer satisfaction, positive word-of-mouth, and purchase intentions, *Journal of Business Research*, **54** (1), 11–24

Maxham, J. G. & Netemeyer, R. G. (2002a) A longitudinal study of complaining customers' evaluations of multiple service failures and recovery efforts, *Journal of Marketing*, **66** (4), 57–71.

Maxham, J.G. & Netemeyer, R. G. (2002b) Modeling customer perceptions of complaint handling over time: The effects of perceived justice on satisfaction and intent, *Journal of Retailing*, **78** (4), 239–252.

McCollough, M. A. & Bharadwaj, S. G. (1992) The recovery paradox: An examination of consumer satisfaction in relation to disconfirmation, service quality, and attribution based theories, in *Marketing Theory and Applications*, Allen, C. T., Madden, T. J., Shimp, T. A., Howell, R. D., Zinkhan, G. M., Heisley, D. D, Semenik, R. J., Dickson, P., Zeithaml, V., & Jenkins, R. L. eds. Chicago: American Marketing Association, 119.

McCollough, M. A., Berry, L. L. & Yadav, M. S. (2000) An empirical investigation of customer satisfaction after service failure and recovery, *Journal of Service Research*, **3** (2), 121–137.

13

McQuilken, L., McDonald, H. & Vocino, A. (2013) Is guarantee compensation enough? The important role of fix and employee effort in restoring justice, *International Journal of Hospitality Management*, **33** (1), 41–50.

Metzger, M. J., Flanagin, A. J. & Medders, R. B. (2010) Social and heuristic approaches to credibility evaluation online, *Journal of Communication*, **60**, 413–439.

Michel, S. & Meuter, M. L. (2008) The service recovery paradox: True but overrated?, *International Journal of Service Industry Management*, **19** (4), 441–457.

Petty, R. E. & Cacioppo, J. T. (1986) The elaboration likelihood model of persuasion, *Advances in Experimental Social Psychology*, **19**, 123–205.

Schamari, J. & Schaefers, T. (2015) Leaving the home turf: How brands can use webcare on consumer-generated platforms to increase positive consumer engagement, *Journal of Interactive Marketing*, **30**, 20–33.

Sen, S. & Lerman, D. (2007) Why are you telling me this? An examination into negative consumer reviews on the web, *Journal of Interactive Marketing*, **21** (4), 76–94.

Skinner, B. F. (1969). *Contingencies of Reinforcement*. New York, NY: Appleton-Century-Crofts.

Smith, A. K., Bolton, R. N. & Wagner, J. (1999) A model of customer satisfaction with service encounters involving failure recovery, *Journal of Marketing Research*, **36** (3), 356–373.

Tax, S., Brown, S. W. & Chandrashekaran, M. (1998) Customer evaluations of service complaint experiences: Implications for relationship marketing, *Journal of Marketing*, **62** (2), 60–76.

van Noort, G. & Willemsen, L. M. (2012) Online damage control: The effects of proactive versus reactive webcare interventions in consumer-generated and brand-generated platforms, *Journal of Interactive Marketing*, **26**(3), 131–140.

van Noort, G., Willemsen, L. M., Kerkhof, P. & Verhoeven, J. W. M. (2015) Webcare as an integrative tool for customer care, reputation management, and online marketing, in P. J. Kitchen, & E. Uzunoğlu (Eds.), *Integrated communications in the Postmodern Era*. London: Palgrave Macmillan UK.

Vermeulen, I. E. & Seegers, D. (2009) Tried and tested: The impact of online hotel reviews on consumer consideration, *Tourism Management*, **30** (1), 123–127.

Ward, J. C. & Ostrom, A. L. (2006) Complaining to the masses: The role of protest framing in customer-created complaint web sites, *Journal of Consumer Research*, **33** (2), 220–230.

Weitzl, W. & Hutzinger, C. (2017) The effects of marketer- and advocate-initiated online service recovery responses on silent bystanders, *Journal of Business Research*, **80**, 164–175.

Weitzl, W., Hutzinger, C. & Einwiller, S. (2018) An empirical study on how webcare mitigates complainants' failure attributions and negative word-of-mouth, *Computers in Human Behavior*, **89**, 316–327.

Willemsen, L. M., Neijens, P. C., Bronner, F. & de Ridder, J. A. (2011) Highly recommended! The content characteristics and perceived usefulness of online consumer reviews, *Journal of Computer-Mediated Communication*, **17** (1), 19–38.

Willemsen, L. M., Neijens, P. C. & Bronner, F. A. (2013) Webcare as customer relationship and reputation management? Motives for negative electronic word-of-mouth and their effect on webcare receptiveness, *Advances in Advertising Research*, **4**, 55-69.

13

Index

Printed in the United States
By Bookmasters